Praise for Breathe

"Reading *Breathe* is inspirational oxygen! You will inhale the words of this book and exhale hope. This isn't the story of one woman; it is a call to action for all women to listen to our bodies and souls."

—VICTORIA CHRISTOPHER MURRAY, number one *Essence* best-selling and award-winning author

"You won't be able to put down *Breathe*! It is inspiring and another real example that God is still performing miracles. The hope in this book will stay with you long after you turn the last page. A must-read."

—EARNEST PUGH, Stellar Award-nominated gospel singer and songwriter

"Angela's story will stay with me. Of all of the rights of women, the greatest is to be a mother. Learning that women around the world are dying to have this right when they don't have to is unthinkable. Thank you, Angela, for sharing your story, reminding us to have faith, and shedding a light on this crisis."

—MALINDA WILLIAMS, Image Award-nominated film and television actress

"As a cohost of the TV show *Exhale*, I understand why women need to *Breathe*! Angela's story is just another example of how important it is for all women to listen to their bodies and God, and to put their health first. I applaud my colleague and friend for sharing her story with the hope that it will help many."

—RENE SYLER, host of numerous talk shows, including former host of CBS' *The Early Show*; author, speaker, and founder of GoodEnoughMother.com

"As the editor in chief of the website www.momspark.net, connecting with moms and sharing stories is what I love. When I heard about Angela's story, I knew of the difference it would make, and I was reminded of the incredible "spark" that moms have. This spark makes a difference in our individual homes and in the world. I am so grateful that Angela is here to share this story, and grateful that readers around the world can be helped by it."

–AMY BELLGARDT, award-winning parenting
and lifestyle blogger at www.momspark.net

"I created my blog, Mocha Dad, to be a resource to help men be better dads. Although I didn't grow up with my father, I had a loving mother who nurtured and molded me. Mothers add critical value into the lives of children and are the cornerstones of our society. I am so thankful that Angela and Samson Logan have shared their story. I know that their story will inspire, and it will make a difference in the lives of families everywhere."

–FREDERICK GOODALL, cited by Cision, Babble,
and others as one of the top dad bloggers

"Motherhood has been a life-changing experience for me. My son has inspired my new career and ability to work online instead of in a newsroom. Angela's story has far-reaching relevance for moms and the families who love them. I can't wait to get my copy."

–JOYCE BREWER, Emmy Award-winning TV journalist
and parenting blogger

Breathe

WHEN LIFE TAKES YOUR BREATH AWAY

ANGELA BURGIN LOGAN
SAMSON LOGAN

BroadStreet
PUBLISHING

BroadStreet Publishing Group, LLC
Racine, Wisconsin, USA
BroadStreetPublishing.com

Breathe: WHEN LIFE TAKES YOUR BREATH AWAY

ISBN-13: 978-1-4245-5302-0 (softcover)
ISBN-13: 978-1-4245-5303-7 (e-book)

Some names and other details have been changed to protect personal identities.

All Scripture quotations are taken from the King James Version of the Bible, which is in the public domain.

Stock or custom editions of BroadStreet Publishing titles may be purchased in bulk for educational, business, ministry, fundraising, or sales promotional use. For information, please e-mail info@ broadstreetpublishing.com.

Interior by Katherine Lloyd at theDESKonline.com

Printed in the United States of America
17 18 19 20 21 5 4 3 2 1

This book is dedicated to Samia.
You are our reason for breathing!

It is also dedicated to every mother, father, and child
whose story may not have been heard but is no less
important. If you have gone through a similar experience,
and you feel like your voice wasn't heard, then this
book is for you. It is your voice, your anthem,
and your reminder that God hears all.

CONTENTS

1

The Beginning of the End

(From Angela)

Now that I'm dying, I wonder if my doctor will finally listen to me. That was my thought as I watched my doctor saunter into my chaos-filled room and take one look at me. His already pale skin seemed even more translucent as all color drained from his face, making him look like a ghost. Or maybe as if he'd seen a ghost.

I'd tried to tell him. For months I'd been trying to tell him that something was wrong. But no matter what I said, his response was always the same: "Nothing's wrong. This is your first time. Pregnancy is hard. You have to toughen up."

Over the months, he'd convinced me that I was nothing more than a high-strung mother-to-be. He was right; this was my first time being pregnant. What did I know? Maybe pregnancy was much harder than I imagined.

Even earlier tonight, I had heard Dr. Walters in my head and I told myself that what I was feeling was nothing, even though I knew it was something. Something was wrong.

The day didn't start out that way, though. It had been uneventful enough. I had spent most of the day in my chair, the one I'd been in for what felt like eternity, but it had really only been the last three months. That chair was my constant companion. I sat in it, ate in it, read in it, surfed the Internet in it, and yes, I even slept in it. With all the pain I was in, I couldn't do much else. I'd tried to go back to my bed, but I always ended up in that chair.

I wasn't used to sitting. I was used to moving, running, walking, and sometimes even flying by the seat of my pants. But now I had to live in this chair because, if I tried to sit or lie anywhere else, I couldn't breathe.

It was because of this life inside of me, a life that took my breath away, both figuratively and literally. At least that's what this little life I was carrying seemed to be doing.

It was ironic, really. Eight months earlier, the pregnancy test had turned pink and the baby I had wished for and prayed for had finally been conceived. Once I knew for sure that I was pregnant, she became the reason I *wanted* to breathe! She was my wish granted, the beginning of a new chapter in my life.

And my baby was a "she." I was being presumptuous by being so definite, but I was absolutely sure. I don't know if it was my intuition or if it was just that I wanted my baby to be a girl, all I knew was that I sensed "her" almost immediately. I was sure my little girl was going to be something with her daddy's looks and her mommy's personality. That's what my husband, Samson, always said too. "Our little girl is going to be a little me without the goatee," he joked.

Yes, our little girl was the most wanted baby in the world. I couldn't wait for her to get here, not only because I couldn't wait to meet her but because I wanted to get my life back. I needed to breathe again.

My husband jokingly blamed the pregnancy challenges on me. "You never do things the typical way, Angela," Samson said often. "You have to do everything the hard way." We laughed whenever he said that, but in a way it was true. Samson had told me that he'd fallen for me because I was a little different, unusual, even extraordinary. But he wouldn't have minded if this pregnancy was the complete opposite: uneventful, plain, and simple.

I squirmed a little in my chair, trying to find a way to be comfortable, when Samson looked over at me. "You okay?" he asked, pausing for a moment from stuffing his shirt into his overnight bag.

I nodded. What else was I going to say? I wasn't going to tell him about this mild headache that seemed to be crawling slowly toward becoming a migraine. I wasn't going to tell him about the contractions I'd felt earlier this morning that seemed to have gone away. And I wasn't going to tell him about the aches in my body or the pain in my limbs. Samson had heard it all before. So I said nothing and pretended that I was fine.

I once again found a comfortable spot in the chair, then watched my husband finish packing. He was full of excitement and flashed that smile I loved so much.

"This gig up in Toronto is going to be hot," he said.

I smiled at him, but the truth was that I was sad. I didn't want him to leave, not even for one night. But I knew he wanted and needed to go. And as a good wife, I wanted to support him.

This concert had been planned long ago and was the last event Samson had scheduled before our baby's due date. There was no way I could begrudge him. So I put on my brave face, even though I felt anything but brave.

With his bag in his hand, Samson said, "Okay, I think I have everything."

I smiled again.

"You sure you gonna be okay?" he asked.

"Of course," I said, telling him yes in as many ways as I could. "Definitely. I'll be fine."

Samson helped me stand up, then he held my hand as we slowly walked to the door. He kissed me on my forehead and then my lips. "I love you," he said.

"Me too."

"Call me if you need me."

"You know I will," I assured him.

He kissed me one last time, then I watched him retreat down the driveway, hop into our Cadillac, and slowly back out.

A deep longing filled me as I kept my eyes on the car. With the way I was feeling, you would have thought that Samson was leaving for a world tour instead of just an overnight gig. I stayed by the door until I couldn't see the car anymore, and only then did I back away. But before I closed the door, I glanced up at the darkened sky that was filled with masses of billowy black clouds. The clouds seemed to be gliding toward me and were so apropos as they matched my mood.

The storm that the weatherman had promised was making its way into Buffalo, and I hoped Samson would make it over the bridge in the quiet that always came before the storm.

It took a few minutes to waddle back to our bedroom, and once again I settled into my chair. I shifted until I found a spot that would keep me comfortable, at least for a few minutes, then I opened up my laptop and went to work.

About an hour later, I heard the whistle of the wind and the rustling of the leaves. Minutes after that, the branches of the young weeping willow we had planted began to tap on the side of the house. It sounded like this was going to be some storm.

I glanced up and shuddered but then turned my attention back to my computer. Maybe if I focused on something else, that would help. But it was hard to concentrate. Soon the taps of the branches turned to thuds. It felt as if the whole house were shaking.

I began to tremble along with the house. *Come on, Angela,* I thought, *there's nothing to be afraid of.* I tried to calm myself down, but it was difficult. I was still getting used to the sounds in our new house, and now as every branch hit the house or fell to the ground I shook in fear.

The Beginning of the End

Maybe if I stand up.

I pushed myself off the chair and made my way to the window. But then the glass began to quiver. Next came the rumble of the thunder that matched my headache that was now pounding against my temples. I tried to breathe deeply to relax, but when I heard panting I panicked.

What is that? It took me a couple of seconds to realize that the panting I heard was mine. My breathing had been so heavy in these last few months that I hardly recognized myself.

"Okay, Angela," I said to myself. "You're stressing yourself out for nothing." I figured if I talked to myself aloud, I'd be able to get this under control. "Just relax," I told myself again. I grimaced and laughed at the same time. Relax? Seriously? I hadn't been able to do that in …

Boom!

I screamed as the sound of a cannon filled the room and then the light that followed brightened the entire space. In the light, my shadow loomed large against the far wall—the only thing was that there were two shadowy figures on the wall. I whipped around in a panic, trying to see who was in the room with me. Blinking quickly, I tried to focus but couldn't. The room had started to move, and in seconds it was spinning. I tried once again to get control of my emotions.

Maybe if I sit down.

With the banging of the tree limbs, the whistling of the wind, and the roar of the thunder, I slowly walked back to the chair and then eased into it. But the moment I sat back, my throat constricted, as if someone had grabbed me and was squeezing the life out of me.

I put my hands on my throat, trying to rid myself of the choking sensation that was enveloping me. As the room filled with light, and then darkness, I couldn't get away. I couldn't breathe, and now I was consumed with pain too.

"Oh, God!" I screamed.

Through the pain, I pushed myself up once again. *If I can just make it to the phone that was on the nightstand.* But when I tried to take a step, I couldn't move. No matter what I did, I was frozen. Had fear gripped me so thoroughly that I could not will my legs and feet to walk? I closed my eyes and prayed, then moved my left foot, then my right one. My steps were short, slow, and heavy. Each step was filled with pain.

If I can just make it to the phone.

Between the chair and the nightstand, there was a table I looked to as my savior. My plan was to get to the table, then I could drag myself to the nightstand. But when I leaned on the table, a searing pain cut through me like a knife.

Was that a contraction?

Then a bolt of lightning. Next, the crackling roar of thunder. I screamed.

That fear seemed to drive me and I dragged myself to the nightstand and grabbed the phone. I pressed 9, the first number I needed for an emergency. But then I wondered what I was going to tell the police. That I was being attacked by lightning? That I was afraid of thunder? So I hung up and then dialed another number. I called the person I knew would rescue me. The man who always did.

My fingers were stiff as I dialed the number. After the third ring, I heard his voice. "Hello."

I only got out a breathy, "Dad!"

"Angie!" he exclaimed. Concern was already in his voice.

I wanted to say more, tell him everything that was going on, but I couldn't speak through my labored breathing. "Dad," was all I could say. That was all he needed.

"I'm on my way!" he shouted. Then I heard the dial tone.

My father didn't know what was going on, but it didn't matter. My protective and doting father was coming to save me. I collapsed on the side of the bed as the pain once again gripped every part of me. I needed my father here. I needed to get to the hospital.

2

(From Angela)

As I sat waiting for my father to show up, I tried to figure out exactly what I was feeling. One minute my heart raced, the next it slowed down. Raced, then slowed. And in between I was scared—not so much for me but for my baby.

Was this just pregnancy nerves? No, it couldn't be—there was too much pain surging through my body for it to be nothing more than my nerves. Something was wrong and I had to do everything I could to save my baby.

In one of my slower-heart moments, I pushed myself from the bed, then waddled toward the closet. I tried to ignore the sounds of the storm that crashed through the walls. All of my attention, all of my energy, needed to be focused on getting to my closet so I could be ready when my father came, so he could get me to the hospital.

My hospital bag had been packed for weeks. For a while now, I'd wanted my doctor to induce labor because I'd been in so much pain, and because I was having such a tough time breathing. But, as always, whenever I complained about my symptoms, Dr. Walters merely said, "Toughen up."

With the way I was feeling now, I wasn't going to let anything stop me. I was going to get to the hospital, and this time they were going to take care of me and my baby. I was moving slowly, but my steps slowed even more as my world became unfocused. I blinked, trying to get my vision clear, but when I opened my eyes I was still unstable. I was surrounded by two images of everything: two chests, two chairs, two doors. I glanced over my shoulder—two beds. And then black spots appeared.

"Oh, God!" I whispered.

My dad didn't live far away; it would only take him minutes to arrive, and then less than five minutes for us to get to the hospital. But still I wanted to meet him at the door with my bag so that we could leave right away.

It felt like an eternity had passed by the time I made it to the closet, but I had to lean against the door to catch my breath and garner some strength. In that moment I seemed to have every symptom that I'd had throughout my pregnancy: I was dizzy, my feet were swollen to the point where they were cracked and bleeding, and I was having a hard time breathing.

I'd never had all of these symptoms at one time. But tonight, every symptom, every pain, had descended on me. It felt as if I were moving in circles even though I was standing still.

"Maybe I should call an ambulance," I said aloud. But then Dr. Walters' voice spoke to me with the words he always said: *It's all in your head.* Dr. Walters' voice was louder than my own, and so I decided that I didn't need the ambulance. I could wait for my father.

That's right. I heard Dr. Walters' voice again as if he were in the room with me. *This is probably just the beginning of labor. This is your first baby. This is how you're supposed to feel.*

Even as the doctor spoke in my mind, I knew what I was feeling wasn't right. Just like all the times when I spoke to him in his office, I knew what he was telling me wasn't right. But he was the doctor. He was the one with the medical degree. What did I know?

I grabbed my bag and made my way out of the room. The breathing exercises that I'd learned from Lamaze were helping, but I wasn't doing them for contractions. I was doing those exercises just so I could keep breathing. How long had it been since I'd been able to catch my breath?

It's in your head. There was Dr. Walters' voice again. One side of me agreed with the doctor. My baby had probably just shifted, pushing herself against my lungs. Maybe that was why all of my air seemed to be seeping out of me.

Finally, I made it to the door. I dropped the bag there, then collapsed at the edge of the stairs. I sat up. There was no way I was going to lie back down again. Time moved slowly as I listened to the passing seconds of the grandfather clock inside and the roaring storm outside. With each passing second, I breathed in, then tried to breathe out. It took every bit of my strength to do so, and I wanted to pass out because of the pain.

Then I heard it. The sound of rescue. The car tires screeched into the driveway and then a few seconds later, "Ang'!" My father called out before he even got to the front door. "I'm here. I'm here!" he yelled.

"Dad!" I felt as if I were screaming, but the word came out as a whimper. I was grateful I'd given my father a key to our house when we moved in—you know, just in case. Especially since I was pregnant. If my father didn't have a key, I would have never been able to make it to the door.

My dad was wearing a raincoat, but he was still soaked, as if he'd been standing in the rain. It must've been coming down hard out there. Then I saw his face. My father's cocoa-colored skin seemed too pale as he looked at me. I guessed I was quite a sight, sprawled out at the end of the stairs.

"I was trying to get to the door to wait for you," I told him. "But this is as far as I could get."

"That's okay, baby," he said. "I'm here now."

"I don't know if I can walk."

My father stood there for a moment; both of us knew this was trouble. I had gained at least a hundred pounds during this pregnancy, and I didn't know how my father was going to get me to the car. In the next second he squatted, then hoisted me up into his arms. With a strength I didn't know he had, he carried me (though he staggered a bit) through the rain and into his car.

"My bag!" I said as we sped out of the driveway.

"That's okay," he said. "I'll come back for it. I've got to get you to the hospital."

Even though we weren't far from the hospital, every few seconds my father asked me if I was all right. I kept telling him that I was okay even though I wasn't. He knew that. My father could hear me breathing … or rather struggling to breathe.

As my father drove, I felt every move of the car, every bump in the road. *I'll be okay once I get to the hospital.* That's what I kept telling myself. That's where I kept my focus.

My dad screeched to a halt in front of the glass doors to the emergency room. He jumped out and waved his arms, yelling, "Help me! Help me!" In just a few seconds two nurses ran out, one rolling a wheelchair.

"What do we have here?" one of the nurses asked.

"My daughter," my father said. "She's pregnant. I think she's in labor, but she's having a hard time breathing."

"Okay, let's get her inside."

I was grateful the rain had let up. It now felt like a shower as the nurses scooped me from the front of my dad's car and settled me into the wheelchair. I was going to be okay now. It was all going to be okay.

I was already preregistered at the hospital for my delivery, so when my father gave my name to the admissions attendant inside, she told my father, "You can roll her right up to labor and delivery."

Calm was returning as my father and one of the nurses pushed me into the elevator. "I have a new admit here," she said to one of the nurses at the desk on the third floor.

The nurse pointed and my father wheeled me right into a room.

When the nurse settled me into the bed, I told her I had to call my husband. "Go ahead," she nodded as she covered me with a sheet.

"Dad, can I use your phone?" I asked since I didn't have a thing with me.

"Sure, baby," he said. He handed me his phone and I dialed as quickly as I could. If I was having this baby, then Samson had to be here for the birth of our daughter.

I was both surprised and relieved when Samson answered after just a couple of rings. I wasn't sure what he'd be doing, though I knew he was close to being on stage. From all the background noise, I could tell that the club where he was performing was packed.

"Baby, it's me," I said.

"Angie!" he said. "What's wrong?"

"Nothing now," I told him. "But I'm at the hospital. Dad brought me here because I was having a hard time breathing. I wanted to make sure that everything was all right with the baby."

"What?" Sam said. "Ang'! I can't hear you. What did you say?"

I sighed. The music was too loud. Would he ever hear me?

"Ang'!" he said again. "What's wrong?"

"I'm at the hospital," I repeated, a bit louder this time. "I can't breathe!"

The phone went dead. I wasn't sure if Samson heard everything or not, but I had a feeling that he would be right here. He was only about ninety minutes away and he wasn't going to let me go through this by myself.

A young blonde doctor entered the room just as I was handing the phone back to my father. By her youthful appearance, I figured she was a resident. "What's going on with you, young lady?" she asked me. She seemed rather chipper for someone who was on the late-night shift.

I managed to force a smile. "I hope that I'm having a baby tonight," I told her, "but I'm actually here because I'm having trouble breathing."

"Well, let's get some labs on you and see what's going on," she said in a tone that was filled with concern.

Once I was back in the room, the doctor asked a nurse to draw some blood while she examined me. When her hands gently squeezed my legs, the smile on her face faded away. She lifted the sheet and inspected my legs and feet. "You're swollen," she said.

"I know. I've been this way for months," I told her.

With the sheet drawn back, she squeezed my leg again and when her hand left an imprint, her smile completely disappeared. "Okay, let's get a fetal monitor in here," she ordered.

Within seconds, a machine appeared. After she hooked me up, she did a pelvic exam. "You're two centimeters dilated," she told me. Then she added, "Did you know that you were having contractions?"

"Not really," I replied. "I'm just trying to breathe here." We both laughed a little.

"I'm a little worried about your blood pressure," she said, "which is quite high right now." I nodded because I didn't know what she wanted me to say. "Let me get the results from your labs and I'll be right back."

When she left the room, my dad made his way to me. "You're in the right place now," he said while patting my hand. "They're going to take care of you." He was always the reassuring father. He stayed by my side until the resident returned just a few minutes later.

"Well, I've got some news," she began. "I'm recommending that we induce labor."

My head fell back and I looked up toward the ceiling. "Thank you," I whispered to God, to the doctor, and to myself. Finally! Relief washed over me. Tonight would be the night that my baby was going to come and I was going to feel better.

As she held the paperwork in her hand, the doctor explained, "We found protein in your urine, your blood platelets are low, and with your shortness of breath and high blood pressure I think it's a must that we induce you."

"Okay," I said, nodding my head as hard as I could. I wanted to make sure she knew I completely agreed with her.

"All I have to do is confer with Dr. Walters," she told me, "and then we can get your Pitocin started."

The doctor stepped out of the room and the small smile on my face went away. *Oh, God! She has to talk to Dr. Walters? Why?*

"What's wrong, baby?" my father asked. We were so close, so tuned in that my father could feel the change in my mood. I shook my head as if I were okay, even though the hope I felt a minute ago began to fade.

Knowing Dr. Walters, he was going to stop it. He was going to tell the resident that it was all in my head. That I was a first-time mother who just needed to toughen up. She was going to walk back in here and tell me that I'd have to do this for another month. And I knew that I wouldn't make it. Not for thirty days. I wasn't sure if I could make it through another day.

Please, God. Please, God. Please, God!

When the doctor returned to my room, I wanted to cover my ears. She said, "Well, Dr. Walters said that since you're here and admitted, we might as well induce you."

If I'd had any energy, I would've pumped my fist into the air. I could tell by the resident's tone that it hadn't been an easy call. Dr. Walters was probably hesitant, still wanting to leave me in all of this discomfort and pain. But he had finally said yes and I was going to have my baby.

"I'm going to send in the nurses who'll get you set up and going," she said. "And then I'll be back to check on you soon."

Between my slow breaths, I thanked her. I was sure she could hear my relief. I waited until the doctor stepped out of the room before I turned to my father. "Sam's not here," I said. "If they're going to induce labor … suppose he doesn't get here in time?"

Just the thought of Sam not being with me made my breathing more labored. I couldn't do this without him. After all we'd been through with this pregnancy, I wanted—I needed—him here.

"Calm down, honey," my dad said. "Don't get excited. I'll give him a call and find out where he is."

"Okay," I said.

Inside my heart I called out for Samson. And then I heard him shout my name: "Ang'! Ang'!"

I thought I was imagining it. Hardly an hour had passed since I called him. There was no way he could have gotten to me this fast. Then I heard him again: "Ang'!" he yelled.

My father grinned. "He's here." He moved toward the door to greet my husband.

But before my father could get to the door, Sam burst into the room in full panic mode. "Baby, I'm here," he gasped as if he were out of breath. As if we were in a movie, he rushed into my arms and we held each other. My heart had called out to him and he appeared.

Samson stepped back as if he didn't want to get too far away. "What's wrong?" he asked, looking from me to my father and then back to me again.

I broke it down into the fewest words as possible. "I couldn't breathe," I told him, "but it turned out that it was probably just contractions."

"Contractions?" he shouted.

I nodded and tried to take a couple of deep breaths. "They're going to induce me."

He leaned over and squeezed me even tighter. As he held me, I could feel his relief. "So we're going to have the baby tonight?" he whispered.

"Our baby is coming," I said as I nodded.

When Sam sat on the edge of the bed, I turned to my father. He was smiling, but his eyes were weary. He had to be tired. Not only had he rescued me, but he'd had to endure my pain, which was something he wasn't good at. He could take a lot, but he couldn't stand to see either of his daughters hurting.

"Dad, why don't you go home, get some rest, and then come back," I suggested.

My father frowned as if he had no intention of going anywhere.

"You know how long these things usually take," I continued. "It'll be a couple of hours, and now that Sam's here, he'll call you when it gets closer to the time."

"Are you sure?" he asked.

"Yes." My father's tiredness was only one reason I wanted to send him away. I wanted him to go because if he'd had a hard time watching me already, I didn't know what was going to happen to him when I had a contraction that I could actually feel. Between breaths I tried to smile to reassure him. "It's okay," I said. "Really. We'll call you when I get to seven centimeters."

It took my father a moment to agree. "But I'm not going home," he said. "I'll go get some coffee, but I'm going to be close by." He leaned over and gave me a hug.

"Thank you, Daddy," I whispered.

He kissed my forehead, hugged Sam, and then left us alone.

Sam picked up my hand and held it between his. "So this all happened right after I left?" he asked.

I wanted to answer him, I wanted to tell him everything, but a contraction seared through my body much like the pain I'd had at home. I had to focus on breathing.

"Baby?" Sam whispered.

I closed my eyes and tried to breathe more deeply. I had a feeling that if I thought my pregnancy had been difficult to this point, it was about to get much harder.

Just as the contraction subsided, two nurses entered my room. "Okay," one of them said to me. "We need to insert a Foley catheter."

I only had two thoughts: *You need to insert a what? And you need to insert what where?*

The nurse must've seen Sam's and my confusion because she

went on to say, "This is standard procedure with labor and delivery. I just need for you to lie back."

"Lie back?" Sam and I said together. I hadn't lain flat on my back in well over three months because whenever I did I couldn't breathe. That was my biggest complaint to Dr. Walters, but I could never get him to listen to me. I couldn't get him to believe me.

"No," I said, shaking my head at the nurse. "I'm already having a hard enough time breathing. You have to find another way."

The two nurses looked at me as if they were not about to allow me to make their jobs more difficult. "This is the way that we do it," the nurse who had been doing all the talking said. "It won't take long. We'll be done in a minute or two and then you can sit right back up."

"Does she really need the catheter?" my husband asked. "Isn't there another way you can do it without her lying flat?"

The nurses gave us a look that said, *Look, we do this every day and you're trying to tell us what to do?*

Finally, the other nurse spoke: "The doctor said you have to have the Foley."

"What about my breathing?" I asked. "I haven't lain flat in months."

"You won't be lying down for long," the other nurse said as if none of this were a big deal.

Why did I have such a hard time getting anyone to listen to me? "I came to the hospital because I was having a hard time breathing," I told them. "I'm afraid this will make it worse."

"Listen," a nurse said, "if it's pain you're worried about, I'll give you some numbing gel and you'll be fine."

The other nurse added, "Like I told you already, this will only take a couple of minutes, but we have to do it now."

I was so tired of fighting. And the numbing gel sounded good. I looked to my husband for his opinion and he shrugged. "I guess we have to do it," he said.

Breathe

The nurse closest to my bedside hit the button for the bed to recline. As I slowly went back, I grabbed Sam's hand and focused on the relief that was coming. In just a few hours this would all be over. Our baby would be born.

The bed continued its slow recline until I was flat on my back. I took a deep breath and waited for trouble to come, but my first thought was about how good it actually felt. I hadn't been in this position in so long and my thoughts went to all the nights when I'd tried to get a good night's sleep while propped upright in a chair. It was impossible and uncomfortable, especially after all of these weeks of being in the chair.

I felt gloved hands pushing my legs apart and then the cool gel was applied. "Now, you might feel a pinch," one of the nurses said, though I couldn't see which nurse was speaking.

I closed my eyes, squeezed my husband's hand, and stayed focused with positive thoughts of my baby.

"Okay, it's in," she said.

Instantly I was relieved. Like the nurses had promised, that hadn't taken much time. And I was okay.

"We can lift you up now," the nurse said.

I heard the buzz first and then felt the slow rise of the bed. I waited a couple of seconds before I unpeeled my eyes and looked into my husband's. "That wasn't too bad."

He smiled. And then …

I gasped and choked and struggled to get one breath out of my body. Fear and panic filled me. I opened my mouth, trying to pull air inside. But that didn't work. I turned to my husband with my eyes wide. I fought to breathe. I fought to speak. It took a moment, but three words finally squeaked out of me: "I. Can't. Breathe!"

Sam's smile turned upside down. "Ang'! What's wrong?"

"I. Can't. Breathe!"

We turned to the nurse, and together we said, "Help!"

I had a feeling that single word might be the last word I would ever speak. Every fiber of my being knew that life was leaving me. Rapid-fire thoughts passed through my mind. But it was strange—even though I was fighting to stay alive, I was more alert than ever. Every one of my senses were working overtime.

This is it! my mind told me.

The nurses looked at each other and practically rolled their eyes. One of the nurses walked over to Sam and the other to me. At almost the same time, they patted us on our backs, patronizing us as if we were children.

"She's having a panic attack," the nurse who had gone to my husband told him.

I guessed the fact that I was dying meant nothing.

The nurse who hovered over me said, "There, there," in a voice that was supposed to be soothing. "The Foley is in. You'll be okay now."

My eyes bulged inside my head. "I. Can't. Breathe," I repeated. I felt like I was screaming, but my words were no more than a whimper.

My nurse shook her head and waved her hand at the same time. "You're going to have to calm her down."

Samson took his job much more seriously than the nurses. He turned to me. "Ang', calm down," he said. "You're okay." Those were his words, but in his expression I could see his panic—the way his eyes widened, the shallow breaths that he was taking.

"I. Can't. Breathe!" I told him like I'd told everyone else. If anyone would believe me, it would be Samson.

"Calm down, Angela," one of the nurses said in a sterner voice than she'd been using. As if being stern was going to save my life.

I wanted to scream again, but I didn't have enough air to say another word. My mind took over and began to play out the many scenes of my life. As life drained from me, I was reminded of all I'd lived. At the same time, I saw everything I would never see.

Like my baby! *Dear God, my baby!*

Would my baby live? I prayed she would. And Samson would

take good care of her since I wouldn't be there for her. He would be a great father.

Father! My father! What would he do when he found out that I'd died and he wasn't by my side? He would never forgive himself. "Get my father!" I struggled to say to my husband.

As life drained from me, I wanted my father there. If I was going to die, I wanted the last people around me to be my father, my husband, and my unborn baby.

Hold on, Angela. Hold on. Even though that's what I kept saying to myself, I didn't think I'd be able to hold on until my father got there. I was fading fast. I fought to scream again. "Help me, please! Somebody help me." I was filled with such desperation that I barely recognized my own voice.

When the nurses didn't respond, Sam went into action. He pushed past the nurses and went screaming into the hall. "We need help!"

In less than a minute, more nurses rushed into the room, rolling machines on carts, then pushing needles and tubes into me, hooking me up to life machines. As soon as I was connected to the machines, they shrilled warnings that something was wrong. The machines told the nurses what I'd been saying. I was in trouble.

I heard the patter of running footsteps and the room filled with more hospital personnel. "What's happening here?" I heard someone yell. If I could have answered, I would have told him that I was struggling to live. But the words wouldn't come out as I held myself up using the bed rails.

Chaos filled the room. Nurses pushed in crash carts. The doctor yelled out orders. And the whole time I screamed, "Help me!"

Another nurse ran into the room and her eyes locked with mine. "Hello, beautiful," she said as she shone a light into my right eye, then my left. Her words, her tone, showed me kindness. "I'm going to help you," she said. "Tell me what's happening."

The weight of my head was too much for me to hold it up, so I let my chin fall to my chest. "I. Can't. Breathe," I wheezed.

Over her shoulder, I saw another woman rush into my room. Her eyebrows were bunched together as if she were trying to assess the situation. "Where's her labs?" Her tone was stern, but then she looked at me and her expression changed. She was warm and inviting.

She glanced down at my chart before she moved toward me, wearing a gentle smile. "We're going to help you," she said softly as she placed her hand on my leg. But when she touched me, her smile went away. "She's got at least a plus two edema." As she backed away and shouted orders, she nodded to a couple of nurses who turned to my husband.

"Mr. Logan, we have to ask you to step out of the room," one of them said.

"No!" he shouted. I knew Sam would never leave my side.

"Mr. Logan, please." I watched as two nurses pulled Samson away.

"Ang'!" he yelled. "Ang'!"

I garnered enough strength to hold myself up, keep my head still, and lock eyes on my husband. Suppose this was the last time I ever saw Samson? I wanted his image solidly in my mind.

As Samson was dragged through the door, another man came in pushing a cart. He didn't speak a word, but he looked at me. His eyes spoke to mine without uttering a word. His gaze said, *I am here to help*, as he eased his cart next to the bed. He lifted my arm and I'm not sure what he did next.

Then … I saw *him*! Actually, it was more like I sensed him. I managed to turn my head and there he was, entering the room. Dr. Walters. My doctor.

Slowly, my eyes made their way up his blue-mist-colored scrubs, to his face that seemed to be growing paler by the second. Then our eyes locked. He seemed transfixed, though he kept moving toward me. It was as if he were being pulled into the chaos, drawing closer to me and closer to the truth that this was all happening because of him. It was happening because he hadn't listened to me. It was happening because he hadn't treated my symptoms.

Even though what I was going through was Dr. Walters' fault, I was desperate, and so my mind pleaded with him: *Please, help me!* But just as quickly, the plea in my mind was followed by, *I tried to tell you that I couldn't breathe. And now, because of you, I'm dying.*

Dread and doom were in his eyes as I labored to breathe. And he labored the same way. As the air left my body, it seemed to be doing the same to him. He broke his gaze and his eyes took a slow tour around the room filled with frenzied doctors and nurses. When he turned back to me, his entire essence seemed to say, *What have I done?*

I wanted to scream that this was all his fault. He was the reason I would never see my baby. It was because of him I wouldn't get to love my husband anymore. It was entirely his fault that my father would blame himself for the rest of his life.

But I couldn't scream any of that because that was the moment I felt it. My last ounce of strength was being squeezed from me. In my mind and my spirit, I knew this was it. This was the end. I had to conserve my remaining energy and this moment wisely. With all the strength I had left, I lifted my head and raised my eyes toward the ceiling. I inhaled, then exhaled, calling out, "Jesus, please help me."

That was it. My fingers relaxed, and with nothing to hold me up I crashed back on the bed. I heard the thud as I fell back. I was in the position I feared the most—flat on my back.

This time, I didn't want to scream. I felt no pain. All I did was close my eyes and give in. I gave in to the white light.

3

The Rider on the White Horse

(From Angela)

In that white light, I drifted back to memories, drifted back in time. Back to Samson's and my beginning—September 1999.

My family was planning a wedding for my younger sister. Kristy and Pete had been dating for a while and I was excited about my brother-in-law to be. I'd known Pete since grade school. In Mrs. Jones' sixth grade class, we sat next to each other in the front row. We were both in our awkward stage then—me with my Coke bottle glasses, and he with his braces and chubby cheeks. But now his boyishness was gone, and he stood handsome and ready to marry my sister.

Kristy and I were more than sisters—we were best friends. As her maid of honor, I was involved in every aspect of her wedding planning. Actually, Kristy's wedding was an event that had already been conjured up in her mind since she was a flower girl in our cousin's wedding many years before. When the time finally came for Kristy's wedding, she didn't need a year to plan. Three months was all she needed.

I wanted to do something special for my sister's wedding. For weeks I wondered what I could add to make the already grand celebration even more special. Pete was Italian, and according to his family traditions, this wedding was going to be a big party with lots of food, lots to drink, and lots of fun. I needed to add something to all of that.

It took me a few weeks to figure it out, but I finally came up with an idea. I would bring in a national recording artist to sing at Kristy's wedding. That would be the perfect gift. My first thought was that I could get Brian McKnight. He was from Buffalo, and though I didn't know him, I knew people who did. I was hoping that the six degrees of separation theory would work and so I started calling people. But after a few weeks of no response, I had to admit it wasn't happening.

I told my dilemma to one of my best friends, April, who'd grown up with Kristy and me. April was Kristy's best friend; we were all as close as sisters.

"If you can't get Brian," April asked me, "what are you going to do?"

"I don't know," I told her. "That's why I'm calling you. You have to help me think this out."

"What about Samson Logan?" she asked.

"Hmm," I hummed, giving it some thought. I'd heard about this guy, mostly from my sister and April, who always talked about him. He was a rising star who was beginning to have a lot of buzz, especially in our city, since he was from Buffalo too.

"Yeah," April said. "I think he'd be good. His songs are getting a lot of play time in New York, and I heard he's actually doing a project right now with Devante." That had to be good—Devante was part of Jodeci. "And," April continued as if she were his publicist, "you know his signature song is 'Ribbon in the Sky.' That would be the perfect song for Kristy's wedding."

I hadn't heard Samson sing, but from what Kristy told me, every time she heard him she melted. "Yeah, yeah," I said going over all the checkpoints in my head. "He would be great."

"I'll get in touch with him," April said.

I hung up the phone feeling good because April had known Samson over the years and I figured she could make it happen. But when I didn't hear anything after a few days, I called her.

"What's going on?" I asked her. "Have you got ahold of Samson yet?"

"Don't worry," she assured me, "I'm on it. We're gonna get him."

So I left it all in April's hands and went back to focusing on my life. Things were really good for me at that time. I had just bought my first home and I was feeling good in my own skin for the first time in a long time. I didn't judge myself as I'd done so harshly in my teen years, criticizing every curve, noticing every blemish. I was finally appreciating me—both the good and the not so perfect. I was beginning to embrace myself and love myself. I was really happy.

This introspection came at a time when I was going through what I termed "the change," or "men-o-pause." At my age, it wasn't the natural order of things to give up dating guys, but it was necessary. I actually hadn't dated much, but the relationships I'd been in had gone far south. So I decided to take some time to focus on taking care of me instead of everyone else, especially a man.

This wasn't easy at first. My men-o-pause came with the typical symptoms: mood swings, irritability, crying jags, even night sweats. It was something I had to do, though. In my last relationship, I'd given everything—my love, my time, and my commitment to my man—because I'd wanted to be a considerate, caring, loyal woman who would eventually become his wife. But that breakup had left my emotional pitcher empty. I had nothing left to give to myself, let alone another man.

As the days moved on, I began to feel content, something I hadn't felt since my college days at Syracuse University. While there I was often struck with a feeling that I was in the right place, doing the right thing, at the right time. I was never able to explain why I felt that, but I did, and I felt it deeply. Even though things weren't always perfect in college, I still had contentment and peace.

This gift hadn't stayed with me, though. After graduation, there were times when I felt everything but being sure of myself. I often wished I could have bottled that feeling so that I could have sampled it and shared it whenever I needed. But, of course, I couldn't, and after college I can't say I felt that feeling too much.

So when this feeling came back to me, I knew I was doing the right thing by taking this break to focus on me. During this time, I became a homebody and I loved it. Even though I spent a great deal of time alone, I was completely content and happy with not meeting any guys and not dating.

Kristy and April didn't agree with my decision to take this break, however. For the two years I'd taken this sabbatical, they were constantly telling me I had to get out and meet people. "No one is just gonna drive up to your house, knock on your front door, and find you," Kristy said all of the time. "You have to get out some time."

I told them every time they tried to drag me out someplace that I was fine. Kristy and April didn't really understand all that I'd been through. I'd had a couple of relationships with men who had a little notoriety. It always started out good but always ended up bad. I wanted to be free from all of that. Plus, I trusted God. I believed his timing for me to meet someone would be perfect.

I certainly wasn't looking for any man that September day. The weather in Buffalo can be weird at times, and there are many Septembers that already feel like winter. But this day was sunny and bright. With the temperatures in the seventies, I figured it would be a good time to wash my windows. I put on a T-shirt and jeans, pulled my hair back, and went outside without makeup, of course. With a bucket, a couple of sponges, and towels, I went to work.

Not only did I love my house, but I loved my neighborhood too. It had all the sounds of home: the rustle of leaves in the wind, children's laughter carried by a breeze, the melody of a jogger's feet, the whish of a stroller along the sidewalk. I even enjoyed the panting of Chance, my neighbor's dog. Even though I was used to the melodies and harmonies of my neighborhood, I wasn't used to the sound I heard as I finished washing the first window.

Where in the world is that coming from? Those bumping drum-beats were not the norm on this street. Turning around, I spotted the culprit—a shiny white Mustang rolling down the street. And I mean *shiny*. Everything on this car sparkled—from the windows to the rims. I watched as the car eased up and parked in front of my house.

I wasn't expecting anyone, so dropping the towel onto my porch, I trotted down the steps to check out who it was. As I got closer, the man slipped out of his car, and my eyes widened. "Oh my gosh!" I said with a grin. "Sam!"

He walked up and I threw my arms around him, giving him a huge hug. I couldn't believe it. April had done what she promised. Sam must've been so excited about the invitation to sing at Kristy's wedding that he decided to come and speak to me in person.

"So April got in touch with you!" I said.

"April?" he said with a confused look on his face.

"Yeah. April," I said, starting to sound confused myself. "She told you about singing at my sister's wedding."

"Your sister?"

"Yeah," I said, taking a couple of steps back from him. He sounded like he had no idea what I was talking about. "Aren't you here because of my sister's wedding?"

"No," he said as he shook his head. "I have no idea who your sister is. I stopped because I saw *you*." My smile slowly melted into puzzlement. "I stopped because I saw you on the porch and I said to myself, 'Oh my gosh. That's my wife!'"

I nearly put my hands on my hips at those words, but I caught myself and shifted my stance instead. It took a moment for his words to make sense. *He hadn't come to talk to me about the wedding? He just drove up in front of my house?* It was hard to believe, so I backed up and started all over.

"I thought you were here because my friend, April Jones, had gotten ahold of you."

"No," he said, shaking his head and beginning to grin.

I could tell he thought I was just coming on to him, but I wanted him at Kristy's wedding, so I told him everything. I told him about April and Kristy and how I wanted to hire him to sing at Kristy's wedding.

His eyes widened as I talked. "You're Kristy's sister?" he asked. "I didn't even know that Kris had a sister. Especially not one this beautiful." I glanced down at his words, hoping that his flattery meant that I was going to get what I wanted. When I looked back up into his eyes, I waited for him to say something about my request.

"Okay," he said, "I might be able to do that. But first we should go out and talk about it."

"Go out?" I asked. Now I was the one thinking he was coming on to me. "We don't need to go out. I just told you about it. All we need to do is make plans for the wedding. It's in a little more than two weeks, on October eighth. I can give you all the information on where it's gonna be and the time—"

He held up his hand. "No, we have to go out and talk about it."

I sighed but gave in—this was too important. What else was I going to do? We exchanged numbers, but I had no plans to call him for anything except Kristy's wedding.

Before I turned away to go into my house, I asked him, "So if you didn't just ride up to the front of my house for my sister, why were you here?"

He pointed down the street. "My sister Tonnie just purchased a house down there. I was in New York and came home for the weekend to check her out." Then he said, "I'll hit you up later." Then he got in his car and drove away.

I had to ask myself, *Really? Had I just really met Samson Logan?*

Just like he said, Samson called me the next day. "Let's go out," he said. "And while we're out, we can talk about your sister's wedding."

Besides the fact that he'd given me a line about being his wife, I could tell he was genuinely interested in me. But I wasn't interested in him. I was fine by myself. Plus, if I was to get into a new relationship, I was going to do it with a regular guy who had a regular job, someone who wasn't in the limelight. "I really don't want to do that," I said, trying to be as nice as I could because I still wanted him to sing.

"Okay, I'll call you again tomorrow," he said as if he hadn't heard me. "We'll work out the details."

He wasn't hearing me. I wasn't going out with him.

After we hung up, I called April and told her what had happened. She was excited about me meeting Samson, but she was even more excited when I told her that he wanted to go out with me.

"Ang', you should do it," she told me.

"No," was all I said.

"He's a really nice guy," April said. "Go out with him."

"No," was all I said again.

"I really like him. I really think you should go out with him."

I didn't know how many times I had to tell her no. She was as bad as Samson. Everyone needed to know that me going out with Samson was never going to happen.

The next day, Samson called again. "Hey," he said. "Tomorrow's my birthday, so it's gonna be real cool when we go out so that we can talk about your sister's wedding."

"I'd rather just tell you everything you need to know over the phone," I said, telling him the same thing I'd said the day before.

"Well, if you're not going to go out with me, then I'm not gonna be able to do it."

Inside, I screamed. *Blackmail? Really?* I wanted to yell at him, but all I said to him was, "Okay! Fine!"

"Great!" he said as if he hadn't just twisted my arm.

As we made plans on where we were going to meet, I had an idea. "Okay, and just so you know," I told him, "April will be with me 'cause she's my sister's wedding planner," making up the story quickly. If April was with me, I'd feel much safer.

"Okay, that'll be cool," he said.

I hung up, called April, and noticed it didn't even take a minute to convince her. She couldn't wait for all of us to get together.

The next day, April and I drove to where Sam told me to meet him. He told me he was going to be with a friend named Flute by the food court at the mall. It was easy to find them when we arrived. Even though we'd come into the mall on the first level, as we rode up the escalators, we could hear Samson and Flute three stories up. They were laughing and cracking themselves up, and as I soon found out, they were like that all of the time.

When we got to the mall that day, I didn't know they were the ones making all the noise. Once I realized this, I shot April a glance that simply read, *Seriously?* April grabbed my arm and whispered, "Don't worry," even though she was glaring herself.

Sam noticed us approaching before his friend did. "Hey," he said, popping up out of his chair and pulling out chairs for April and me. As he stood, I took in the black jeans and tight-fitted shirt he wore that showed off his physique. It wasn't hard to see there was no body fat on him. And then there was his chiseled face, his strong jawline, and his broad smile framed by a well-groomed mustache and goatee. His hair was curly on top and glistened under the florescent lights. He definitely had movie-star looks and a musician's swagger. I could see how my sister and other women swooned during his shows.

Once we sat, I got down to business, telling Samson all about the wedding, the plans that were in place, and how wonderful it would be if he sang to my sister and Pete. After just a couple of minutes, Sam agreed to sing "Ribbon in the Sky." I wanted to lean over and hug him.

Breathe

After we left the mall, Samson didn't stop calling me. Between September 23 and October 8, he called me just about every day. Don't get me wrong: I thought he was a really nice guy and he was certainly more than a little bit attractive. He was six feet tall, brown skinned, and very fit. His smile just added to the whole package.

He had it going on professionally too. He was working with quite a few recording artists—he was a rising star. The world was going to hear a lot more from Samson Logan. And it was because of that that I wasn't interested in him. When I was ready for a relationship again, I was going to meet a regular guy—not someone who was known by others. There was nothing regular or ordinary about Sam.

However, he wasn't getting any of my messages. And it was hard to say no to his phone calls because every time we talked we had a great time. I felt as if I'd always known him. Our talking wasn't just on the phone, though. Between our first meeting and the wedding, we went out a few more times to talk about the details of the wedding—at least that was the excuse Sam always used.

On the day of Kristy's wedding, I tried to keep all of my thoughts on the occasion. But as the girls in the wedding party dressed at my house, there was a nagging tug in the back of my mind: I wanted to look good ... for Samson. That realization made me giddy even as I tried to suppress the feeling.

I was able to take my mind off Samson long enough to enjoy my sister's wedding. It was amazing—from the way our dapper dad escorted her down the aisle to Kenny Lattimore's tune "For You," to the way my sister expressed her joy through a smile and spontaneous laughter rather than through the tears that everyone expected. The ceremony was beautiful, sentimental, lovely, and short, which was fine with me. I couldn't wait for the reception and my surprise guest.

The reception was held at Rich's Atrium, a spectacular venue where the guests had to cross over a pond on a small wooden bridge adorned with sparkling white lights. Luscious green plants flanked both sides of the bridge. When we walked into the room, we were assaulted with the fragrance of all the food. Servers wandered through the crowd with hors d'oeuvre trays and champagne. And guests marveled at the display of cakes that was a gift to my sister and her husband by Pete's aunt Linda, who was one of the best bakers in the state.

When Kristy and Pete arrived, the reception was already in full swing. It was a party and everyone was having a great time ... everyone, except our father. Our dad was a ball of nerves as he got ready to do his toast. He went over the four lines he'd prepared, at least one hundred times with me. I was nervous too because I had to give my own toast, and then sometime after that I'd be introducing Samson. Both my father and I were pacing back and forth.

It wasn't that I thought Sam was going to do anything wrong; it's just that I wanted everything to go right. This wedding was the blending of two cultures and the uniting of two families. I wanted Samson to be another addition to make the wedding even more fun and enjoyable than it already was.

It's going to be fine, Angela, I kept telling myself through my toast and then through my father's.

When I got word that Samson had arrived, I stood at the door and waited. And then ... oh my gosh. Samson walked in. And as he moved toward me, it was like a halo hovered over him. He wore a dark suit, but jazzed it up a bit by wearing just a white tank top underneath. He looked extra good. As he strutted into the room, I could hear the whispers:

"Who's that?"

"Oh my gosh!"

"Is that Samson Logan?"

He was causing such a stir that I had to go ahead and make my surprise announcement before Kris and Pete figured out what was going on. I signaled the DJ, then quickly made my way up to the stage. The lights dimmed and the room was bathed in the soft red up lights while yellow and orange textured lights illuminated the dance floor.

As I stepped onto the platform, I was set aglow by a delicate spotlight that looked like white mist. When the DJ totally stopped the music, I stepped to the mic. "If there is one thing that sisters know how to do," I said, "it's how to keep a secret. But keeping a secret from each other is one of the hardest things to do."

I turned and looked right at Kris. She looked amused but puzzled. She was trying to figure out what I was doing since I'd already given my toast.

Because of the emotion of the moment, I had to turn away or else I wouldn't have been able to continue. "It's no secret that Kris means the world to me and that I am now proud to call Pete my brother. Since they announced their engagement, I've been searching for a way to express how special their love is. I couldn't do it with words, so I figured that a song would be appropriate."

At that my sister started laughing so hard I thought she was going to fall out of her chair. She apparently thought I was going to belt out a tune! So I laughed and said, "My special gift to the beautiful couple is a serenade for your first dance from national recording artist Samson Logan!"

Kris fell back in her chair. Her white gloved hands cupped her mouth and her eyes widened in amazement. Pete held onto her and beamed. On cue, Samson strutted across the dance floor as low fog hovered around his feet. His pianist began the melody and Samson had barely sang the first line, "Oh, so long for this night I prayed ..." when my sister's laughs turned into tears of joy. Her new husband hugged her and led her onto the dance floor.

It looked as if Kris and Pete were dancing on a cloud to Samson's soulful singing. With each word he sang, I began to feel the song, the moment, and *him*. By the time he hit the last high note, there wasn't a dry eye in the house.

My guard was slipping. I saw why my sister swooned when Samson sang, and as I listened to her and the other girls talk about Samson, I began to see him through their eyes. And I had to admit, I loved what I saw.

4

The Reception

(From Samson)

The wedding reception was winding down, people were beginning to leave, and I knew I didn't have much more time to make my move. *It's now or never*, I thought to myself. I had always been confident, but I wasn't so sure about Angela. She had been so standoffish from the day we first met. That didn't stop me, though. I strolled up to her trying to look as cool as I possibly could.

Her eyes were on me as I made my way across the ballroom. She stood there, waiting for me to approach. That surprised and pleased me. When I was finally in front of her, I reached out and simply took her hand. "What are you doing for the next forty years?" I asked, then got what I wanted from her—a smile.

"Forty years?" she asked, and then looked up as if she were considering the question. "I'm not sure."

"Well, let's start with tonight," I said. "I heard there's a little after-party going on. Can I be your date?"

Her eyes rolled a bit and she cocked her head to the side. But still she kept her smile. "An after-party is definitely not my idea of a date," she said, "but you can come with us." That was all I needed to hear. I followed the group over to Kicks Nightclub, where the party continued. Dancing wasn't my thing, but if hanging out at this after-party was what it was going to take to get Angela to really go out with me, then I was game. As I stood on the edge of the dance floor, I could see Angela watching me out of the corner of her eye, even as she was dancing. She was checking out the other girls as they came over to talk to me. A couple of them even asked me to dance, but I told them all the same thing: "I just want to watch."

I was watching all right. I was watching and waiting for the right moment to make my next move. It turned out I didn't have to move much at all. My moment came when Angela, who was dancing and laughing, stumbled and fell into my arms. I was in the right place to catch her.

She was still laughing and trying to catch her breath from all that dancing. "Whew!" she said. "I can't even breathe."

I was still holding on to her when I said, "Well, let me do it for you."

"Do what for me?" she asked as she wiggled from my arms.

"Breathe," I said as I pulled her back into my arms and held her a little closer. Looking into her eyes, I then said, "When I breathe, you breathe." As if on cue, the DJ put on a slow jam. We wrapped our arms around each other and swayed to the music. I pressed my body against hers and her body seemed to be following my orders.

I took a deep breath in, and she followed. I did it again, and so did she. That made me smile. I pulled her even closer; now we were dancing cheek to cheek. Slowly I exhaled and gently blew into her ear. And she did the same to me.

"In and out," I whispered as I took in another deep breath. "That's much better, right?" I leaned back, and even in the dim light, I could see the flush in her cheeks. I wasn't sure if that came from the dancing she'd been doing or if it was from the heat that was between us.

She answered me with a nod and a smile.

I still held her, but now I stared into her eyes as we kept swaying to the beat of the music. I spoke softly, "Now let me take you on a proper date."

"What's your idea of proper?" she asked. Her voice was just as soft as mine.

With the way she said that, I knew I had her. "I have an idea that I know you'll like, but you're gonna have to wait and see. So tomorrow at six?"

It was a question, but I didn't give her a chance to answer. I stepped back, turned away, and without another word I walked straight out of that club. I didn't even look back. It was a suave move, but it also didn't give Angela a chance to say no.

I went home that night, and though I hate to admit it, I could hardly sleep. I wasn't kidding when I told Angela that when I saw her that day I knew she was going to be my wife. All I could think about was making sure that everything was perfect for our first date. If this was right, then there would be many more to come.

I woke up the next morning with the date on my mind. I made all the calls, all the preparations, and when I showed up to her place promptly at six, I got traditional on her. When she opened her door, I didn't even say hello. All I did was present her with a single rose.

"Thank you," she said.

"A beautiful rose for a beautiful woman." It sounded like a corny line, but I meant every word.

"So where are we going?" she asked coyly.

I wanted to keep the surprise going a little longer, so I said, "If you ask me that again, I'm going to have to blindfold you."

That seemed to satisfy her enough to sit back in the car and enjoy the short scenic drive to what I believed was going to be our perfect time together.

When we got to Niagara Falls, I had reservations at the Skylon Tower. We rode to the top of the world-famous landmark and sat at our window seats in the revolving dining room. As the restaurant slowly rotated, we took in the view we had sitting high above Niagara Falls and Great Gorge.

After dinner, I couldn't wait to take Angela for a stroll around the Falls. It was romantic as we held hands, strolled, and talked. I knew I liked Angela, but now I was sure. There was no doubt she was alluring. She was beautiful. Her curves were that of the anatomy of my dream girl. But it was beyond her body—Angela was much more than that. It was the sparkle in her eyes, and when we talked her words reached in and touched my mind, body, and soul. She was confident yet humble. She was smart, funny, and driven—all the things I wanted in a spouse.

By the time I took her home and gave her a kiss at her front door, I knew I had succeeded. Her guard was down, and now we were free to pursue what was already growing between us. I couldn't wait to talk to her again, so I didn't wait until the next morning to call—I called her as soon as I got home.

And that night was our beginning.

5

Whirlwind

(From Angela)

Samson and I were caught in a whirlwind. We spent as much time together as we could, which was a bit of a challenge since both of us had such busy lives.

I was a marketing manager for a Fortune 500 consumer packaged goods company in Buffalo and worked with a lot of local accounts, though I always had a bag packed since I had to spend much of my time in Boston, New York, Chicago, and several other regional offices. And Sam, of course, was on the road performing. This meant that our time together was limited, but maybe that was one of the reasons why it was so wonderful when we were together.

Most of the time we had to meet somewhere on the road, which was fun to plan because Sam and I loved to do the same things. Neither of us were the types who wanted to go to the beach and just stare at each other and the ocean. Instead, our time together was about exploring the sights of the city. In those few months together, we created so many memorable times. Like when we went out to dinner at Fanny's and Sam and I were talking about our dreams.

"Look at this," Sam said, taking out his wallet and pulling a picture from inside. "This is the house I want to live in. I've been visualizing this for a long time." I stared at the photo as he continued.

"I love to drive around and look at homes," he told me. And then he described the new community that was being built in one of the suburbs of Buffalo.

A lump grew in my throat and butterflies fluttered in my stomach as I listened to him talk. It was as if Sam were speaking all of my thoughts out loud. He loved to do what I loved to do. I'd been driving around looking at houses ever since I was sixteen, when I got my license and my dad bought me my first car—a Buick Skylark. If there was a beautiful street to see or new development going up, I wanted to see it. I loved seeing how other people lived, what was beautiful to them, and what new trash-to-treasure I could find.

"Oh my gosh!" I said as I stared at his picture.

"What?" he asked with a confused look.

"I did the same thing," I said. Then I told him all about my first car, about how my sister and I went around neighborhoods, shopping as if we had money and were ready to buy. Samson laughed and I continued, looking up from the picture. "I always imagined that I would have a house on Judge's Row."

"And you did it." Sam smiled and nodded his head slightly. "That's where you got your first house."

His hand had been gently resting on mine. I moved my hand up his and spread my fingers, so my hand intertwined with his. As we held hands, I thought about all the talks we'd had and just how much Sam and I had in common. It was time to quit listening to all the stop signs in my head and to follow my heart.

The lump that had been in my throat was easing its way down to my pounding heart. "Yes, my first house." I nodded. "And that's where I met you."

Sam was silent for a moment before he lifted my hand and kissed it. "Since looking at homes is one of my favorite things and one of your favorite things … why don't we start looking at houses together?"

"Isn't it amazing that we both love to do that!"

The corners of his mouth tugged up and became that broad smile I was beginning to love. "See?" he said. "We were meant to be."

There were so many times like that, times where we discovered how much we had in common, or how fate had brought us together. We were each other's destiny.

During our time of discovery, I also came to know Samson as a caring and loving man. He planned an amazing trip for us to Paradise Island in the Bahamas after I told him how much I loved that place.

"I do too!" he said. The next thing I knew, Sam had planned a three-day getaway filled with all kinds of romantic adventures, including a sunset cruise around the island on our first night. From the island cocktails, to the lavish hors d'oeuvres, to the way Sam wrapped his arms around me as we watched the Caribbean sky light up with the magnificent shades of the sunset, I knew this was the beginning of one of the best nights of my life.

By the time the boat docked back at the resort, however, the night would take a drastically different turn. I had been rubbing my hands over my arms, believing it was just the ocean breeze making me shiver as the boat glided across the water. But once we docked, my shiver turned into an itch and my normally satiny skin began to feel more like leather.

As we stepped onto the dock, Sam stopped walking and made me stop too. As he examined my arms, the look on his face changed.

"What?" I spun around, thinking some exotic bug had landed on me.

"Ang', you're breaking out."

I took a look at my arms, and then my bare legs that were exposed from the roll-up shorts I was wearing. "Oh my God!" was all I kept saying as I looked up and down my body. I had broken out in hives and was swelling up, looking like one of the red lobsters they had served at dinner.

"You must be having an allergic reaction to that seafood you ate on the boat," Sam explained. The same thing had happened to him years before in Japan.

That night I learned how much of a caring man Samson Logan was. He got me settled into bed and made sure I was as comfortable as I could be before he went on an hour-and-a-half hunt through the humongous resort in search of Benadryl. Once he found the medicine, he rushed back to the room and covered me with the ointment, nursing me back to health.

It was not the night he planned, nor the night I wanted. But it was the night I needed. God showed me another side of this man. He showed me that Samson would take care of me, and Samson Logan was the man I was supposed to be with for the rest of my life.

No matter where we were, our time together was always special. Even the bad times were good when it was only the two of us. Sam often told me he loved it when we were together because he could just be—he could let his guard down. He said being with me was like being home: "When you're with someone you can be this comfortable with, you're where you're supposed to be—you're home."

It was the same for me.

While being away on our mini-vacations were good, we also loved being home too. Those were the times when we were able to do all the normal and regular things, like go to a movie or dinner or just hang out. Being at home wasn't always as romantic as our times away, but they were just as sweet. Every time we were together, we found out something else about the other that drew us closer.

Our best times together came when we were with our families. My parents liked Sam, and of course, my sister and April already adored him—especially after his serenade at Kris' wedding. April and Kris' only question was when Sam and I were getting married. I guess we moved too slow for them. I'd taken my time getting back into dating and I'd taken more time dating Sam. April and Kris were just going to have to wait, even though they were ready to be aunties.

When April, Kris, and I were together, they joked about hearing an alarm going off—my biological clock. Though they kidded me about marriage and kids, they were serious when it came to my heart.

One night, April and Kris actually cornered Sam, asking him about his intentions. They dropped all kinds of hints about marriage. Their quick talk ended with a threat—they would hurt him if he ever hurt me. I understood how much my sister and April loved me, but I guess their takeaway from my men-o-pause was that I didn't take heartbreak well.

Their covert operation was blown later that night when Sam and I were alone and Samson laughed as he told me about what they'd said. At first I was embarrassed, but then Samson said, "I think it's great the way your family cares about you so much."

Having Samson meet my family was the easy part. I was a bundle of nerves when it came time for me to meet his. There were a lot of people to meet since Sam had four sisters and two brothers. To top off the meet-the-parents anxiety, his parents were pastors.

Samson told me his parents loved him dearly but sometimes wrestled with his choice to pursue secular music instead of the gospel songs he'd been singing in church since he could hold a Bible. They knew his heart was always with God, but they worried about his choices and where those choices would lead him, especially his choices about women.

Of course that revelation put extra pressure on me, and it didn't help when Sam told me about his parents' personalities. His father, Raymond, was going to be easy enough, I thought. According to Sam, his dad was easygoing and his pastoral style was the same—he was laid-back. But his mom, Earnestine, gave me more than a little concern. Sam said she had a spirit of excellence and was a tell-it-like-it-is kind of woman. All I could think about was, *What if she doesn't like me?* They were well-respected and much loved in their community, parental figures to many, and even Sam's friends called them Mom and Dad.

When I finally met Samson's parents, it was a blessing that his mom liked me right away, because she would have certainly told us if she didn't. She was on my side from the beginning. In our world, Samson was the one with the fans, but in our relationship, Mom Earnestine was my fan. She was always praying with me and for me, cheering me on. From the start, she was excited about Samson and I being together.

While Sam often told me how he was already in love with me, I knew it was true once he did two things: when he invited me to go to church with him (where he first began to refer to me as the first lady), and when he introduced me to his son.

I had known Samson had a son early on. He gushed about what a wonderful child little Sam was, and how he believed that I would really like him. Once we met, little Sam spent a lot of time with us. Seeing Sam and his son together was just another insight into a side of Sam I had not seen before.

Sam was an amazing father. He had never been thrilled that he'd had a child out of wedlock and he had some guilt over the situation. He never felt good about the fact that little Sam would never have the benefit of having both parents in his household nurturing him. But even with all of that, Sam did everything he could for his son. Whenever he was in town, picking up little Sam was his first stop. Even though Sam wasn't with his son constantly, he made it clear how much he loved him. And the best part was that little Sam knew he was loved.

One of the best things about Sam already having a son was that it would make it easier for us to have a little girl. I always dreamed of having a daughter, and with Sam already having a son, I figured he'd hope and pray for a girl the way I did.

Watching Sam with his son helped me see he was the man with whom I always dreamed of having my little girl. It showed me that what he'd always told me was true—he was a family man and he adored the people he loved. That was the kind of man I wanted in my life.

It was because of all of these moments, and many more, that I fell in love with Samson Logan. It was so easy. And the fact that he wanted the same things out of life only made it that much better. I just never expected to have so many challenges along the way.

6

The Best-Laid Plans

(From Samson)

I hated whenever I was away from Angela, but, interestingly enough, my travel schedule actually made our relationship much better. After each of my shows, we'd talk on the phone for hours. I'd tell her about my day and she'd tell me about hers. We'd talk about everything and nothing at all.

I never wanted to hang up, and many times she fell asleep while still on the phone. I always felt bad about that; Angela had a serious work ethic and I knew she had to be up early for work. She didn't play when it came to her career. But the thing was that it was so easy and we would lose track of time. That's how it always was for us. We just couldn't get enough of each other.

Talking to Angela was wonderful, but it was tough at times too. It was a reminder that the road was lonely. It was hard not having someone around I could fully trust; it was hard not having someone around who allowed me to be myself, not a celebrity. I didn't have to put on a show for her. I could just be.

One night when I called Angela, the sound of her voice gave

me joy and peace. That was when I realized that Angela was more than the girl I loved; she was becoming the best friend I'd ever had.

"Are you listening to me?" Angela asked as I was caught up in my thoughts.

"What?"

"I just asked you about your show tonight and you didn't say anything."

"Come and see me," I said suddenly. The thought had just come to me and that was all that I wanted in that moment. I wanted Angela with me, by my side.

After she asked what I had said, I repeated, "Come and see me."

"You know I can't do that," she insisted. "I've got to work."

That simple truth took away all the joy I'd been feeling in that moment. Then I said, "Yeah, I know. You're right. It's just that I won't be home for another six weeks and that's way too long not to see you."

"I know," she said with sadness in her voice. "And I'm sorry."

Something inside told me not to give up. "I know you, Angela, Miss Workaholic," I said. "When was the last time you took a vacation?"

"We just went to Disney World, remember?"

"Only for a few days," I reminded her. "When was the last time you really took some time off—like a whole week?"

"I ... I ..." She just stuttered.

I didn't let her do that long, though, before I said, "Take a week off and come see me. I miss you."

She didn't say anything, but I could tell she was beginning to soften and think about the idea. "You're going to be in Cleveland soon, right?" she asked.

"Yeah, next week."

"Well ..." she began slowly as if an idea were forming in her mind. "Maybe I can work from our Cleveland office that week."

"Yeah, and we can see each other every night!" I said, trying not to sound too excited. But it was too late—she had to have heard my excitement.

"I might be able to do that," she said. "Let me see what I can work out."

For the rest of the week, I was filled with anticipation. My expectations kept building, and when Monday rolled around I could hardly contain myself. I knew this was going to be the best week ever. Too bad I would be proven wrong.

7

Baggage

(From Angela)

I was excited to see Samson, but there was also a rumbling in my spirit that felt a little bit like a warning. I tried to ignore it. I was sure it was nothing but leftover mental baggage from past relationships. That had to be put out of my mind so I could focus on what Samson and I had. Our relationship had nothing to do with anyone else. It was just the two of us.

That's what I was thinking about as my car came to a stop outside of my hotel where Samson was waiting for me. We held each other and kissed as if we hadn't seen each other in forever. It sure felt like forever, even though it had just been three weeks.

"I have a great week planned for us," Samson said once we were in the hotel lobby. "We're gonna go shopping and then have dinner every night and hang out at some of the spots."

"What about your shows?" I laughed.

"Oh yeah," he kidded. "I do have to work, huh?" Then he paused as he thought. "Of course you're going to come to all of my shows, right?"

"Definitely!" I said, though that was the part I was least excited about. Not that I didn't love hearing Sam sing and watching his shows—I absolutely loved his performances. What I wasn't so fond of was all the women who hung around. Don't get me wrong, the whooping and hollering was fine and I even laughed when I was at a show and women screamed out, "Take it off!" That was all part of the business. What I didn't like were the groupies who always seemed to be around.

"What we are going to do now," Sam said, interrupting my thoughts, "is a little bit of shopping."

That wasn't a surprise. I'd learned early on in our relationship that shopping was something he loved to do. It was therapy for him, his escape on the road. When he called me at night, he told me about the spots he found in every city, and it seemed that Cleveland was no different—we hit all the shopping spots, both big and small.

I was exhausted by the time he took me to my hotel.

"We'll have dinner after the show, okay?" he said.

"Of course," I said with a smile.

I went to the show with Sam, watched him perform, listened to the women screaming, and watched the groupies stalking him. At the end of the night, Samson Logan left with me, which was the only thing that counted. And we enjoyed our time alone.

The next day, we did the same thing. We spent the day together, went to the show, and then spent the night together. We did that the next night too, and this week was turning into a dream for me. The time alone with Sam was special. When it was just the two of us, Sam wasn't Samson Logan. He was just Sam, my boyfriend, the man I loved.

I was looking forward to the Friday night show. No matter what city they were in, Samson told me Fridays were always a sold-out house. And it seemed that it was the same way in Cleveland. The State Theatre was bumping and there were even a few Cleveland Cavaliers in the house. I understood why the ballers were there: the place was packed with ladies. Many of them were dressed as if they were on the hunt.

Sam performed as he always did, and the women screamed the

way they always did. But my eyes were on Samson the whole time. I could listen to him sing all night long. When he closed the first half of the show with his soul-stirring song "Atmosphere," I was proud when he got a standing ovation.

During the intermission, Sam did what he always did—he went into the lobby to sign autographs and take pictures. That was his time with the fans, so I would just watch from the back of the lobby. Our routine was the same each show: I'd stand there and watch Sam, then before he headed backstage for the second half of the show, he'd give me a hug and a kiss. I knew he did that because he wanted to, but I always had a feeling he did it to make it clear to anyone watching I was there with him.

On this night, however, I had to make a quick run to the bathroom before I went into the lobby. Who would've thought that making a pit stop would have changed so much for me.

8

(From Samson)

I rushed out from behind the stage to get a quick glance at Angie before I had to meet my fans. But when I glanced at the back of the lobby where she always stood, she wasn't there. I figured she was in the restroom, but I didn't have a lot of time to think about it because I was swept into the fan frenzy that always met me during intermission.

Girls were shouting, jockeying to be the first in line to get my autograph and take a picture. This was one of my favorite parts of the business—meeting the women who supported me. I did what I did because of them, and I always wanted my fans to know how much I enjoyed them and how grateful I was for their support.

I was grateful. Angie understood that. She knew I was doing what I had to do. Not only that, but I went out of my way to let Angie know I was trustworthy. I had been consciously trying to show her that even with all of the temptation, I knew what I wanted and it was her.

Making her feel secure was important because, though we didn't talk a lot about our past relationships, I knew Angie had been through some things. Not that I'd been a saint in my past, but this preacher's kid knew that what I'd done in my past was not what I wanted for my future. I wanted one woman. I wanted the one who would be in my corner when the lights went down. I wanted the one who would be cheering me on when there were no screaming fans waiting at every show.

"I'm next, Samson," a girl in gold lamé pants said. "How you doing?"

"Hey, baby," I said, using that pet name as a generic term of endearment. It was all part of the package my fans expected. I'm sure these women knew that when I called them baby, it was different from when I said that to the woman I loved.

"Hey, yourself." The girl giggled, as I signed her program and then took a picture with her.

After that girl stepped aside, I greeted the next lady in line, female after female after female. And then …

"Hey, Samson."

I recognized her voice before I even saw her face. I couldn't believe it. It was Raven—again!

"Hey, Raven," I said. My eyes instantly rolled. "What are you doing here?"

As I asked her that, there was a chorus of, "Umm, excuse me!" from the other girls in line. Raven had pushed her way to the front, and the girls who'd been waiting were not too pleased. But, of course, that didn't bother Raven.

"I just happened to be here," she said.

That couldn't be true. This New Yorker was a long way from home. Cleveland wasn't just around the corner. But I can't say I was surprised to see her either. Raven was an old flame who loved to pop up every once in a while. We'd had our good times in the past, but it was clear to me that Raven wasn't the one for me.

In fact, I was pretty sure she was a bit on the crazy side. Every time she popped up, she proved that I was right. No matter how many times I'd told her our relationship wasn't working, no matter how many times I told her that it was over, Raven went out of her way to find me in city after city. I guess she figured if she was with me enough on the road, something would start up again. But that wasn't going to happen.

Not only was she not the one, but I had found The One. That made me glance quickly around the lobby again. Whew! Angela still wasn't anywhere in sight.

"You told me that you were going to be in Cleveland, remember?" Raven purred, stopping my thoughts.

"Yeah," I said, sorry I had told her that, though, knowing Raven, she would have found out anyway. It was true that I did talk to her every now and then. It was hard for me to avoid her since she constantly blew up my phone. And I didn't see any harm in talking to her—at least not until this moment.

"Aren't you glad to see me, baby?" she asked. "When we talked on the phone last week, you seemed to miss me so much that I decided to come out and see you."

"What? Girl, you're trippin'," I said. "It wasn't like that."

I knew Raven wasn't going to be deterred. All kinds of thoughts were going through my mind, but the first one was that I had to get this girl out of here before Angela came back. Only the Lord knew what this girl might say or do if she saw Angie.

"No worries," she whispered. "I came to help you remember how it was with us."

Before I could say another word, Raven had her hands on my waist and her mouth on my lips.

For a moment, I was frozen with shock. But then I grabbed her hands and tried to push her away from me. "Raven," I said, "you're gonna have to get out of here."

While I was pushing Raven away, I backed up at the same time. I wanted to put as much space as I could between the two of us. When I backed up, I bumped into someone. Or maybe it wasn't a bump because it felt more like a shove.

"Baby!"

I closed my eyes. *Angie!* Angie was behind me. I turned around as fast as I could, but all I saw was the back of her head, stomping away from me. This wasn't happening!

"Hey, Samson," one of the girls shouted out, sounding as if she were annoyed. "There's a whole bunch of us still waiting!" And she should've been. Raven had taken up too much of my time and now she had me in serious trouble.

"Ladies," I said, already walking away from the group and from Raven, "I'll be back after the show. I promise." Then I took off. I only had a few minutes before I had to get back on stage, but I had to get to Angie.

"Angie!" I yelled through the crowded lobby. "Ang'!"

My eyes took in every corner, and then I spotted her at the door. I pushed through the mass of people, some of whom tried to stop me to talk. But I didn't stop. The only person I wanted to talk to was Angela.

I caught up to her. "Hey, hey," I said, reaching out to grab her arm.

The moment I touched her, she spun around. Her eyes were filled with hurt, and in her voice I heard her anger and pain. "Let me go!" she said through clenched teeth.

"No," I told her. "I can't 'cause it's not what you think."

She rolled her eyes as if she were sure my words were a lie, and she yanked her arm from my grasp.

"This is what I do." I started talking as fast as I could.

It wasn't fast enough, though. Before I could get anything else out, Angela yelled, "This is what you do? Meet women in every city?"

"No, it's not like that," I shouted back in frustration. I had tried so hard to convince Angela that what we had was real and she never had to worry about me. Because of one little incident, everything I'd done seemed not to matter. "Look, this is my business," I told her. "What do you want me to do?"

Before she could answer, the stage manager called out to me: "Sam! Sam! It's time to hit the stage, man." I glanced over my shoulder to look at him, turned back to Angie, then back to the stage manager and once again back to Angie. I was torn.

"One minute, man," I finally said to the stage manager.

"Now!" he shouted. "You've got only one minute before the show starts again. You've got to go." He grabbed my arm, pulling me away from Angela.

"Ang'!" I yelled out. "Just do me a favor and go back inside. Sit down and we'll talk after the show. Please!" I begged as I was being dragged further away. But when I hit the stage for the second half, I had a bad feeling. It was hard for me to concentrate, hard for me to perform. I did the best I could and it seemed to be enough because the girls were still screaming at the end of it.

I hardly noticed, though. All I did was rush to find Angela. But just like I thought, she wasn't there. She was gone.

9

Jesus, Take the Wheel

(From Angela)

My mind and my heart were racing, but not quite as fast as my feet. I started speed walking out of the State Theatre, pushing past the crowds, through the turnstile, and then finally onto the street.

Is this what's been going on? Has it been just a turnstile, a revolving door of women with Samson in every city? I only had questions, no answers as I took the brief sprint down the street back to the hotel. Once I busted through the lobby doors, my mind quickly shifted from questions to purpose.

I am out of here! That was the only command my body seemed capable of following. I flung open the door to my room, ready to grab my belongings and get out of there in record time. But I took two steps inside, then stopped.

My eyes suddenly filled with tears. In front of me were all of the memories. All of the moments Samson and I had already created on this trip. Every surface was covered with something—bags from our shopping trips along with trinkets and souvenirs I'd picked up from our excursions around the city. Then there were all the clothes Samson had bought for me. It was all a reminder of what we'd done and what could have been.

How could it have changed so quickly? Just hours before, I'd left the room full of love for Samson and full of the hope I had for us. But now I knew the truth. As painful as it was, I had to pack up these memories and get out of there.

Moving as fast as I could, I tossed my bags onto the bed, then crammed everything I could inside. There was no order, but how could there be? My mind was garbled; I couldn't capture a single thought. So I packed in a state of confusion, and it looked that way. I had no idea how much time had passed, but it didn't take me too long to get myself together and out of that room. I had to be gone by the time Samson was finished.

I dragged my bags downstairs, then waited impatiently by the door for the bellhop to bring my car around. Then I did something I didn't want to do—I glanced down the street to the State Theatre and I stared at the bright lights on the marquee. I could almost hear the applause and the laughter floating down the street, mocking me.

I thought I was going to the theater to see a performance, but it seems I was the one who got played. As I stared at the theater, my eyes widened. People began spilling out of the doors while I was still waiting for my car. *What?* I watched to make sure it wasn't just a few people leaving early. When more people poured out, I realized the show had to be over.

I had to get out of there. There was no way I wanted to look at Samson, much less talk to him. I was so busy looking down the street, fearing that I would see Samson, that I didn't even feel the first tap on my shoulder.

"Miss?" I turned around and the bellhop was standing there. "Here are your keys," was all he said, though he looked as if he wanted to ask me if I was all right.

"Thank you." I breathed, relieved.

Breathe

As he shoved my bag into the trunk, I ran around to the driver's side of the car, slipped inside, and took off. I was grateful to be on my way, except for the fact that I had to drive down Euclid Avenue, which went right past the theater. My eyes took in the posters plastered all around with Samson's face. Seeing them made my heart sink.

I didn't have to do much thinking to get on the road. My Taurus had taken me to and from Cleveland so many times that it seemed to get on 90 Eastbound almost by itself.

Once on the open road, I finally felt safe. But that didn't slow me down. I wanted to put as much distance as I possibly could between me and what had happened.

What just happened back there? How could my dreams for a life with Samson come to an end just like that? How could my hopes dissipate that quickly? Wasn't Samson the man I'd been waiting for? Wasn't he the man I was meant to be with, my life companion, my soul mate?

My questions didn't stop. I found myself in another argument, with the other man in my life—God. "God, what just happened?" I prayed as I drove. Not that I expected to hear an audible response, but I waited a few seconds before I let the questions roll. "How could you let this happen? *Why* did you let this happen? Why would you do this to me after everything I've been through?"

Then I turned the subject to be more directly about Sam. "Why did he do this to me? Why would he betray me? Are all men jerks?" I interrogated God with question after question. Every possible question I could think of I turned over to God. I let him know I was angry and hurt and filled with sadness.

"Remember my men-o-pause, God? I was doing that because of everything that I'd been through. But really I was doing it because I thought you wanted me to. I thought you wanted me to wait on someone truly special.

"I thought I was doing it your way, God, setting myself aside, taking the time to work on me. I was pruning and getting ready, protecting and saving my heart for that special man I believed you would send to me.

"And then I really believed you had sent him. Because, who has ever had a man, a knight in shining armor, simply roll up to their house? Samson and I meeting the way we did had to be you, right?"

I let my mind wander, driving in complete silence. I wanted to hear my thoughts. And they were there, pulsating in my mind like a soft beating drum. As my thoughts continued, the drumbeat grew louder and deeper. Even though I was sitting still, my body began to shake. I couldn't stay silent any longer.

"Why, God?" I cried out.

Sure, I'd made my share of mistakes in the past by not listening to God. Whenever I did that, I always felt I deserved whatever situation in which I found myself. But this time I was absolutely sure I had heard him and followed him.

Even once I met Samson, I tried to stay close to God. I was hesitant, resistant at first, because I wanted to be sure this was it. I wanted to make sure that Samson was a man with a heart for God. I knew that kind of man would love me and inspire me, and that I could do the same for him.

"I was so sure," I cried out to God. "I was so sure about Samson. I mean, he's a preacher's kid! If anyone should know how to treat a woman, it should be a PK, right?"

How could this go so wrong? I thought about all the times Samson and I were together, all of the long phone calls, all of the great outings and trips together. How could I have been so wrong about him?

My thoughts weighed me down, made me feel so broken. I laid out all of my feelings and all of my questions to him. When I felt exhausted, when it felt as if I had no more questions, there was one that still lingered. I had been shouting my questions to God, but this one I thought about for a while, and then I asked softly, "Who am I that you should care about this, God?"

I let that question settle not only in the quiet of the car but also in the center of my soul. That made me slow down, think, and begin to question myself.

I knew God. I knew he always had a purpose behind the problems. But as I thought about this, what kind of purpose could there be? I couldn't understand it. Or maybe I didn't want to understand it.

As I passed the sign for Erie, Pennsylvania, I was halfway home, and not referring to the distance to my destination. I was halfway home in terms of understanding what God was doing. I really wanted to surrender completely to God. I wanted to surrender and wait for his answer.

I trusted God would help me. Falling in love with Samson had been easy; falling out of love with him would not be so easy. But I had faith in God and I believed in me. I had been an independent woman and I would be one again.

As I edged off the interstate, I let out a sigh. I really loved Samson, but I didn't love him because I needed him; rather, I needed him because I loved him. That thought made my heart ache. By the time I pulled into my driveway, I decided I was bruised, but not broken. I'd have to give this whole situation to God and he would help me get through it. At least, that's what my mind said, though my heart felt differently.

My mind kept drifting back to the one question that had settled inside of me: *Who am I that you should care about this, God?* I turned off the car's ignition. I sat there and continued to turn that question over and over in my mind: *Who am I that you should care about this, God?*

There were wars all over the world, hunger and poverty, and natural disasters that left people homeless and penniless, and I was coming to God with this drama? Because my feelings were hurt? This was so trivial, so beneath him, and I began to feel bad about my tirade. I felt horrible for the way I'd gone to God and complained, shouted, and cried. But I couldn't let that question go: *Who am I that you should care about this, God?*

Then it hit me! I suddenly knew why I had gone to God with everything, why I had poured all of my emotions out to him, and why I expected him to answer my questions. It was because I knew him as God the Father, and I knew that somehow, someway, however small my drama might be, God actually cared. He would be right there with me as I got over Samson.

I slid out of the car, leaving my bag in the trunk. I'd get it in the morning. Completely drained, I headed into my house. Whether or not I was ready for it, I was starting a new chapter in my life—one that wouldn't include Samson. And although that thought caused me to hurt, I would eventually be okay.

It didn't take me long to undress and crawl into bed. I was ready to sleep. When I laid my head down on my pillow, however, I felt a whisper in my spirit. It was the answer I had been waiting for, the answer to all of the questions I'd asked God, the answer that had taken hours for me to finally hear.

He said, *You are mine.*

10

Real Men Pray

(From Samson)

As the stage manager pulled and prodded me to go backstage, I couldn't help the sinking feeling that was coming over me. I had performed at the State Theatre so many times that I knew it well. I also knew that this historic theater was once known for having the world's longest lobby. That understanding was now part of my anguish.

What am I walking away from? I kept asking myself, as I looked over my shoulder, trying to keep my eyes on Angie. But I lost sight of her in the lobby that was still bustling with people, smiling and laughing and calling my name.

I wasn't willingly walking away from Angie, but while she was running toward one end I was being dragged to the other. The space between us felt like it was never-ending, though somehow it felt as if we were the only two there. The crowd and their noise faded into the background and all I heard were my shouts for Angie to come back.

Right before I stepped onto the stage, there was another sound. It may have only been in my mind, but I was sure I heard the slam of the theater door, the door that Angie was closing on us. I was torn, but I had a job to do; people paid money to see me perform.

As I rushed to put on my microphone, I was about to do some real acting.

One of my greatest loves is performing, especially with faith-based projects. Expressing myself through singing and acting is one of the ways I minister to people. But that night I was the one who needed to be ministered to. I had blown it. There was nothing I could do, nothing that would allow me to fix what had happened. So I did the only thing I could do in that moment—right before I rushed onto the center of the stage and the bright light that would be shining on me, I raised my head and my heart to God. I whispered, "Lord, please don't let me lose Angie."

That prayer and God were all I had in that moment. Moments after, I took the stage and put Samson (and all of my drama) aside and became the character I was being paid to play. But there was no way for me to really let go of what had just happened, not even for a few minutes. I tried to push away those thoughts, but Angie was still on my mind. I could imagine what she was thinking; I didn't want to think about what she was doing.

Thankfully the audience didn't seem to notice that I wasn't at my best. They roared with laughter at the right moments, talked back to my character when I said something they agreed with (or didn't), and then leapt to their feet during my closing song.

However, hardly a moment went by when my mind wasn't on Angie. I tortured myself with questions I couldn't answer: Would she talk to me? Would she give me the chance to explain? Angie had to give me a chance because I wasn't all wrong (though I wasn't all right) with how things went down. Raven showing up was a surprise to me. But then again, I should have made it clearer that I wasn't an option for her.

When the curtain went down, I was escorted to the lobby with the other actors in the show to meet and greet our fans. Of course, my wish was that somehow, for some reason, Angie would have come back. Of course, my wish wasn't granted. I kept smiling, though, through every handshake, every hug, every picture. What I was doing was probably the best performance of my life; it certainly felt like the most grueling.

After over an hour, I breathed with relief when I was finally able to leave. As I gathered my belongings, I tried to gather my words too. What was I going to say to Angie? I had no idea. But I had to get to that hotel and face her.

That wasn't what it looked like. No, that seemed too obvious.

I didn't know she'd be there. No, that seemed too dumb.

I didn't really know her. That was a complete lie, and I wasn't going to ever lie to Angie.

My thoughts changed from what I was going to say to Angela to what I'd told God: I want a good wife—I *need* a good wife. I'd taken that request to God because I had some big plans and having the right life partner by my side was an important part of my overall plan.

Although I'd prayed to God to bring me my life partner, I hadn't been in any rush. My plans were *long* term, so I didn't have to have a wife right now. And I'd been happy with where life had taken me in the time before I met Angela.

As I took what felt like the longest walk to the hotel alone (I'd told my castmates that I'd catch up with them later), I thought back to the day when I'd met Angela. It had been a great day already. I had just landed a music project with Devante and was floating. As I was driving down the street, my thoughts were on making a name for myself, not *giving* someone my name. Traveling the country and taking trips overseas had been fascinating for me. It was a great life and I was grateful for the blessings.

But like everyone knows, home is where the heart is. I'd been away for months and had been so happy to be back in Buffalo, even if it was just going to be for a few days. It was the perfect time to be back too. There are few places in the world that could challenge the beauty of Western New York at the beginning of fall.

When I'd hopped in my car that day, all I was going to do was cruise through a couple of my old stomping grounds, and then visit with my family. Little did I know that I was driving toward my destiny. My last stop was at my sister's house. I couldn't wait to get there and see the fixer-upper she'd moved into while I'd been gone.

When I got in my car, I popped in a CD and was humming happily as I drove. I was feeling the bass when I turned down Burke Drive; her house was a couple of blocks down this tree-lined street. My head was bopping as I passed the brick ranches, Tudor styles, and mini-mansions on Judges Row. There was even a quaint-looking brick church on one corner that caught my eye and I pulled over to get a better look at it.

Wow, I thought. This could be the perfect neighborhood for our new church. Checking out churches wasn't on my list of things to do, but that didn't matter because I always had church on my mind. I guess that was because church was where I grew up. I'd had a Bible in my hand and a hymn in my head since I could remember.

Even though I was a singer, I wanted to help build the ministry that my parents started. The church my parents pastored had been helping people in the Masten District for twenty-five years. We were outgrowing the location that he and my mother had built. The time would come when we would have to move, so I was always on the lookout for a new facility.

I got out of my car, but since there wasn't any kind of For Sale sign up on the building, I lingered in front of St. Michaels and All Angels Episcopal Church. As I walked around, I imagined what it would be like to have a ministry right here. It was the perfect location, a quiet location. And the church itself was magnificent with a beautiful sanctuary I could see through the huge glass front doors. When I walked around the side, I peeked in the windows and saw a couple of offices, a few classrooms, and all the way in the back was a large fellowship area that looked like it was set up as a dining hall.

After walking around the entire building, I jumped back in my car. I'd definitely have to tell my parents about this place. I wasn't quite sure what I would say since it wasn't for sale, but I figured I'd worry about that later.

I hopped back in my car, put it in drive, and cranked up the music again. Then I glanced up so I could take off—and that's when I saw *her*. That was all it took—one look. This beautiful vision was standing outside her home washing her windows. Her long hair was pulled back in a ponytail and all she had on was a T-shirt and jeans.

Something made her turn around. Her big brown eyes locked right on to mine and a slow smile came across her face. I was already smiling. It wasn't only seeing *her* that made me smile; it was what happened a moment after I laid my eyes on her. God spoke to me: *She's the one. That's your wife.*

I'd heard God's voice before, but this time he was communicating with me beyond mere words. This time he gave me a complete knowing. He filled every fiber of my being with this truth. Even though I was mesmerized, that didn't matter. This woman was the one God had chosen; she was God's pick for me.

This gave me more confidence than I would have normally had. I'm not saying that I wasn't confident to begin with, but what I did next took a holy kind of confidence. I swerved my car to the other side of the street, eased it right in front of her house, and got out. I walked up to her as if we had known each other for eternity.

My first words were, "Oh my gosh, that's my wife." When the words came out of my mouth, confirmation filled my spirit. And even I, a romantic, someone who wrote love songs, was pleasingly puzzled. Had I really just fallen in love with someone at first sight?

All of those memories came flooding back to me in the minutes it took me to walk from the theater to the hotel. Angela was not just *some* girl; she was the one I was going to marry. I had to do something about what had happened. I had to fix it. Now.

Remembering how God had put us together, and knowing how much I cared for this woman, helped me to form the words in my mind that my mouth needed to say. What Angela needed to hear was, "Angela, I love you." That was the truth and that was where I would start.

This wasn't the first time I'd be saying those words to Angie. I'd said them before and I think she knew they were not just words to me. She knew I'd meant them. But tonight I needed to say those words again; I needed to tell her and I needed to show her that I loved her.

When I entered the hotel my heartbeat quickened, and when I got to her hotel room I pounded on the door the way my heart was pounding in my chest. Yet there was nothing. "Angie!" I called as I knocked again.

No response.

For a moment, I stayed quiet, pressed my ear closer to the door, and listened for sounds on the other side. It didn't take me long to figure out she wasn't in the room. Turning around, I took the stairs down to the lobby. Maybe she was waiting there for me. When I ran into the lobby, my eyes scanned the massive space—twice. There was no sign of Angie.

I didn't know if it was the expression on my face, or the way I was standing, looking like I was lost that made the bellhop come over to me. "Hey," he said, making me look up and face him. "You need anything?" he asked.

I couldn't remember his name, but we'd been pretty friendly with him since our arrival. "Yeah," I said. "The woman I was here with this week, have you seen her?"

"Yes sir, I have."

My hope rose.

"She checked out about a half hour ago."

My heart sank. It took every bit of energy to muster a thank-you before I turned away and headed up to my own room.

Angie had checked out—had she checked out on us too? That was my only thought as I rode up the elevator. This was not what I wanted. I needed Angie here so we could see each other face-to-face. I needed to look into her eyes and know she believed me. And she needed to look into mine and know I was telling the truth.

Now that she was gone, I wasn't going to wait until I saw her again. She needed to know this now. A phone call would have to do. The first thing I did when I got to my room was drop my bag, pull out my cell phone, and dial her number.

And I called. And called. And called.

No answer.

Finally, I had no choice but to leave a message. "Angie, where are you?" I said. "I want to speak to you. I need to talk to you." I left that message over and over, half expecting that she would come back and come knocking on my door. But as each hour passed, my confidence dimmed. She'd left the hotel. She was heading home. She'd left me.

In the first few hours, I was angry. "Doesn't she know who I am?" I kept asking aloud. Angie had to realize I was Samson Logan. I was accomplished, so I was sought after by women. What did she expect? Of course that had nothing to do with us. I was all in with her. I loved her. Didn't she know me?

But then my mind answered that question: No! Angie really didn't know who I was. And not only that, she didn't know why I loved her—that one of the reasons I loved her was because she had never set out to catch, tame, trap, or change me. Truth be told, she wasn't even trying to date me. At first I wasn't sure I was going to be able to get past all of those times in the beginning when she said no to us going out.

She didn't know that one of the reasons I fell in love with her was because she was a woman who was about her business. She was all about being the woman God called her to be and she was all about being the woman who would wait for God to bring her the right man. She radiated with a knowledge that the right man would answer that call and he would be the one her soul would love.

I leaned back on the bed and remembered one of our many dates to one of our favorite places: Niagara Falls. We'd sat on a blanket, simply enjoying each other's company and the beauty that surrounded us. The awe-inspiring sound of four million cubic feet of water falling at what seemed like our feet was like a soothing melody. Through the mist, we saw a rainbow arching its way over Bridal Veil Falls. My heart knew then what God had told me before—I was sitting with my bride.

I'd asked her that day as we sat so quietly, "What are you trying to do? Change me?"

She squinted at me and grinned with the sun in her eyes. "What good is change without transformation?" she asked. I didn't have a chance to ask a follow-up question because she was on her feet and beginning to walk away from me.

I stood up to follow her, when she glanced at me over her shoulder, and said, "Since we're talking about change, if you've got a little, you can buy me an ice cream." She had changed the conversation just like that!

I didn't really understand what she meant. Now it was clear to me. Angela had never set out to change me because she was prepared to leave me if it meant changing what she believed in. Sitting in my hotel room alone, I thought about her words and understood that change fixes the past, but transformation creates the future.

She'd always been talking about the future, and now I was in danger of Angie being part of my past. I picked up my cell phone and stared at the blank screen, waiting for that call from her. As I waited, I recalled so many wonderful moments of our courtship.

And with each memory, I prayed that she would call, that she would come back.

I wanted to catch the first plane I could find heading toward Buffalo. But I still had another three weeks to go before we finished the show. Our tour bus was pulling out the next day for Columbus, and I had to be on it.

As hour after hour passed, I didn't bother getting off the bed. I never undressed, never did anything else except sit there and wonder why I hadn't done something sooner to stop tonight from happening. If I knew God had brought us together, what was I waiting for? Why hadn't I acted on what God had told me? Why wasn't Angela my wife?

Angela wouldn't talk to me, but I knew that God would listen. Or at least, that's what I hoped. I hoped he would give me the chance to right this wrong. I hoped and I prayed. And I talked. I knew God would hear me.

I never had a big moment in my life where I "got saved." God was simply always there. I counted on him, I was filled by him, and I knew him in so many ways. Tonight was one of those times when he was God, the Father, and he was listening to his son go on and on. After I talked, I simply listened.

And you know what? God talked to me. He talked to me by helping me see and remember more moments and more things about Angela. He helped me remember how she was shining so bright on the day that I met her, how she got me, how she really understood me. He helped me remember how she found the good in my quirks, even when I got on her nerves. On more than one occasion, she'd said, "I just want to push you off a cliff, then run down and catch you!"

That was love.

I had tried to show her my love too. I told her that I would always put her first. Had I done that? She'd once told me, "Don't put me first. Put God first. A man following God will know how to properly lead a woman." With the way she loved God, I knew

Angela was a woman I could trust with my heart. But now I'd broken hers.

I wasn't quite sure when it happened, but the night had become day once again. As the morning light slowly crept through the hotel window's blinds, I knew what I had to do. I had to believe. I had to believe that the same way God brought her into my life, he'd keep her there.

I was going to have to do my part—I knew that. I was going to have to show her I was serious. I didn't know how I was going to do it being hundreds of miles away from her, but I was resolved to find a way.

When the sun had fully risen, I jumped up, packed my bags, and met the rest of the cast in the lobby. We were on our way a short time later, and I was grateful for my bunk in our sleeper tour bus since I had stayed up all night. It wasn't a long way to Columbus, but I needed to rest my mind for even a short while.

The next three weeks of my tour went by excruciatingly slow. My phone calls went unanswered, and I really missed Angela. I sent her flowers and cards, not knowing whether or not she got them, or whether or not she even cared. I was deflated but never dissuaded from continuing on. Angela had to know I was in this for the long haul. I had to tell her and I had to show her.

One of the final legs of our tour was New York City. We were only there for a few days, and with the tight schedule I barely had time to do what I should have done a long time before. I headed to the diamond district with a purpose. Yes, it was hard to impress Angela, but still I wanted to find the biggest diamond I could afford. Surely that couldn't hurt. But it had to be tasteful. And I wanted the diamond to really mean something.

On Forty-Seventh Street, I walked up one side and down the other, going in and out of all the stores, searching for but not finding the special ring I wanted to present to her. I ran out of time on that first day and had to get back for the show. And the next day, I headed to the diamond district, again returning with no results.

It was my final day in New York, and my Adidas shoes had to be getting close to having a hole in the soles with the way I had walked up and down the streets in search of an outward expression of the inner bond I wanted to pledge to Angela forever. There was one more store and another hour before I had to get back to the Beacon Theatre for my call time.

When I walked into the store, I once again described what I was looking for to the jeweler. This time the man didn't shake his head; instead, he smiled. "I think I have the ring you want," he assured me. "I just finished making a ring like that. Let me get it for you."

I stood there waiting, thinking, and hoping. When he returned, he carried a black velvet box with a small black tassel and said, "Sir, I knew I was making this for someone special. And now you are here. Here it is." When he opened the box, the light caught the diamond in just the right way that the sparkle was almost blinding. He removed the ring and handed it to me. This was it.

Buying a ring for someone who wasn't answering my calls, who hadn't called me back, and who may not ever let me into her space again probably seemed crazy to anyone else. But I didn't care. This was what I needed to do; this was what I should have already done. The next day I boarded a plane back to Buffalo with that ring in my pocket and hope in my heart.

When I landed, I did what I always did: I called Angie to tell her I was back in town and wanted to see her. But like every other time I'd called for the past three weeks, there was no answer. That didn't matter anymore because I was back in Buffalo. She was going to have to see me now; she'd have to speak to me.

After going home and dropping off my bags, I hopped into my car, and with the ring in my pocket went straight to Angie's house. On the drive over, I prepared all the words I was going to say, all the words that would get Angie to forgive me and marry me. When I pulled up in front of her house, I was ready. I jumped out of the car, marched to her front door, raised my hand to knock, then stopped.

For a moment, I wondered why my hand was frozen in midair. Why couldn't I knock? I stood there, for endless minutes, with all kinds of thoughts galloping through my head. I turned around and went back to my car. I sat there for a moment as I figured out what had just happened.

I'd been so anxious to talk to Angie; I truly couldn't wait to see her. But as I stood in front of her house, I thought about all of her rejection over the past few weeks. She hadn't given me one chance; she had completely shut the door on us. What if she did the same thing when we stood face-to-face? At least in that moment I had hope. At least I could imagine that when I saw her again, she'd believe me and fall right back into my arms. I couldn't take the chance of her rejecting me in person. Then it would be over; *we* would be over.

As I started the ignition and pulled away from her house, another plan formed in my head. I'd wait for Angie to come to me. Surely, she wouldn't be able to reject me if she came to me; she wouldn't walk away from all we had become. As hard as that was for me, that's what I did.

Part of my plan was easy because Tonnie lived on the same street, so just about every day I drove by Angie's house. I made sure my car was parked in Tonnie's driveway so Angie would see it if she drove by. Whenever I went to Tonnie's house, I got out of the car slowly, taking my time, hoping that at any moment I'd see Angie. And I did the same thing when leaving.

After days turned into weeks, it finally worked! One day when I was heading out of Tonnie's house, I saw Angie driving toward me. I stood and stared and finally her eyes turned to me. This was it—I'd get the chance to talk to her and explain everything. I waved. And Angie kept right on going. She drove by as if I weren't standing there.

I was mad at myself for getting into this situation and not being able to fix it. "God, what is it going to take?" I questioned as I slid into my car. I felt as if I couldn't breathe without her. I was stuck in this space between loving her and losing her, and it was getting to be too much. I couldn't wait any longer; I was going to have to lay it all out there.

The next day I got into my Mustang and again rode down Burke Drive. Only this time, I pulled right into Angie's driveway, just like I'd done weeks before. When I got out of my car, I slammed the door hard, making sure she knew there was someone outside. My heart was pounding as I walked onto her porch. I took a moment to inhale, say a quick prayer, and then … I knocked.

Within seconds, she appeared through the glass panes. She looked at me and stopped. That was appropriate because right at that moment my heart stopped too. Time passed … one second, two seconds, six seconds … and then she answered the door.

11

A Ribbon in the Sky

(From Angela)

I held onto the door and just stared at him with a steely glare. Samson had no idea I was holding on because I felt paralyzed, as if I wouldn't even be able to stand straight without the aid of the door. Although I felt frozen, I couldn't still my mind. Thoughts warred within. I was locked in a battle between all of my hurt and anger on one side, and on the other side all of my love and longing in my heart.

My grip on the door tightened. It was more than the fear of falling that kept me holding on. I held on to the doorknob because, if I could stand, I wasn't sure what my hands would do. Would my hands turn into fists and strike Samson with blow after blow for each second I'd suffered since I saw him in the theater? Or would my hands betray me and reach for him so that I could grab his shoulders, pull him close, and hold him tight?

As the conflict inside of me continued, I wondered what Samson was thinking because he seemed frozen too, standing stiffly, wordlessly. Even time didn't move. Then his eyes widened a bit as if he were trying to send me a message: *I'll never let you go*, he seemed to be saying.

My eyes yelled right back at him: *Why did you hurt me like that?*

I never meant to do that, his eyes answered back.

With those unspoken words, a thousand pins pierced my skin, beginning at my toes and inching up along my legs and my torso, pulsating up my neck, then down along my arms, finally reaching my hands. The sensation jolted me out of my trance. I tried to make my body do what my mind wanted to do: take two steps back so I could slam the door in his face and run the other way.

Even though that's what I wanted, I couldn't do it. I had run from this moment for too long. All of those times when I saw Samson or his car down at his sister's house, I'd run every single time afraid to have this showdown. But we were here now and it was time. I had to face this so I could move on with my life.

All I was feeling inside seeped out of my eyes in a long, slow eye roll that moved with me as I turned and headed inside my living room. I paused to reach for a box on the floor. My back was to Samson, but I heard him step inside and move behind me. And then when I no longer heard him, I felt him. He hadn't touched me, but we were so in sync that I knew he was about to say something. I couldn't allow him to speak first, so I let my words come rushing out.

"I've got your things," I said with my back still to him.

Over the past few weeks, I had gathered everything that belonged to Samson. I hadn't packed it all at once. No, I'd tortured myself and spread out the pain. Every time I had a thought like, *Samson must think I'm stupid*, I'd go in search of something that he had left behind. The first things I'd gathered for the box were his favorite basketball and his Adidas sneakers that he kept by the back door for those neighborhood pick-up games that boys would ask him to play whenever they saw his car in my driveway.

That's when that thought turned to, *How could I have been so stupid?* I gathered all of the photos we'd taken together: from our day trip to Toronto where we'd shopped and dined and had a blast, to the photo from his mother's annual New Beginnings gala that she held every New Year's Day, and all of the pictures of the two of us dressed to the nines and of him performing for the crowd. I tossed every one of those pictures callously into the box.

When I began yelling at myself that *I should have known,* I went after the gifts I'd given Samson, especially the cherished autographed picture of Peyton, Archie, and Eli Manning I'd given him after we played sand football with the trio for an event I organized in the Bahamas. I hurled that into the box.

And when I asked myself, *Why didn't I see this coming?* I found every trinket and keepsake he'd given me and I tossed them all into the box.

There was one photo, though, that I kept—the picture of Samson singing at my sister's wedding. Every time I tried to toss it into the box, I stopped, as if I couldn't throw it away. I couldn't because that was the first time I'd *really* seen Samson, so handsome, so charismatic. Even now, as I stood there, holding this box, I remembered that night and the tender side of the man who sang:

Oh, so long for this night I prayed,
That a star would guide you my way ...

I remembered feeling as if he were singing to me. While my head knew that the two of us had to part, my heart wasn't ready to let completely go. So I'd kept that photo and hoped that one day I'd throw it in the trash too.

Leaning over, I heaved up the box and turned toward him. When I faced Samson, I had to pause and blink a few extra times. I don't know why, but it felt as if I were back there again—at my sister's wedding—and Samson was singing:

This was not a coincidence,
And far more than a lucky chance ...

On that day, those weren't mere words. I'd believed everything that Samson sang. I believed it wasn't just a coincidence; we were supposed to meet and to be together.

I pulled the box closer to my body, but only for a second. Then I stretched out my arms so he could take that box and our life together away from me. My hope was that he would just grab the box and go. But Samson didn't say a word; he just stared at me.

My emotions were bubbling. I felt like Mount St. Helens ready to blow. I fought to hold back everything—every emotion, all of the hurt. I didn't want to cry, I didn't want to scream, I didn't want to do anything. All I wanted was for him to take the box and leave.

Finally, he reached out for the box and touched my hands as well. "My things?" With a confused look, he glanced in the box. Maybe he didn't realize how much of his life he had left with me. He took the box with one hand and with the other he picked up one of the framed photographs. In an instant, the expression on his face said it was all beginning to compute for him.

With a shake of his head, he let go of the box and it hit the floor with a thud. I looked down; he didn't. He took the couple of steps that brought us closer together. He hesitated, then took my hand and pulled me close to him. "I didn't come here for my things," he said. "I came here for the one thing I know that I need and I want. And that is you."

That was all it took. Mount St. Helens erupted! I snatched my hand from his grasp and with as much force as I could muster, I pushed him away. "Just take your stuff and go!" I screamed. "You obviously don't know what you want or who you want!" I paused just long enough to catch my breath. "Or maybe you do. Maybe you just want to have your cake and eat it too."

His eyes were on mine when he shouted, "Angie, stop it! It's not like that! It wasn't like that! You didn't even give me a chance to explain!"

"Explain?" I jumped in. "Why would I need your explanations? What I saw was explanation enough!"

"What!" He hurled his words back to me. "I had no idea that girl was coming or would do that. She was on me before I even had a chance to say anything."

In my head, the questions I'd been asking for weeks came back. *Did Samson think I was stupid?* I turned away and yelled, "Whatever!" All I wanted was for this man to go so I could begin to heal my heart and learn to live my life without him.

His voice was softer this time when he said, "Angie, I was wrong." His apology stopped my heart. Made me turn to face him. "She should have known and everyone should know, for that matter, that I am taken," he continued. "I should have made that clear. The only woman I want in my life is you. I thought you knew that!"

I held onto my anger with a vice grip. "Clearly, you don't know what you want," I said. "If you did, what happened would have never happened. If you just want to have someone on your arm, you can have anyone … except for me."

"Angie—"

I didn't let him say anything more because I wasn't finished. "I want something that is real, Samson. Something that I can feel. And I used to feel like I could trust you with my heart. But now you've broken that trust. That trust that I worked so hard to believe in again. You broke it! You … happy … now?" I stammered.

"Just go," I told him, trying to brush away my emotions and the tears spilling from my eyes.

Samson nodded and moved, but in the wrong direction. He walked toward me when the door was behind him. When he was close enough, he reached out his hand again. "Please don't do this," he said. "Give me another chance; give *us* a chance. I can't stop thinking about you and I miss you so much. I miss us."

I looked toward the heavens, trying to figure out why he wasn't hearing me. "Were you thinking about us back in the theater?" I asked. "Did you think about what your actions or lack thereof would do to us?"

"Stop! Just stop it," he said as if he were tired of me taking us back to that same place. "Nothing happened. I already told you that. And I also told you that you are my first lady. I've told you, I've told everyone we know, and it's time now for me to tell everyone else."

"First lady, huh?" I said. "What are your plans? Do you have a second lady, and a third lady lined up too?"

"What?" His expression was a mixture of confusion and disgust. "I don't know how many times I have to tell you this; I don't know how many ways I can say it before you hear me: what you saw wasn't what you thought."

"What I thought," I began, "was that we were on the same page." I'd chosen those words carefully because those were Samson's words, something he believed in, something he said all the time about the two of us. I knew those words would make him stop. And they did.

He stood silently before me before he took a deep breath as if he had to swallow what he wanted to say. Then he exhaled. "Ang' … let's get on the same page. I want you on my page." His voice made me focus on him again. "I'm still on the same page, Ang'. I never got off of it." He lowered his head and shook it.

When he looked up, there was an emotion in his eyes I'd never seen. He put his hands together as if he were about to pray. "There are so many things that I could give you to try to make up for hurting you. I've tried sending you cards; I've sent you all these flowers." He gestured with his hands. "Look around, this place looks like a flower shop."

Without my permission, my head turned and begrudgingly I glanced at the red roses, yellow gerbera daisies, pink tulips, and white lilies in stunning vases that had come to me in four different deliveries. They were all so beautiful, I couldn't talk myself into throwing the flowers away.

"But no gesture"—his words made me face him once again—"nothing I can give you would be better than my word." He paused for just a moment. "I can't breathe without you."

My pulse quickened.

"There's nothing that I want more than having you in my life," he said.

My heart stopped.

"I pray that you will come back to me. I pray that you will give me a chance to show you that the only page I want to be on is yours."

My heart melted, but my mind revolted. I wasn't prepared for this. I didn't want this. Although I was prepared to leave Samson, was I now going to be prepared to trust him again?

He must've been able to see the fight that raged inside. His words were still soft, but he spoke a little faster. "I want to show you that I can be the man you have waited for. I know that you are the woman I have prayed for."

I shook my head as if that would make him and his words go away.

He reached for me and cupped my face between his hands. Then he began to hum. His humming was something that I was used to; I always loved it, but right now I didn't want to hear it. Especially not this song.

I reached up to pull his hands away and push him away.

"We can't lose with God on our side ...," he sang.

That stopped me.

"We'll find strength in each tear we cry ..."

When he'd sang that at the wedding, I'd fallen for him that day. And now I'd fallen again. I knew right then I had to give Samson Logan another chance. No matter what my head said, my heart won.

12

Rules To Live By

(From Angela)

We spent the next hour standing there holding each other. I was grateful to be nestled into his chest with his scratchy goatee grazing my forehead and the familiar scent of his favorite cologne filling my nostrils. I was caught up in the stillness of being in his arms, completely caught up—as if God had touched my heart and allowed me to love Samson all the way again. That is the only way for me to explain how I'd forgiven Samson completely. It had to be a God thing.

"I can't breathe," he whispered.

"I know," I said. I understood what he meant. This moment was taking my breath away too; his words made me squeeze him even tighter.

"No, Ang'," Samson said, his voice sounding strained. "No really. I *can't* breathe. You're holding me too tight!"

I busted out laughing, but Samson didn't laugh until I released him. I let go in every way. The weight of the anger I'd carried all of these months like a boulder wrapped around my shoulders lifted off of me, and in its place was joy and love. The joy of being with Samson and the love I felt for him.

"I'll be right back," he said once our laughter had subsided to chuckles. He jogged down the hallway toward my home office before I could ask him where he was going or what he was doing.

I was puzzled. He hadn't stepped into my house in weeks and now he was searching for something. I wanted to tell him he wouldn't find anything in there; I'd tossed everything that belonged to him into the box. But he didn't give me a chance. He was gone before I could say anything.

As Samson went on his hunt, I lifted my eyes to the heavens and whispered, "Thank you, God." I had to thank him because the feeling of relief that had washed over me felt like grace. I had needed it, and I was so grateful God knew it too. The Lord knew I'd been too hurt and too stubborn to do this on my own.

Without moving my lips, I thanked him again. And again. And again. Until Samson came back into the living room with a pen and one of the small notebooks I kept on my desk.

He didn't say a word as he flipped through the notebook until he found an empty page. "Take a seat," he directed me.

I did as I was told, even more amused now. What was Samson up to? I watched as he jotted something onto the page and then I leaned forward, trying to peer over his arm, but he said, "Not yet," then shifted so I couldn't see what he was writing.

Eventually, he turned the notebook around for me to see the bold letters he'd written across the top of the page: *The Rules*.

"What?" I said.

"We're going to get on the same page," he said. "Tonight!"

That made me giggle, but Samson was serious.

He kept on, "We've got to have some relationship rules to live by so this never happens again."

Once he said that, he seemed to catch my case of the giggles and we laughed together, unable to stop. "Okay," I said, finally able to get words out in between my giggles. "I'm down."

"Cool! And I get to make the first rule," he said.

"No way," I protested, even though I didn't mind. "I'm going first."

He shook his head. "My idea, so I get to go first."

I paused for a moment and marveled at how quickly we'd fallen back into step. This is how it had always been between us—good times filled with laughter. Somehow I knew this was how it would be forever. God wouldn't have brought us together the first time and then fixed us this time if this wasn't what he wanted. "Fine!" I pretended to pout. "But it better be a good rule since it's the first one."

"Rule number one," he said, scrunching his nose as he wrote on the page. He was silent for a moment, as if absorbed in thought, before he began writing: *Pray together and put God first!*

My laughter went away and I was filled with surprise. I don't know why, but I'd expected Samson to write something silly to stay with the moment. I guess he really was in the moment because his focus was on God.

Looking up from the book, he turned to me. "Let's face it," he said. "You and I can't make it without God!"

We both nodded, then laughed together once more.

"Rule number two," he said.

"Nuh-uh." I jumped in and reached for the notebook. "I'm supposed to go next!"

Samson twisted and held his arm away from me so I couldn't reach the notebook. "No, my idea," he said. "So I get to go first and second."

I stood and put my hand on my hips, giving him my best pouting face, but it didn't faze him. With his head down, he began writing again. A few seconds later, he said, "Rule number two: Talk every day," and then in parentheses he added: *No matter what.* Looking up, he asked me, "Can we do that, ma'am?"

I knew the "no matter what" part was in parentheses because of me and the way I had stubbornly refused to speak to him for weeks. I pretended to think about it for a moment and then told him yes in a tone that sounded like I was exasperated. "Now my turn," I announced and reached for the notepad again.

But just like before, he pulled it away. This time, though, he stood, as if he knew that if he stayed seated I'd somehow wrestle that book from him. He moved to the opposite side of the coffee table in front of us. "Not yet," he said. "I have one more."

"That's it!" I shouted. I ran to the other side of the table, but he ran from me.

"I promise," he said, still running. "I just have one more and then I'll give it to you!" He'd slowed down when he started talking, so I caught him, pushed him onto the sofa, and tickled him, making him laugh uncontrollably. But that didn't make him relent. "I promise, I promise," he said between giggles. "My last one."

If tickling didn't make him give up the notebook, then nothing would. "Fine," I said once again, too exhausted from all of our laughing and running to say or do anything else.

He sat up, cleared his throat in a serious manner, and began to write. When he was done, he said, "Rule number three: What I say goes."

When he looked up with that sheepish grin, I shouted, "What!" and I leaped onto him and grabbed the notebook from his grasp. I snatched the pen away, prepared to cross out rule number three, when I looked down and read what he'd really written. "Rule number three: Believe in each other," I read slowly. I looked up at him.

He shrugged. "Oh yeah. That's what I meant to say."

My eyes had been filled with water from all of our laughing, but now my eyes were filled with the mist that came from my emotions. "That's a good one," I managed to get out.

He paused for a moment, as if he knew I needed a second to get myself together, then he said, "Although this was my brilliant idea, you may have a turn." He sat back as if he were royalty and circled his hands in the air, motioning for me to write.

I rolled my eyes but then focused on the notebook. After a couple of seconds, I said, "Okay, I only have one." And I did the same thing Samson had been doing to me—I hid the notebook so he wouldn't be able to see what I was writing. When I was done, I cleared my throat loudly. "Rule number four: Keep your word." That's what I said, but I'd also written in parentheses: *Do what you say you are going to do.*

I turned the notepad around for him to read what I had written and watched his eyes move as he read my words.

When he looked up at me, I said, "If you say you're going to pray with me and put God first, then do it. If you say you're going to talk to me every day, do it. If you say you're going to believe in me, then believe because I believe in you."

He hesitated, then said softly, "I will." It was Samson's turn to get a little emotional. He stood up, pulled me into his arms, and when he kissed me it felt like the first time.

I don't know how many seconds or minutes passed before I finally pulled away. "Now go!" I said, giving him a gentle, playful shrug. "I have to work in the morning."

He glanced at his watch. "It's after midnight," he said as if he couldn't believe that much time had passed. He looked up. "Okay," he said. "I'll go, but not yet. I have just a few things left to do." He then reached for the notebook with our rules and ripped out the sheet we'd written on. Next, he grabbed my hand and practically dragged me behind him into the kitchen.

"Samson! What are you doing?"

He didn't answer. Instead, he led me to the refrigerator where he used one of my many collector magnets to secure the paper on the fridge. "Now we are officially on the same page!" he announced.

I chuckled. "Okay. I agree. Now go."

He shook his head. "Nope. Still more to do."

He let go of me this time, and I followed him back into the living room. He was searching again, but I had no idea what he was looking for.

"There it is!" He stomped across the room to the cardboard box that held all of his worldly possessions he'd left with me. He lifted the box, then one by one he removed each item, putting it back in its place: the photos he returned to the mantel, his shoes he put in the mudroom by the back door. He paused for a moment when he held the autographed football, looking at it as if he were in love.

Abruptly, he turned to me and said, "I need to add an amendment to our rules."

"What?" I asked, squinting my eyes, trying to figure Samson out.

He headed toward the kitchen. "Rule number four: Do not toss the autographed football into old boxes."

I stopped him before he reached the kitchen. "Oh no, you don't!" I shouted. "That's not a rule and I have to go to sleep!"

"All right." He walked over to the display case in the living room and opened it, gingerly placing the football back inside.

As he stood there admiring his prized possession, I knew I'd have to take this matter into my own hands. "Good night, Samson," I said, gently nudging him toward the door.

"It has been," he said, leaning against the door.

I stood on my toes and kissed him.

He said, "I've made you sad, mad, and—I hope—happy, all in one day." Then he walked out the door and down the path to his Mustang that shone in the moonlight.

The midnight hour was still and quiet and beautiful. All I could do was smile as I watched my man walk to his car.

He opened his car door and before he got inside, he looked back at me. "I'm gonna just focus on making you happy for the rest of our lives, okay?"

My heart skipped several beats. That was okay with me.

13

The Gift

(From Samson)

J slowly backed my car out of Angela's driveway, filled with relief, purpose, and gratitude. I could finally breathe again. It felt as if I had inhaled anxiety for all of these weeks, and now I could exhale all of the doubts and worries. Finally.

When I stopped at the red light at the corner, I reached inside my pocket and retrieved the small black velvet box I still had tucked away. I'd been fiddling with it all evening, not sure what to do. I flipped open the box at the traffic light, tilted it, and a cascade of colors danced across the dashboard and the roof of the car.

I was supposed to give this to her—that was my intent. I wanted to propose. But when the moment came, it didn't feel right. Other things needed to happen first. How could I give Angela a symbol of my love when I needed her to trust me and my sincerity?

Angie needed to believe in me before I slid this ring on to her finger. She needed to believe in me and she needed to believe in us. And what she needed most of all was some space between tonight and what had happened these past few weeks. When she told our children the story of our engagement, I wanted it to be a time of joyful memories. I didn't want our memories to be tainted with the trauma and tension of what had happened.

The Gift

I paused my thoughts. *Our children*, I thought. That made me smile. I loved the idea of Angie and me having children together. I glanced down at the ring once again.

Angie.

Our children.

Looking at this ring, thinking about Angie, imagining our future—all I wanted to do was whip the car into a U-turn, crash into her driveway, storm to her door, and be down on one knee when she opened it. We were on the same page once again, and I couldn't wait to start our next chapter together. I couldn't wait for us to be a family.

It wasn't until I heard the honk behind me that I snapped out of my trance. I pressed the accelerator and the car lunged forward. Even though I was heading home, my thoughts went back to Angie.

We had built a great relationship in our short time together. To some, it probably seemed as if our courtship had been long. But because of my long stints on the road, we only saw each other every few months, and then it was only for a few days at a time. Being in each other's face and in each other's space was something we both cherished. It was how we'd developed our relationship, by talking and treasuring our time together.

It wasn't just the time I spent with Angela that mattered; it was *how* we spent that time together. When it was just the two of us, I didn't have to be the leading man, the soul singer, the performer, the minister, or the life of the party. I could simply be. Whenever I was with Angie, I truly became the best Samson Logan I could be, because she embraced the part of me that was strong, and she encouraged the parts of me that sometimes felt weak. She was the one person I could talk to about anything.

Looking up to the heavens, I said a quick prayer of thanks to God for the grace he had given to me. I thanked him for Angie's forgiveness and for her acceptance.

As I pulled up to my place, I paused for a moment. I was still overcome with anxiety, though it was much different now. The knots that had earlier been in my stomach had been replaced with flutters of anticipation. When I slid out of my car and approached my house, I knew exactly what I had to do.

It was Indian summer in Buffalo and the temperature made it feel as if we were approaching Labor Day rather than the holiday season. Thanksgiving was coming up and Christmas was just a little over a month away. Though the weather was warmer than usual, the feel of Christmas was in the air. The apple and oak trees in the yard were bare, their fragrance replaced by the pine trees that were everywhere.

This was my favorite time of year—especially this year. With what Angela and I had been through, with us back together, with what I planned for our future, I was going to do everything to make this a Christmas that Angela would always remember.

That wouldn't be difficult. Everyone knew how I was; I turned into a kid at Christmas, shaking presents that made their way under the tree early, sneaking around searching for presents that had been stashed away with my name on the boxes. Every year I was the one who put on the full Santa suit for all the kids in the family, and with the whole family around I told the *true* story of Christmas before we passed out the gifts from under the tree.

Honestly, the presents really were my favorite part of the holiday. But while I loved getting presents, my joy was in giving them. The reactions of my family as they opened the presents was always heartwarming, and this year I couldn't wait for my biggest gift ever—for Angela. I knew her reaction was going to be priceless.

I would only have two days with Angela before I had to head out on the road again for a four-week stint that would have me away for Thanksgiving, but back home a week before Christmas. I had the perfect ruse to throw her off the fact I was going to propose. I was going to talk about what *I was going to get* this year, keeping the focus away from what *I was going to give.*

The next morning, I was back at Angela's house and we went to the mall. As we wandered through the Walden Galleria, I made sure I stopped at some of my favorite spots. "Oh, look at those shoes," I said, pointing to a pair in the window at Aldo's Uomo, one of the most exclusive stores in the mall. Next we went to Lord & Taylor's and as we walked through, I started showing Angela everything I wanted under the Christmas tree. She took note of everything I pointed out, totally falling for my plan. I didn't keep the focus totally on me, however; we picked up some gifts for my son, our parents, her niece, and my nephews.

The whole time we chatted excitedly about Christmas, sharing our family traditions. It was great to see the way our families had melded together; both sides had embraced each other. For the past few years since we had been dating, we'd have Christmas breakfast with Angela's side of the family and then Christmas dinner with my family. What was especially exciting about this year was that Angela was hosting the Christmas breakfast at her home. As we shopped, she selected a few festive ornaments, garland, stockings, and a beautiful centerpiece for the table.

I was glad I was home to do the shopping with her. Because I was going to be away, we wouldn't be able to decorate together, but when we selected a new star for the top of her Christmas tree, I told Angie, "We'll put the finishing touches on everything when I get back home."

For two joyous days, Angela and I hung out together as if we had never been apart, and then the time came for me to have to leave. As usual, she drove me to the airport, but this time it felt different. Usually I would hop out of the car, always eager to hit the road because there was never a time when I wasn't grateful for the opportunity to perform.

But I didn't have those feelings when Angie stopped the car at the airport. Instead, I was filled with a bit of sadness and our parting was difficult. We usually shared a quick hug, but this time that hug turned into a lingering curbside embrace. She held on to me tightly, as if she didn't want to let go. She held on to me the way she did two nights before, squeezing me a little tighter with each passing moment. I had to say, "Angela, I can't breathe." We both burst into laughter as she released me.

I wiped away the single tear that rolled from her eye. "I'll be back before you know it," I told her. She nodded and I walked toward the revolving door. Just as I got inside, I turned and yelled, "Don't forget to wrap my presents!"

She just shook her head, smiled, and waved.

When I got to Houston and caught up with the rest of the cast, I was once again in that place where I felt good about being on the road, but it was different. Yeah, I was happy, but I was more aware of the joy that filled me rather than the happiness. I felt God's presence, as if he were enveloping me, following me with every step I took. Being surrounded by God that way let me know I was where I was supposed to be, doing what I was supposed to be doing—not just with my career, but with my heart also. With Angela, God had given my heart a place to live. Our love was special and our love was a gift I would never take for granted.

It was fitting that I was doing a show called *Whatever She Wants*. Each night the crowd roared in laughter and applause as I took the stage in Je'Caryous Johnson's play alongside Vivica Fox, Boris Kodjoe, and others. Even though Angela wasn't there with me, I felt her presence.

Four weeks flew by and it was time for my winter break. Like I always did, I called Angela the moment my plane landed. We always had the same routine: I'd call and then she would head to the airport and meet me curbside. That gave me enough time to disembark and make my way to baggage claim. As I passed the waiting area, the bag on my shoulder slipped down and fell to the floor. I bent down to pick it up and was met with another hand trying to help me gather my belongings.

"Thank you!" I said with my head still down.

"You're welcome!"

I was grinning before I even had the chance to look up. There was Angie, wide eyed and smiling. "What are you in doing here?" I asked with surprise in my voice as I hugged her at the same time.

"I couldn't wait to see you!" she said coyly when we finally backed away from each other.

"Angela, you couldn't wait another ten minutes?" I joked.

She shook her head and in all seriousness said, "Nope, not even another ten minutes!"

She sent the butterflies in my stomach fluttering once again. Seeing her and knowing what was about to happen made my anxiety rise through the roof. We laughed as we gathered my bags and talked about Christmas.

"Now that you're here, I can finish up my decorations," she said.

"Perfect!" I said. "Did you wrap my presents yet?"

She smirked and folded her arms. "You know what I was thinking? That maybe it would be nice if this year we didn't buy each other gifts and just focused on the reason for the season."

"Hmm ..." I said, putting as thoughtful of a look on my face as I could. Then I shrugged and patted my stuffed suitcase. "I guess I'll have to send back all of these gifts I bought for you on the road!"

"Oh no, you don't!" she said, trying to grab my bag from me.

But I didn't let her get anywhere near my luggage, because I knew she'd try to peek inside. "Hey, it was your idea," I told her. As she kept trying to grab my bag, I added, "Okay, okay. I guess exchanging a few gifts wouldn't be a bad idea as long as we truly remember the reason for the season."

The tips of her lips seemed to reach her ears as she smiled. "Well," she said, "if you insist."

We chatted on the ride to my mother's. I was so glad to be

home—because of Angie, of course, but I also couldn't wait to see my family. I hadn't told anyone when I was coming home, so this was perfect. It was Sunday evening and that meant that the whole family would be at my mother's house for dinner.

When Angie and I walked in, everyone was thrilled to see us. Of course, I'd stopped by to say hello, but I had another motive for going to my mom's house. I had hidden the ring there for safe-keeping while I was gone.

After we all said our hellos and greeted everyone with hugs and kisses, we gathered in the living room. We sat and talked and sipped on Mom's famous eggnog that she only made during the holidays. Everyone was so engaged that no one saw me slip out of the room.

The small velvet box was where I'd left it, and when I opened it, the sparkle of the ring seemed to be even more brilliant. I tucked the box into my pocket. When Angela and I said good night that evening to my family, I knew the next time I'd see them Angie and I would be engaged, which made me even more excited.

It was hard for me to sleep that night. Early the next day, I was back at Angela's place with the ring in my pocket. When she opened the door, I had to pause for a moment. She looked like she had the day we'd first met. She was wearing a T-shirt and jeans with her hair pulled back and no makeup on. But she could still rival any fully made-up fashion model. Angela glowed. This was the perfect day to get engaged.

We hugged and then she pulled me inside to the chaos of the boxes of decorations and lights strewn about the room.

I stepped around and over all the boxes. "It's looking good already in here!"

"Thanks, but the tree still needs a bit of work," she said, looking around the room. "Something is missing. Can you help me put up this garland?"

I shrugged my coat off my shoulders and then we went to work. We started with the garland, then strung up some lights. The whole time I fidgeted, constantly checking my pocket. Every time I felt the velvet box, I said to myself, *It's still there.* I'd done that about a dozen times before Angie looked at me.

"You okay?" she asked.

"Huh?" I was nervous, but I had to hide my feelings.

"You look a little flushed."

"Do I?" I shrugged. "I probably just need some water. Could you get me some?"

"Sure," she said, sounding a bit unsure and a little concerned.

When she headed to the kitchen, I sprang into action. I pulled the ring box from my pocket and placed it between some garland near the lighted Christmas village she had on display. It blended in perfectly, almost looking like a building in the village. Once I had the box set, I sprinted back to the tree, kicking a few boxes along the way. Thump ... thump!

"You okay in there?" she called out from the kitchen.

"Yes!" I replied, trying to sound nonchalant. "I just need that water."

The concern was still on her face when she came back with the glass. She watched me take a few sips as if she were trying to figure out what was wrong.

"Better," I said, reassuring her.

She let out a sigh, her expression returning to calm.

"I think I found what's missing in here," I said.

"Really?" She looked around the room that was now twinkling with Christmas lights and was fragrant with the smell of vanilla and pine. "What do you think we need?"

I casually pointed to the Christmas village. "Maybe we should add something more to the village," I told her. "It looks like there is a blank spot over there."

She walked over to the display.

When she didn't seem to see the box, I suggested, "Maybe you could just rearrange it a bit."

With a slight shrug, she picked up a few of the caroler figures and moved them, then she reached to pick up the lighted church but stopped. Her hand paused in the air just above the box as if she were trying to register what she was seeing. "I don't remember putting this here," she said. Just a couple of seconds later, she gasped. She turned with her hand cupped over her mouth. She stared at me, standing frozen as I made my way to her.

With one hand I held her hand, and with the other I picked up the box. Tears were already in her eyes and she began to sob. As I opened the box, the light from the star on the top of the tree hit the ring and made the diamonds sparkle. The whole room glowed! It may have been the Christmas tree, the village, and all the decorations that did that—or it may have been just me and Angela and the fullness of the moment.

I took a deep breath that seemed to send away the butterflies that had filled me for weeks. All I felt now was assurance. "The only thing missing in this room," I whispered, "is this ring that I would be proud to place on your hand. If you will have mine."

She simply gazed at me in amazement.

Her silence gave me room to tell her what had been in my heart for so long. "I know that I have found the one that my heart loves, in you," I said. "These last few years have been wonderful. And I'm hoping that you would spend the next fifty with me." I lifted the ring from the box. "I have a diamond for each of the next fifty years," I said, pointing out that the ring was mounted with fifty princess-cut diamonds. I then slipped the ring onto her finger. "Angela Burgin … will you marry me?"

She looked down at her hand, then back up at me, back at her hand again, and then back at me before she finally wrapped her arms around my neck. Her embrace seemed to be as much to steady her trembling body as to show me the love she was feeling in that moment.

The Gift

A few minutes passed and I realized she hadn't verbally answered me. So I teased her, wanting to bring a smile to her face through her tears. "Are you free for the next fifty years?" I asked again.

This time she nodded. "Let's start with the next fifty years," she said, "and end with forever."

14

The Perfect Man

(From Angela)

It was well after midnight, but I still couldn't fall asleep. Thoughts swirled and I wanted to reflect on every one of them. For so many years it felt like my love radar had been stuck in the off position, and I definitely needed help in the romance department. But what I'd discovered, even before I met Samson, was that every woman can find the perfect man. The big secret is that he isn't hiding. He's within us and I only had to look inside to see him and hear him. It took some time, but I came to realize that I needed to *stop praying for the perfect man* and *start praying to God.*

Once I did that, I became empowered in ways I didn't realize. At first I questioned what I was doing. Was I giving up on love? But as quickly as that thought came to me, I shut it down, knowing that I wasn't giving up—I was giving in. I was doing everything I could to have the faith and courage to truly let God have control. And once God had control, he worked it out. I was in love, not with the perfect man, but with the perfect man for me. All because of God.

I sighed and raised my hand in the air just so I could see my ring again. Even in the midnight blackness of my bedroom, the stones sparkled and the colors danced against the wall as if the ring had a life of its own.

It was kind of crazy the way I felt now. That feeling made me giggle because there'd been times when I felt crazy and stupid about love. I'd never been *that girl* who would plot, plan, and pull a guy. But being stupid about love was not a sin; staying stupid was. In that moment I was authentically crazy stupid in love and I felt wonderful about it.

Being with Samson made up for all of the heartbreaks I had suffered before I met him, heartbreaks that made me believe that love was over for me, that it was simply something that was unattainable. But look at God—he put together the pages of a new love story just for me!

There was no doubt that Samson was a serious plot twist in my love life. It still amazed me how God had orchestrated our meeting. *Angela, no one is going to come just knock on your door!* How many times had I been told that? How many times had Kris and April told me that I had to "get out there" and meet someone? Thinking about that made me laugh.

Rolling over again, I wondered if I would ever fall asleep. It's hard to sleep when you feel giddy, like a kid at Christmas, but I guess that was appropriate since there were not too many days before Christmas. I was so grateful Samson had chosen this season to propose.

This season of joy I was entering into and experiencing was all God's doing. This was all his grace and his mercy. Bringing Samson into my life was God's way of pouring more of himself into me. And to think that a few weeks ago I could have never imagined this moment. I thought it was over because I wasn't going to tolerate a relationship where I couldn't trust my partner. But I guess the craziness of our lives and our love made it interesting. And the way Samson and I had worked through our issues and worked them out made our lives and our love more meaningful.

"I can't believe this," I whispered, grateful there was no one in my house to hear me say that for at least the thousandth time. I kept saying it because it was hard to believe. It was no secret that I'd wanted to marry Samson. We'd talked about it on numerous occasions and there were times when I was absolutely sure his proposal was on the way. Those were the times when I got prepared—my hair done, nails done, everything ready.

Samson's proposal came when I least expected it. My hair wasn't done, my nails weren't done, and I wasn't ready—at least not physically. I was ready in all the ways that mattered, though. I may not have looked picture perfect, but the moment was picture perfect.

I had been in complete shock. That was the only way to describe it when Samson put that ring on my finger. It wasn't until he asked me again that I realized I'd never answered him.

"Are you free for the next fifty years?" he had asked.

I had nodded and managed to say, "Yes! Let's start with the next fifty years and end with forever."

From that point on, I couldn't stop crying and grinning; I could hardly get out any words. But Samson and I were able to communicate in our own love language. I knew that my fiancé and God understood all I wanted to say.

It took hours for me to get myself together, and once I was able to talk again (without crying) Samson and I hatched a plan for unveiling the news to our families. We couldn't wait to share with them, of course, but it was important to us that we did it at the right time.

"Let's give this news as a gift," Samson finally said.

"What do you mean?" I asked.

"Let's do it after everyone has exchanged gifts."

I thought about his suggestion: After everyone exchanged gifts? Yes, that would be perfect. Just when everyone was settling down, we'd rile them up again with this news. I clapped my hands. Both of our families would be thrilled.

Keeping the secret of our engagement for the next few days made it even more romantic. The joy belonged to the two of us alone and it felt like this earth, this life, was made just for me and Samson.

Then the day came.

It started with my family first. I could hardly get through our Christmas gift exchange (which we always did before breakfast) without bursting with the news. But finally when everyone was sitting down at the table enjoying the grits, eggs, and bacon I'd prepared, I made a beeline for my bedroom. I'd hidden my ring inside my nightstand drawer and I slipped in on to my finger.

Taking a deep breath, I strolled back to the table, took my seat, glanced at Samson, and then released the biggest yawn I could muster. Of course, I had to cover my mouth, and when I did the light from the chandelier above hit the ring so the rainbow of colors spun through the air.

At first there was silence. And then pandemonium filled with excitement:

"Oh my gosh!"

"Are you engaged?"

"Get out of here!"

The words came at me so fast I couldn't tell who was saying what. Soon the chatter was so loud I couldn't understand the words at all. But I understood the sentiments—there were congratulations and hugs and handshakes all around.

"We've got to call April," Kris said, pushing my cell phone into my hand.

I agreed. April was with her family, but I wanted her to hear the news from me. I had hardly gotten the words *I'm engaged* out of my mouth before April and Kris began planning the wedding.

"This is going to be the wedding of the century!" April exclaimed.

"Yes! Can you imagine," Kris said, "Sam will enter the church in a helicopter or something."

April and Kris laughed as if that were the funniest thing they'd ever heard.

I guess April felt like she had to top that. "No, no," she said. "He's going to rise up from the floor in a glass elevator."

That was pretty funny because Sam always did have a flare for the dramatic. There was no way I would dare mention any of the jokes, especially not the one about the helicopter, because I was fairly certain Samson would get right on the phone, seeing how he could make that happen.

For at least an hour, I basked in the joy with my family. We hung out there for the rest of the afternoon until it was time to leave for Samson's family celebration to do it all over again.

Before we stepped into his parents' home, I slipped the ring off my finger and tucked it into my purse. Once inside, I had to again hide my excitement as everyone opened their gifts.

When we sat down for dinner, I snuck the ring back to where it belonged, and once again had one of those big yawning moments. Once again my ring shone and flashed beneath the light of Samson's mother's two crystal teardrop chandeliers. This time, Samson played along, pretending to be blinded by the light.

It was déjà vu all over again. Everyone stared, then everyone cheered. There were congratulatory shouts all around, and once again I was hugged and kissed as everyone began talking about the wedding.

Sam's mother was ecstatic. "This wedding is long overdue," she said, letting us both know that it was about time. "We're going to have a big wedding. A big red wedding," she said, making everyone laugh even though we all knew she wasn't kidding. Red is Earnestine's favorite color.

By the time Sam dropped me off later that evening, we were both exhausted. But he still had one more surprise for me. At the door, he tried to tease me. "Now I know that you didn't really want to exchange gifts this year, right?"

I was puzzled by his words. I mean, yes, I knew he was referring to our discussion at the airport, but I didn't know why he would bring this up now.

He continued, "You wanted to remember the reason for the season, right?"

"Yes," I said slowly, still unsure of where he was going.

Then he got serious, which was unusual for him because Samson spent more time joking around than being sentimental. With tenderness in his voice, he said, "Well, the first time I saw you, when I drove up to your house, God said to me, 'That's your wife!' I'm so thankful I listened." Samson took my hand. "He is the reason for this season in our lives."

And just like that, I was back to bawling. Samson's words were as precious to me as the diamond. As I recalled these past few days, I teared up, knowing how special it was that the two of us had found each other. And once again, I thanked God for the many blessings he'd given to me, especially my future husband.

The words that Samson had spoken to me before he left rang in my ears: *I know that it will not always be easy, but it will always be worth it.* Then he had added, *I can't wait for you to officially be my wife!*

I had been smiling ever since he said that. As I finally closed my eyes, I knew I'd fall asleep with that same smile on my face.

15

Vegas or Bust

(From Angela)

The next few months were a blur of chiffon, cakes, venues, and never-ending questions. Now that we were engaged, the questions and the requests kept coming in:

"When's the wedding?"

"Can I invite Willie? You remember, he's my third cousin."

"Do you want me to wear anything special?"

"What kind of food are you going to be serving at the reception?"

"How many are going to be in your bridal party?"

I had planned swanky events before, had been in a wedding or two or a thousand, and had cried my way through lots of weddings on TV. So I thought planning my own wedding would be a breeze. But the planning of my wedding was slowly becoming more of a burden than a blessing. Things weren't coming together exactly the way I thought they would. I began to worry.

The only part I was having fun with was looking for a house with Samson. We had dated and waited, and now that the time had finally come where we would have a home and begin to build a family of our own, I was ready to sell mine. So I put a For Sale sign on my house.

Samson and I loved real estate and everything about the house-hunting process. We became emerged in finding the perfect dream home, and if we found an MLS listing we liked, no matter the time of day or night, we'd drop everything to go look at it. We had to do that because between my work and Samson's travel schedules, we never knew if we would miss seeing a great house as we waited for an appointment. So we'd get into our cars and drive by houses, sometimes as late as two in the morning.

That was the only part of this process that was fun for me. When it came to us poring over wedding pamphlets in search of a venue that would accommodate our growing guest list, all of that fun seemed to fade. There was something gnawing inside of me. Maybe it was because I didn't share everyone else's excitement. The truth was that I'd always been enamored with weddings, but had never dreamt of mine. My dreams had always been about my husband. What had played in my mind's eye were the days leading up to the wedding and then the days after that. I thought about the months, the years, and the decades I would spend as a wife.

I figured that was why I was having a hard time with the planning of the ceremony, but I forged forward, feeling sure that once I shopped for my dress, I'd be ready to tackle the entire event. Turning my focus to the dress made me smile, but dressing up my curves with the right mix of chiffon and lace wasn't going to be easy. There were so many beautiful dresses to choose from—how was I going to decide?

I perused wedding gown photos in magazines for weeks and finally narrowed down the field to a style I really liked. I made my first appointment, taking my sister and Shelby, my niece, with me. After greeting us and then discussing the dress styles I liked, the bridal shop owner lined up ten gowns for me. She hung all of the dresses on a rack, where I looked them over for a few minutes before selecting one.

Inside the dressing room, with the help of an attendant, I slipped into the wedding gown. The moment she zipped up the back, I heard the words of friends who'd already gone through this process.

You just know, they had said. *When you see the dress, you know.*

I understood those words the moment I stepped in front of the mirror. This Mori Lee dress was it! The V neck, embroidered lace, and body-hugging net drop-waist gown was perfect for me. When the two-tiered elbow-length veil with scalloped edges was added, I knew this was the right dress for my new beginning.

When I stepped outside of the dressing room, my sister inhaled. "You look beautiful," she whispered.

I checked out myself again in the triple-view mirror. "I'll take it," I said after only a couple of moments.

Kris and my niece were shocked. "Angie, you're not going to try on anything else?" they asked.

"Nope!" I said, smiling at my reflection. "When it's the one, it's the one." Turning to my sister, I added, "Isn't that what you told me?"

With tears in her eyes, she nodded. Looking me over once again, her lips formed a big smile. She too knew this was the dress.

While the selection of my dress was simple, quick, and easy, nothing else worked that way. There were obstacles getting in the way of everything else for the wedding ceremony—especially the main thing, which was the venue.

After visiting every mansion, villa, country club, and banquet hall in the area, we'd finally decided that Salvatore's Italian Garden would be the place for us. It was one of our favorite restaurants and the beauty of their grand ballroom could not be beat. However, when Samson and I made it to our appointment to do a full tour of the ballroom and to review the menu, we were hit with a major disappointment. All of the dates we had in mind were already taken!

We left Salvatore's feeling dejected, and together Samson and I lamented over dinner. "With this huge guest list," I said once we were seated in the restaurant, "I don't know where else we can go. What venue will accommodate us?"

He shook his head, looking as sullen as I felt.

I really wanted to tell him how I was feeling about our wedding and how I couldn't get into planning it. I couldn't wait to marry him—that wasn't the issue at all—but I wasn't married to the idea that we had to have a big wedding. That realization honestly surprised me. What woman didn't want a fairy-tale wedding? I guess I could have been one of the first ones.

We held hands as we discussed our situation and looked forlornly out the window, hardly touching our dinners.

In the middle of us trying to figure out what to do, Samson said, "If our wedding gets any bigger, our dream home is going to go from that"—he pointed to a huge corporate building right across the street from us—"to that." He then pointed to a business right next door that sold sheds.

We burst out laughing, but Samson was right.

"Vegas is looking awfully good right now," I said. I'd spoken those words flippantly, but we both stopped and looked at each other. Then together our eyes widened as if the realization slowly came to both of us at the same time.

Samson turned back to the window and stared at the corporate building and the sheds before he looked at me once again. Neither of us said a word, sitting and staring, as if we were afraid to speak what was on our minds.

But then Samson broke the silence. "Why don't we do it?"

"Are you serious?"

"Yes, why don't we get married in Vegas?"

I wanted to jump up and down, clap my hands, and say, "Yes, let's do it." But there was one thing I knew could stop us, one thing that was huge in our lives. "What about our families?"

As if he had already been thinking about that and had the answer, Samson said, "But what about *us*?"

We allowed the silence to return, looking at each other once again. Then, as if we were in sync, a slow smile spread across our lips and all the joy that I'd felt when Samson asked me to marry him snuck back into my heart.

"So how about it?" he asked after a moment. "Will you marry me in Vegas?"

It didn't take me a second to respond. "I will."

Samson and I hugged and he had no idea that he had just solved every problem that lurked in my mind since we began planning the wedding. I still didn't know how we were going to do this and what we would say to our disappointed families, but it didn't matter. I would be able to face everyone as long as Samson was by my side.

Leaning back, he said, "Let's do this."

I grinned and we sealed our agreement with a kiss. We were going to get married in Las Vegas.

16

When You Fall

(From Angela)

The decision we made that night forever changed our lives. I had no idea at the time how much our world would shift. It all made sense after Samson and I decided to elope. We would have a destination wedding, in Las Vegas, just the two of us. An elopement was the wedding I never knew I always wanted!

As we drove home, we chatted about our decision. There were so many thoughts going through my head about what we decided to do, all of them positive. Getting hitched without going into that huge financial hole was definitely appealing. And the idea of being whisked away by my love to exchange our vows was definitely romantic. Everyone who knew me and Sam said we liked to "go big or go home." Well, we were still going to do it big, but now it would be big on our own terms.

Besides the financial reasons, Vegas was perfect for so many other reasons. I always knew that when the right man came along, I would gamble it all for love. Love was a gamble and the stakes were high. It was an invaluable commodity because what price could be placed on your feelings when giving someone something as precious as your love? While I knew love was a gamble, I also knew it was a sure bet too. I couldn't lose. Of course I knew there would be times when love could hurt, but no one could ever go wrong while serving others through love.

After a failed relationship or two, I'd learned there was a big difference between *gaming* and *gambling* on love. Some people are out there playing the *game* of love, having fun and not risking or truly investing in a relationship. But when you *gamble* on love, you have to invest every part of yourself, you have to risk your feelings in order to reap any real benefits. When it comes time to jump the broom, that's when you have to throw in all of your chips. In order to get all that God has for you in marriage, you have to give it all that you have. I was ready. I was ready to gamble, to throw in all of my chips, and to reap the reward of true love.

By the time we got back to my place, we had decided on what we were sure was the perfect venue. We were going to continue our happily-ever-after at the Bellagio! We'd both visited that grand hotel and we agreed it was the perfect place to exchange our I dos.

"Okay, so what else do we need to plan?" Samson asked as he picked up one of the magazines I'd had stacked on the living room table. With excitement and anticipation, I sat down next to him and we flipped through the pages. For once I had fun going through the pictures. The pressure was gone; the stress had dissipated. I felt free. But then all of a sudden Samson tossed the magazine aside, jumped up, then grabbed my hands and hurled me to my feet.

"What on earth?" I said to Samson, looking surprised.

"You are ready to marry me, aren't you?" he asked with a mischievous glint in his eyes.

"Yes," I said slowly, knowing that he was up to something. "That's what we've been talking about."

I didn't think it was possible, but his smile became wider. "We've gotten our parents' and our pastors' blessing, right?"

"Yes," I replied again, slowly.

"We've prayed over this for a long time, right?"

"Uh-huh."

"I'm the best thing that ever happened to you, right?" he said with a smirk.

I put my hands on my hips and gave him my own smirk. "That's what you keep telling me."

He leaned back his head and laughed. "Then let's do it!" he said, as if he were revealing some new news. "Let's elope!"

"Hello? We are." Had I missed something? "We *are* eloping. What have we been talking about all night?"

"No. I mean, let's elope *now*," he exclaimed as if he'd suddenly had a brilliant idea. "Let's go somewhere and get married tonight!"

I shook my head. I was willing to give up the big wedding, but I didn't want to do anything so compulsive. And anyway, eloping? Tonight? In this city? That wasn't happening. "Oh no, you don't!" I said. "I mean, I can't wait to marry you, but we're not doing this in Buffalo. This is the city of good neighbors, not the city of lights, remember? Plus"—I glanced at my watch—"do you know what time it is? It's after eleven and that means every chapel and everything else in this city is closed."

I was trying to give him a reasonable answer to his crazy question. But when I finished, he looked dejected. "Is that right?" he said. Then he dropped his head and shook it, as if trying to consider what I'd said.

"That's right," I told him softly before I wrapped my arms around him. "I want to marry you, but I can wait a few more weeks." I pressed my lips against his cheek.

"But I can't. I can't wait," he said, with surprising candor. "I want to marry you now. I *love* you." My eyes couldn't help but widen at his truthfulness and all of the emotion I heard in his voice.

"I love you too," I said, "and I can't wait either. But I promise you, the next few weeks will fly by and before you know it we will be married."

He paused for a moment. "Hmm," he said. "I suppose you're right." There was another pause before he added, "Well … at least … we can practice."

He had confused me again. "Practice?" I said, puzzled.

He stepped a few feet away from me, stood tall, and held my hand before clearing his throat in the most dramatic way possible. "Dearly beloved," he began in the most distinguished voice he could muster, "we are gathered here today to witness the union of Samson Logan and Angela Burgin."

I began with giggles that turned to chuckles that became laughter. I laughed so hard I fell back onto the sofa, and since I was still holding on to him, he fell back with me, landing right on top of me.

His laughter was hysterical at first. Then he cleared his throat and continued, "I take you"—he paused and kissed me softly—"to be my lawfully wedded wife." He stopped so he could kiss me again. "I vow to love you"—another kiss—"and care for you"—our lips met again—"as long as we both shall live."

This time, the kiss was long enough for me to kiss him back. He was out of breath when he leaned away and whispered, "Do you, Angela Burgin, take me, Samson Logan, to be your lawfully wedded husband?"

I couldn't take my eyes away from him. "I do." My soft voice trembled from what he'd said and what we were doing in this moment. His next kiss was just as soft as the others, though it was filled with more urgency. My head was spinning with thoughts and my heart pumped harder with all of the emotions I felt for this man. As his hands roamed over me, I was able to breathe a soft, "What are you doing?"

He leaned back and staring into my eyes with a look that was filled with lust, his voice squeaked, "I don't know."

He didn't give me a chance to respond as he pressed his lips against mine again, and we kissed in a way that felt so different from the way we'd kissed before. We gave in to all the things we'd been feeling. We gave in to the emotions that had been building. We gave in, and although we knew it was wrong, we gave in to the love we felt for one another that night.

17

The Surprise

(From Angela)

I awoke the next day, stretched out on the couch, cradled inside Samson's arms. As the sun began to peek through the window shade, I felt nothing but peace … at first. Then the memory of last night, what we'd done, and the realization of what it meant finally hit me. My eyes were wide with horror as I jumped up. I gathered my clothes that were scattered all over the floor.

"Get up!" I shouted at Samson.

His eyes opened, slowly at first, and then he bolted up, startled. "What's wrong?" The volume of his voice matched mine, but I could tell he was still trying to wake up, still trying to figure out what was going on.

"This!" I waved my arms, gesturing at the half-dressed state of both of us.

It took Samson a moment, but the look of his own realization masked his face. His expression apologized to me before he did. "I'm sorry," he whispered. He stood but didn't come near me, as if unsure of what to do next. "I … I just let my love for you cloud my judgment."

I had to hold back my tears. "It would have been perfect if we had just waited," I said. "And now I feel terrible." The guilt of the sin weighed heavily upon me. "How could we fail so close to getting married?" My voice trembled as I spoke. "We knew better. We should have waited." It was hard to keep the tears away.

He moved toward me and pulled me into his arms. "I'm sorry," he said again. "I can't make any excuses for last night."

I began to cry. "If we would have waited just a few more weeks—"

"I know," he whispered.

"—we could have loved each other all day and all night," I sobbed.

"I know," he whispered again.

"Without all of this guilt."

I buried my head into his chest. I was so mad, yet as he held me I felt so comforted. He was the only person who could console me. Plus, as I cried, I realized I wasn't really mad at Samson; I was angrier at myself. I had let God, myself, and yes, even Samson, down. I should have told him no; I should have been the stronger one.

When my tears subsided, he pulled back, though he still held me, and he looked into my eyes. "We can restart from here, Ang'," he said. "This doesn't have to be who we are. It was just once, and if we ask God to forgive us, I know that we can hold on to what we believe until we're married."

I nodded, wanting to make this right with God, although I knew all I had to offer was my confession and heartfelt repentance. We stood together and softly prayed, asking God for forgiveness and vowing to wait until we were married from this point on. After we prayed and Samson hugged me again, I felt much better. I was so grateful—I was marrying a praying man, a man who understood and wanted to be forgiven by God.

When Samson left me alone, the guilt hovered above me like a dark cloud, a cloud that remained for days. I kept thinking about how I'd let down both God and myself, and I kept praying I would be better from this point forward.

As the days passed, the cloud began to dissipate and I began to feel like myself again. Planning the wedding really helped ease my conscience. What was also easy was passing the planning on to our wedding coordinator at the Bellagio. I felt wonderful about the simplicity of what we wanted, so I turned it all over to her, giving her several dates to choose from.

What wasn't going to be easy, however, was telling our families what we'd decided to do—how we were going to go to Sin City ... by ourselves ... to get married. I cringed every time I thought about that nickname for Las Vegas. It brought back to my memory the sin I was trying hard to forget.

Though our families wouldn't know about our sin, the fact that we were canceling our big wedding and they wouldn't be there would be considered treason among the Logans and the Burgins. I didn't know how we were going to make them understand that we didn't want to wait a whole year for a venue to become available in Buffalo that would coincide with Samson's schedule. We didn't want to wait, and I felt like now, after what we'd done, we *couldn't* wait. Going to Vegas was the right choice before and it really was the right choice now.

I rehearsed the words and my reasoning, getting ready for all I was going to say to our families: How this was the right choice because we had such peace; how the angst I'd been feeling planning the wedding was gone and once again I was filled with excitement and joy; and how although the wedding was going to be small, it didn't take away from its significance.

When Samson and I got together to decide what we would tell our families, we decided we wouldn't do it all at once; we wouldn't make a big announcement. Instead, we'd just drop major hints over our next few visits without revealing our full plans.

While I was anxious about how they would react, everything else was falling into place. Just days after I had the first call with the wedding planner, she called me back, saying, "All of the dates that you want for the wedding are available."

I would have jumped up and danced, but I was at work. When I hung up the phone, I wanted to call Samson right away, but he always called me during lunch, so I waited. Like clockwork, around noon his number appeared on my caller ID. I couldn't wait to tell him the good news.

"Hello, this is the soon-to-be Mrs. Logan," I said as I answered the phone. "How may I help you?"

My greeting made him laugh. "Well, this is your soon-to-be old man," he said. "But I have some news that you may not like."

"What's going on?" I asked, my playful mood completely vanishing.

"Well, I got news that the play I was doing last spring got picked up for three more weeks."

"That's great!" I said, genuinely excited. "What's wrong with that?"

"Well," he said and then paused a moment, "the three weeks are smack dab in the middle of our wedding dates."

Forget about busting a bubble—I felt like my bubble had been blown up. "Oh," was all I could say, thinking that my good news was a moot point now. But if there was anything good about this situation, it was that I could get some practice at being a good wife. So I put on my most supportive voice and said, "Okay … well, we'll have to just wait a few more weeks."

He paused and then asked, "You're okay with that?" I could hear the surprise in his voice.

"Honestly, I can't wait to marry you," I said. "You know that. But I know that this is important for your career." Then, to add a little lightness to the conversation, I said, "And let's face it: I'm expecting a humongous wedding present, so you better keep on working."

He was still laughing when he said, "I'm so relieved. I thought you would be bummed and I didn't want to disappoint you."

"All things work together for good, right?" I said quoting the Scripture as much for myself as for Samson. "I'm sure things will

work out. And another good thing is that I won't have to take vacation time during our team meeting in Chicago now."

"That's good," he said. "I know you really wanted to go to that."
That was the truth. I loved my job and at least I'd be at one of our
major meetings for the year. "And now with it getting so close to the
holidays," Samson added, "with these extra weeks we have to wait,
we could make it extra special and just try to do it over the holidays
or even for the New Year."

"That sounds wonderful," I said, getting excited all over again.
"Imagine how the Bellagio will be decorated for the holidays. It'll
be beautiful."

"Well, what are you waiting for?" he asked. "Hang up the phone,
call the hotel, and book it."

"Are you sure?" I asked. "Suppose something else comes up?"

"Nothing else is gonna come up. No matter what, we will keep
the new date. Agreed?"

"Agreed!" I said, then added a quick "I love you" before I hung
up.

I called the wedding planner back, shared our predicament, and
gave her the new dates in December all the way up to the New Year.
She understood, but her words weren't exactly encouraging: "Everyone wants to get married during the holidays, Angela. I hope I have
a date for you."

"Just check the dates I gave you," I said. "I have a feeling that
you'll be able to find a way."

"Well, I won't keep you waiting. Can you hold on while I check?"

I told her that I would, and when I heard the soft music in the
background, I closed my eyes and prayed.

Almost five minutes later, she came back. "You know you and
Sam are one of my favorite couples, right?"

"Yes," I said, my hopes rising.

"Well," she continued, "I can finagle some things and give you a
beautiful event on December thirtieth. How does that sound?"

I had been really hoping for one of the dates that was sooner rather than later, but being able to celebrate New Year's Eve as a newlywed seemed perfect. "That sounds great," I said. "Book it!"

I couldn't have been happier. When I put down the phone, I pushed myself up to stand, but halfway to my feet I swayed a little and sank back into my chair. It felt as if I'd gotten a few butterflies in my stomach with this news.

"If you're this excited about the date," I whispered and chuckled at the same time, "what are you going to do on your actual wedding day?" I was getting carried away. I waited for a few moments and then tried to stand again. This time, I felt nothing except the huge smile on my face.

Samson was as thrilled with the date as I was, and we both began counting down the days until our wedding. I wasn't able to focus on our wedding, though. I was busy at work, trying to get ahead on many of my assignments so nothing would be on my mind when I went on my honeymoon. Not only that, I'd been angling for a promotion and I'd hoped my hard work would pay off. The company was going to make some organizational announcements at the meeting in Chicago, and I hoped that my promotion would be one of those announcements.

For the first few weeks after we set the date, I worked long hours and the time went by quickly. But then, as it got closer to the Chicago meeting, I started feeling weird, not like myself. *You're just tired,* I thought to myself. That explanation made sense. I'd been working long hours, and even though we had a wedding coordinator, there were still many things I had to do. My focus was split, which took a lot of energy.

I had been overdoing it and decided I was going to use the business trip to Chicago as time to relax. I was going to enjoy the Windy City, even try to get in some retail therapy on the Magnificent Mile.

I decided to even take a half-empty bag with me so I could load up while I was there. Just the thought of that should have made me feel better. But as the days got closer to the trip, I *didn't* feel better, and I didn't look like myself.

Samson kept asking me what was wrong.

"I'm just tired," I said, giving him the same mantra I'd been telling myself. But the truth was that it felt like more than exhaustion. When I found myself dragging on the way to Chicago, I decided I was going to have a physical when I returned home.

When I arrived at the hotel, the first thing I did was slip off my shoes, then slide between the high thread count sheets and the luxurious comforter. I sunk my head into the down pillow and sighed, feeling much better. I didn't plan to sleep for long. Although I didn't have any meetings until the following day, I had plenty of plans for this afternoon. After a power nap, I was going to spend the day shopping.

Just when I felt like every muscle in my body was completely relaxed and I closed my eyes, my stomach churned. *Ugh! Is it time for my cycle?* A second passed. Then another. Right after that, my eyes popped open. I sat straight up. "My cycle. My cycle," I said aloud, as if talking to someone, though I was alone in the room.

I jumped out of bed, grabbed my briefcase, snapped it open, and snatched my calendar. As I stared at the month, a slow realization came. My monthly cycles were regular. All of the time. But not this time. This time ... I was late! I'd been busy and focused on so many things that I hadn't even noticed. I dropped the calendar and sank back onto the bed. My mind was racing with a single thought: *Could this be? Is it possible?* And then, *Oh my goodness!*

I bolted from the bed and dashed to the full-length mirror. I stood there gazing at myself before I found the courage to pull my shirt up, inch by inch, until my stomach was in full view. "You look fine," I said as if I could really lie to myself. "You're just a little bloated." But that caused me to rush back to the bed and slip into my shoes. In less than a minute, I was out the door. The fatigue I'd felt had been replaced by a sudden surge of nervous energy.

In the lobby, I asked the bellhop, "Where's the nearest pharmacy?"

"It's just down the block, miss."

"Can I walk?"

He nodded. "It really is just a couple of blocks that way," he said, pointing.

I rushed outside and hurried in the direction he had indicated. I don't remember walking to the store. I don't remember passing anything or seeing anybody. I was pulled down the street and into the pharmacy. When I stepped inside, my eyes darted around. I was a long way from Buffalo, but I still wanted to make sure no one saw me.

I grabbed a basket and strolled up one aisle and then down another as if I were really just casually shopping. With the way my heart pounded, there was nothing casual about this trip. Finally, I strolled right in front of the shelves that held what I was looking for: pregnancy tests. My eyes darted around once again, glancing to see if anyone was looking.

I didn't want to take too much time, so I grabbed two boxes, two different tests. I could take both of them just to be sure of the results. I had what I'd come into the store to buy, but I proceeded to buy other things too: deodorant, toothpaste, lotion—all things I didn't need. They were camouflage, only to cover up my real reason for coming to the pharmacy in the first place.

At the checkout, I wanted to act casual, unconcerned, as if my purchases were not unusual. The attendant barely seemed to notice me or my items as he swiped each one from the cart. I tapped my foot as he took his time, wondering if he knew that my life could be changing as I stood there.

The world might be a completely different place for me. This could be a huge deal. Those were my thoughts as he moved like a sloth.

He finally got to the pregnancy tests, swiping those the same way he'd done the toothpaste and everything else, and he placed both packages in the bag. "That will be forty-three dollars and seventeen cents."

Forty-three dollars? What did I buy? Not that I cared. I handed him my card, signed the receipt, and grabbed the shopping bag and rushed as fast as I could back to the hotel.

Opening the door to my room, I put the Do Not Disturb hanger on the door, then stepped inside. I flung my shoes in one direction and my coat in another before I emptied the contents of the shopping bag onto my bed. I grabbed both pregnancy tests, then went into the bathroom.

For the first time, I studied the boxes and read the instructions. One of the tests had an indicator that would actually say "pregnant" if the results were positive, so I figured that was the best one to start with. As I tore the package open, I convinced myself I'd gotten worked up over nothing. As I peed on the stick, I thought I'd just been busy and the stress of everything had made me late. By the time I laid the stick on the edge of the sink, I was sure that I wasn't pregnant.

I set my phone alarm for ten minutes, the recommended time to wait for results. And then I walked into the bedroom, closing the door behind me as if I didn't want anyone else to go inside. I paced back and forth. Surely, there was going to be a hole in that carpet before the ten minutes (that were dragging on like ten hours) were up.

The alarm went off, startling me from my thoughts. I walked slowly to the bathroom, pushed open the door, and I stood there and peered inside, straining to see the test. I was too far away to see anything from where I stood, so I stepped inside to look at the test—only because I had to.

I picked up the stick, but then closed my eyes before I could look at it. Slowly, I raised my arm and when it was right in front of my face I took a deep breath and opened my eyes. Pregnant! I dropped the stick as if it were a snake. My legs were weak; I had to sit and the commode was the nearest place to do so.

Breathe

My mind was overwhelmed with thoughts, but it was hard to harness a single one. *Oh. My. Goodness.* That was all I could think, that was all I could say: "Oh. My. Goodness." Those words kept coming out of my mouth.

I was overcome with fear; I was overcome with confusion. But then I was overcome with joy. I finally had new words. "I can't believe it," I said. Now I said *those* words over and over.

One of the things I'd always dreamed about was becoming a mother. I'd wanted a child with my whole being, and now that this was happening, now that I was carrying a baby, I realized what I felt most was joy. Then it hit me. It was as if I'd completely forgotten—I'd gotten pregnant before I'd gotten married.

I'd always prided myself on being a good role model for others. And then there were Samson's parents, the pastors—what were they going to think? This was surely going to be a letdown, not only for them but for my parents too. For everyone.

I sighed and held on to my stomach. I sat there, imagining who was inside of me and what the future would be. And then, for the first time, I spoke to my child.

"Hey, little one," I whispered. "I'm so happy to have you in me. I love you already because I have wanted you so much. I know this may not be the exact way I wanted you to come into my life, but there is something I know: all children are an inheritance from God regardless of how they got here. You are my inheritance, no matter what. That's how I see you, that's what I know. I promise that I will take care of you, that I will always be an example you will be able to respect. And I will spend my life doing anything for you and giving everything to you."

I paused and began to see my baby. I saw *her.* That was in my spirit: *her.* That talk gave me the comfort I needed. I knew right then that whatever was going to come next, I was ready. We were ready. *She* and I were ready!

18

A Tale of Two Cities

(From Angela)

J lay back down in the bed, but rest was not an option. My mind was far too busy, racing with all kinds of thoughts. I tried to process all that was happening to me, all that was happening within me.

Sitting up once again, I picked up my cell phone from the nightstand and scrolled through my contacts. After a minute, I landed on the one I was looking for: Dr. Berman. I tapped the screen to call his number, then wondered if he would still be in his office. It was almost five in Chicago, so I wasn't sure anyone would be in his office since it was almost six in Buffalo.

I needed to make an appointment for a follow-up test to confirm the pregnancy, but it would only be a formality. With every fiber in my body, with every sense I had, I knew I was pregnant. I'd seen the positive test with my own eyes. I'd heard myself whisper the words. And then there was the part I couldn't explain as clearly: I felt different. I *felt* pregnant. I *felt* like a mom.

This pregnancy made sense with all of the things that had been happening over the last few weeks. The way my sense of smell had been heightened, the way my sense of taste was more sensitive. And my daily exhaustion? Bingo! I knew what that was about too.

I smiled. I had evidence. But it was more than that. In just the short time that my mind had the chance to catch up to what was happening in my body, something had changed. I *knew* I was pregnant from the inside out. It's like breathing: you don't know that you're breathing—you just breathe. That's how this was for me. Intrinsically, deep inside my bones, I knew the child I had dreamed of, prayed about, and believed for was growing inside me.

"This is Dr. Berman's office," the woman's voice on the phone said. "How may I help you?"

The familiar voice brought my thoughts back to the present. "Diana?"

"Yes?"

I was comforted when I heard her voice. I'd been seeing this nurse since I hit puberty and started going to an ob-gyn. "Hi, this is Angela Burgin," I said. "I need to schedule an appointment."

"Oh, hi Angela!" she replied. "How are you?"

"I'm good."

"So you want to schedule an appointment. Is there something going on or is this to schedule your annual exam?"

There's definitely something going on. I thought for a moment, then I decided to go ahead and say it: "I'm pretty sure I'm pregnant."

"Oh my goodness!" she replied. "Well, I'll say that there is definitely something going on!"

We both chuckled.

But then she became more serious. "I've got some good news and some bad news for you."

I waited, not knowing where she was going with this.

"We can definitely see you to confirm your pregnancy, but Dr. Berman is no longer delivering babies."

"What?" I was instantly exasperated. "What do you mean? When did this happen?" Dr. Berman had delivered my sister's children, giving me the chance to see him in action, so I knew I would be in capable hands with him.

Sensing the deep disappointment in my voice, Diana went on. "I'm so sorry," she said. "Dr. Berman recently decided to drop his obstetrics practice because of the rising cost of malpractice insurance. He'll be continuing only with his gynecology practice."

Obviously Diana had nothing to do with this, and I could understand Dr. Berman's decision. But, at that moment, it was all about me and my baby. "What am I going to do?" I finally asked.

"I know," she said, trying to sympathize. "I've had to tell a couple of his patients this news and everyone has the same reaction. He just couldn't continue on with it, especially with him being close to retirement. But we have compiled a great reference list of OB doctors for our patients as a resource."

"But, Diana," I actually whined near tears, "I thought you would be with me on this journey!" This woman had been with me through all of my major milestones, including the first time I got clamped onto a table for a pap smear and gynecological checkup.

"Don't worry," she said, trying to soothe me with her tone. "I'll make sure that you'll get a great OB. And at least I'll see you when you come in for the confirmation of your pregnancy."

"Okay," I said, finally reconciling to this idea. "I'm out of town now, but I'll be back over the weekend. Can I come in on Monday?"

"Sure."

Whether or not she had an open appointment, I was sure she would do everything she could to accommodate me since I'd sounded so distraught.

"And I'll have that list for you since you'll have to find a new doctor right away," she said.

"Sounds good." I tried to sound as if I were fine with all of this. But when I hung up, all I could do was release a huge sigh.

That conversation had definitely busted my bubble. From the moment I first went to him, I liked him. Dr. Berman had a terrific bedside manner, he always made me feel comfortable, and he knew my medical history—not just from reading it on some piece of paper.

Now, during this important time in my life, I was going to have to find someone new, and I was going to have to find him or her quickly. Being pregnant meant that I couldn't afford to get on a doctor's six-month waiting list for accepting new patients. My prenatal care needed to start immediately.

I groaned at the thought of all the work I was going to have to do. "There's nothing you can do to change this," I said aloud to myself. "Leave this task until next week because there's something else you need to do right now."

Excitement mixed with a little fear arose within me when I thought about what I had to do next. I had to find a way to tell Samson we were going to be parents!

We were going to be parents.

The thought of Samson and me doing this together made my lips curl upward as happiness welled up inside of me. We had talked about becoming parents many times; it was what we both wanted. But what I didn't know was whether Samson would want a child so soon. We would be going from marriage to carriage quickly!

"Oh, brother!" I rolled my eyes as a thought came to my mind. Then I chuckled. If my neighbors in the room next door could hear me, they probably thought there were two people in my room with all of the conversation that was going on. I'd never been one to talk to myself aloud this way.

Then it hit me. I wasn't alone, I wasn't talking to myself. I was talking to *her*. Every thought I had, every feeling I felt, every word I spoke—all of that would be communicated to my baby. Gently I pressed my hand against my stomach to settle *both* of us. But then I had another thought and I couldn't stop the sinking feeling.

When people heard that Samson and I were going to Vegas to get married, and then when they heard this news, everyone would think this was a shot-gun marriage, which was far from the truth. This time I had a lengthy conversation with myself:

"What are people going to say?"

You can't help what people say, Ang'.

"What if they say bad things about me? About Sam? About what we did?"

Everyone has sinned, Ang'.

"Yeah, but this is a sin that people can see," I said, looking down at my belly.

A sin is a sin, Ang'.

I went on like this for a couple more minutes before I realized that worrying about "they" and "them" was plain silly. This was life and this was real. Sometimes smart people do dumb things, and sometimes godly people sin. I had to stop worrying about what other people would think. If I was going to worry at all, it had to be about me and *him.*

Yes, I had sinned. I had to own I had fallen. But I also knew that by grace I could continue on in the face of criticism from others. I'd be able to continue because of his mercy. So I closed my eyes, bowed my head, raised my arms, and I prayed to *him:* "Heavenly Father, please forgive me. I have done wrong in your sight. I have sinned and I am sorry. I need your mercy and your grace according to your great compassion. Cleanse me of this sin, Father. Restore in me a steadfast spirit. Keep me and my child in this pregnancy, God. Help me in this walk with you, O Lord. In Jesus' name. Amen."

I sat there for a while with my arms outstretched, allowing his grace to wash over me. I knew I could have no doubt about God's love. I knew he was faithful and just to forgive me. If I was going to pray, I had to believe. So right there I accepted his grace.

After my prayer, I tried to rest since I had to be downstairs in the conference room for my breakfast meeting starting at seven thirty the next morning. But with so many thoughts in my head, resting was hard to do. What I really wanted to do was call Samson, tell him what was going on, and talk to him for the rest of the night.

But this was not news I wanted to give him over the phone. This was in-person, face-to-face news. I needed to see his eyes. I wanted to embrace him. I wanted us to share this moment together. I was going to be in Chicago for three days; it was going to be hard to not tell him. But it was going to be worth it. Not only that, but the three days would give me time to think of what I would say.

Hours later my eyes finally closed, but it felt like only a few minutes after that when my alarm went off. I dragged myself from the bed, dressed, and proceeded downstairs. Even though I hadn't rested for long, I somehow felt refreshed. I didn't know if it was adrenalin or what, but I was ready for the day.

I marveled at how everything seemed a little bit different. The world had changed a lot—at least for me—and I saw everything with new eyes.

At the buffet table in the conference room, I bumped into my boss.

"Hey, Angela," he said, sounding pretty chipper.

That's a good sign, was my first thought. I was really hoping to hear some news about my promotion on this trip. There was so much happening with the company; we were going through a lot of changes and I was having some of the best results of my career.

"Morning, Jeff!" I said, trying to sound as chipper as he looked.

"I'd like to carve out some time during the afternoon break to speak with you," he said. "Let's meet in Conference Room B at two thirty."

"Sounds good," I said. Then I made my way to my seat in the large room, feeling hopeful.

The agenda said we were in for a big day of presentations, including hearing about the launch of new items for the upcoming year. As I waited for the first speaker to begin, I thought how this trip to Chicago was gearing up to be one of the best trips I'd ever taken. I'd learned I was pregnant and there was still the possibility I would get a promotion. The timing couldn't be better because, with another mouth to feed, Samson and I would be able to use the extra money.

Looking down at my belly, I chuckled. Here I was, in the middle of a chatter-filled room with a couple of hundred people, and no one noticed I was laughing to myself. But then I raised my head and grabbed my phone. I sent a quick text to Samson: *Have a meeting with my boss this afternoon. Fingers crossed that I will get a promotion!*

I knew Samson probably wouldn't see that text for a couple of hours, however, because early mornings were not his thing. He was used to working half the night in the music studio or performing on stage, so he usually slept in. That's why I was so surprised when he texted back within seconds: *You got this. You've been doing a great job. Go get your promotion!*

With all of the different speakers, the hours flew by and it felt as if no time had passed before I was walking down the hall with anticipation, searching for Conference Room B. I entered the much smaller room and Jeff was already there, seated at a table. But he was not alone—his direct manager was on one side of him, and on the other was a woman I recognized from HR.

"Oh," I said. "Hello."

Was I joining a meeting that was already in progress? I wondered if I needed to wait outside.

"Have a seat, Angela." Jeff motioned for me to sit across the table from the trio. Once I was settled in my chair, he said, "I think you know Robert and Meredith."

"Yes," I said, feeling more positive. "It's nice to see you all again." This promotion was going to be huge if Robert and Meredith were part of this meeting.

"Same here," echoed the two of them, both wearing warm smiles.

So far, so good, I thought.

Jeff launched right into the purpose of the meeting. "I'm glad we have this opportunity to speak to you. You know the company is making some organizational changes and restructuring a bit."

I nodded in agreement and even more anticipation.

"Well, we are pleased with your results. You have consistently delivered an 'Exceeds' performance."

It was so hard to sit still. My hope and excitement kept growing.

"With that being said," Jeff continued, "we would like to promote you to director."

"Wonderful!" I blurted out, realizing I'd practically been holding my breath waiting for him to get to the good part. I felt my grin spread wide across my face.

"But ..." Jeff paused.

My smile faded. *But?* I didn't want him to start with buts now.

"... the position will be in Tampa."

I blinked. *Tampa? Like in Florida?*

Jeff continued through my confusion: "There is a great opportunity in that region and we would love to have your expertise there."

My eyes grew wide at this completely unexpected turn of events.

"So what do you think?" he asked me.

I took a moment because I wanted to say the right thing. I began, "Quite frankly, Jeff, I've been working hard to earn a director's position within this region." I paused to give him a chance to respond, but he said nothing. I continued, "I've been working to learn the nuances of each of my customers and geographies. Now that I have a keen understanding and using that, along with my knowledge, I'd like to drive even better results in *this* region."

This time, it was Robert who jumped in. "We understand that, Angela, and again we've been monitoring your performance and agree that you've done a great job. However, as part of this restructuring, we're eliminating some of the positions in this market. But we do want you to stay on with us; that's why we've offered you this position in Tampa."

My heart sank. It felt as if I'd gone from a promotion to a pink slip in a matter of a few minutes. "I'm pleased that you view me so highly," I said, "but moving to Tampa wasn't on my radar. I'll certainly consider the opportunity, but what are my options if I decline?"

Now Meredith jumped in and suddenly I understood why she was there: "If you decline the opportunity, we'll be able to offer you a severance package since your position in your market is being eliminated." My blank stare must have given Meredith room to continue. "Obviously," she said, "this is not a reflection of your work. It's just the opposite. You're one of a few being given the opportunity to relocate versus being only offered a severance package."

I guessed that was some kind of good news. "Thank you," I mustered. In my confusion and shock, that was all I needed to say. But I did have a question: "How long do I have to consider this opportunity?"

Jeff spoke again. "You'll have a couple of months before we'll need a final decision. By then we'll have the exact date when the roles in this market will be eliminated."

Then Meredith jumped in. "Over the next few weeks, why don't you look into the Tampa area along with reviewing the relocation and the severance package, and your benefits plan. And, of course, feel free to call me with any questions."

My mind was on fire with all of my questions, especially the one that would affect me the most: *Did I just lose my health insurance?* Even though I hadn't told them, I knew Tampa wasn't going to be an option for me. And even though I hadn't spoken that sentiment aloud, I think the three of them sensed that as well.

"I do have a few questions," I said. "I travel all of the time and our customers are everywhere. Can I do the same position from my current location? Are there opportunities outside of Tampa, because Tampa isn't exactly one of our biggest regions? And what happens if I do move there? What would be the next position for me?"

"We can definitely keep your name in play for other opportunities if you're open to relocation," Meredith said. "But right now, the only position we have for you is in Tampa. We want the role to be based there, so relocation is mandatory. And as far as what would happen next, we can't guarantee that another job will open in another location before we eliminate your regional position." She continued, "If you do opt to move to Tampa, most likely you'll be there for two to three years, and then you'd be relocated again. Based on your exemplary performance, I can foresee two to three more moves for your career path."

"Well, I have a lot to think about," I told them. There was no point asking any more questions or trying to come up with a clever way to stay in my current role. The organization had made up its mind and now I would have to make up mine.

The rest of the day was a blur as I hardly heard any words from the rest of the presenters. All I wanted to do was get back to my room and call Samson. This news was something I couldn't hold.

Talk about a tale of two cities. This trip to Chicago had brought the best possible news and now what felt like the worst possible news. Laid off and pregnant was not a part of my master plan. Neither was going into a marriage having to think so much about money.

Even though the stability of having a job was at risk, relocating to Tampa was not the right choice for me. Starting off my marriage away from my support system was one thing, but having my child start her life away from her support system was another thing altogether. I wanted my child to have her papa, nana, grammy, granddad, aunts, uncles, and cousins. I wanted her to be close to her family, to establish unbreakable bonds, and that couldn't happen if we were in Florida. I may have been able to do it for her first year or so, but to move before she was even born?

Back in my hotel room, I called Samson. He answered after just one ring. "Hey," he said. "I didn't think I would hear from you until tonight."

It took me a moment to say hi, but that was all that came out before the well of emotions overtook my voice and body.

"Uh-oh, Ang'." Already I heard concern in his voice. "What's wrong?"

That's when the sobs took over and I could hardly speak. "I think ... I just ... lost my job!"

"What?" I knew he couldn't believe what I'd just told him. He knew how hard I'd been working; he knew about my results. "But I thought for sure you were getting a promotion!" He waited for me to say something, but I couldn't get out any words. "All right," he said, trying to soothe me. "Calm down and tell me what happened."

It took me a couple more moments, but I was finally able to run down how I'd gotten the promotion, but what the ultimate cost would be.

Even Samson was taken aback by the news. "Wow," he said, "I didn't see that coming. Well, with my career I can live anywhere, but obviously Tampa is not something you want."

If he knew we were pregnant, he wouldn't have said that. But I still didn't want to tell him over the phone. All I said was, "Getting married and moving to a different state at the same time is not what I had in mind."

"I know," he said, sounding as dejected as I felt.

"But the thing is ... I love my job," I said. "And I didn't plan on starting our marriage going from the receiving line to the unemployment line!"

He took a deep breath. "Let's not think about it like that. With your degree, your résumé, your skills, you'll be able to find another job or maybe even start your own business."

What he was saying was true. I had my degree from Syracuse University, and with my experience I was now considered a top marketing expert. "Listen," he said, "you don't have to make up your mind tonight. Let's think about it and pray on it and then you can decide."

I agreed.

"Is there anything else going on?" he kidded, trying to take the conversation into a different direction.

If you only knew!

"I think that's enough for tonight," I said.

After exchanging a few I love yous, I hung up the phone and lied down. There was nothing but silence in the room, though it was totally the opposite in my head. Placing my hand on my belly, I said, "Sorry for the swirl of emotions today, little one. Mommy had a crazy day. But don't worry: somehow things will be okay."

When I clicked off the light, I prayed, thanking God for everything, even the news I'd received. No matter how bad I thought it was, the blessing he'd given me made up for everything. So I closed my eyes and fell asleep with my hand resting on my belly.

19

Promotion

(From Angela)

In the morning I woke up and then dressed as if I didn't have the weight of my career on my shoulders. Downstairs at the conference, I wore the same smile I had on the day before as I sat through the presentations, even though all kinds of thoughts and emotions twirled through my mind. It was tough to sit there, knowing that so much would be changing for me. Gratefully our meetings concluded just a little after noon, leaving me free from that point on to do whatever I wanted in the Windy City.

I decided there was no reason to change my original plan. No matter what was going on in my life, Chicago had some of the best shopping, so after changing my clothes I headed down to the Magnificent Mile. While my goal to shop had stayed the same, what I was shopping for had changed. No matter what store I entered, I was drawn to the maternity section, and then right after that I'd stroll through infant clothing.

As I looked at stylish outfits for me and the cutest onesies for her, I wanted to buy up everything, but I didn't settle on anything. Even as the baby's clothes brought out all of the ohs and ahs in me, I knew I really couldn't buy anything. As much as I believed this baby was a girl, I had to admit I really didn't know for sure. So buying a bunch of pink stuff wasn't the smartest thing to do.

Then there was the fact that I couldn't purchase anything for myself. I calculated that I was about seven weeks along, and I was well aware that the first trimester was always delicate. So I didn't want to buy anything until I was past that milestone. That didn't stop me from continuing to look around, though. And as I did, I thought about how I would tell Samson about our baby. I tried to think of clever ways, something that would be different than, "Hey, I'm pregnant," but I couldn't think of anything.

That is, until I came across an adorable onesie that read, *If you think I'm cute, you should see my dad.* The beige and green stripes made the outfit unisex. It would be the perfect prop to help me share the news with Samson! The first present I would ever buy for our little one would be the best way for me to show Samson he was going to be a father.

I left Chicago the next morning and was so happy that Sam was home for once; he'd be able to pick me up from the airport. He was right there at the curb to greet me once my plane landed. His hug was warm and long; he knew what I needed after the news I'd received about my job. When he lifted my bag to place it in the car, he said, "This is awfully heavy for someone who just went away for a few days. You do some shopping?" he asked with a smirk.

All I did was shrug.

"Well, I just hope there is something in there for me!" He slammed the trunk and then opened the door for me. I fought hard not to grin. He had no idea that he was playing into my plan already.

He took me home for a bit before we went out to dinner at Cecelia's. Once we sat down and placed our orders, he took my hand. "You look a little tired," he said. "Let's not talk about your job tonight. Let's just enjoy our dinner and then veg out in front of the TV when we get home, okay? We can tackle it all tomorrow."

I nodded, feeling blessed he was so in tune with me. Plus, he was right about me being tired. Even though I knew the reason, that didn't stop exhaustion from hitting me.

We finished dinner and, just like he promised, Samson and I returned to my place. We'd been sitting there for about half an hour, which I guess was too much for him because he said, "You still didn't tell me why your bags were so heavy."

I'd been waiting for the right time all night long. This was it. "You think my bag was heavy? It felt normal to me," I said coyly, teasing him.

"There was nothing normal about it." He reached up and massaged his shoulder. "I nearly dislocated my arm trying to pick that thing up. Let's see what you bought."

I shot him a confused look.

"Don't try it, Ang'," he said. "I know you bought stuff. You would never come back from Chicago empty-handed. Let's see your haul."

"Okay." I smiled, pushed myself up, and went into the bedroom where Samson had set my luggage. Right away my heart started pounding. I gathered everything and brought my gifts into the living room. I'd made sure to pick up a few things for myself, along with the items I bought for him to go along with my ruse.

As I lined up the packages, Samson rubbed his palms together.

"First," I began, "you know I couldn't leave Chicago without going to Nuts on the Clark." While Sam loved the goodies I always brought back from that famous gourmet nuts and popcorn store, this was not one of the finds that he wanted to see.

"I know," he said with impatience in his tone. His eyes were already checking out the bag with the men's store logo. "I really want to know what's in that one," he said, pointing.

I had to slap his hand away playfully when he tried to reach across me to grab the bag. "You'll see," I said. "Just wait. I'll show you in due time."

He rolled his eyes, but he sat back and waited as I went through each of my purchases.

I dragged it out as much as I could, taking my time describing in great detail each blouse, each T-shirt, each dress I'd bought. And I could tell his impatience was growing. "Oh, all right," I finally said, feigning exasperation with the way he was squirming. With annoyance all over my face, I handed him the bag. "I did bring you back a few things."

He played right into my plan by gleefully pulling out a V-neck shirt with just the right amount of flash for his engagements. He gave me a thumbs up. "I love this," he said. "I can definitely wear this on the road." He had the same reaction with the long-sleeve button-down shirt. "I really love this one. I can think of a million places where I can wear this!" His smile stretched across his face. "Thank you, baby," he said to me and gave me a quick peck on the cheek.

With all of the paper he'd pulled from the bags, the final bag I had for him was barely visible. I casually reached for it and said, "Oh, there was one other thing that I got for you that I thought you would really like."

"Really?" he said, taking the bag from me, but not looking into it yet. "I was just teasing, Ang'," he said softly. "You didn't have to bring me back anything at all." His tone was genuine. Then a second later, he said, "But since you did ..."

He was right back to his old self, smiling as he looked into the bag. He pulled out the mounds of paper I'd stuffed inside. "Hmm," he said as he pulled out the onesie. He unfolded the infant's outfit and read the words on the front aloud: "If you think I'm cute, you should see my dad." He continued to hold it in the air, as if he were trying to figure it out. Then he read it again, the words coming out faster this time. "If you think I'm cute, you should see my dad."

As gently as he could, he put down the onesie, then hopped up, grabbing my hand and pulling me up at the same time. "Da ... Da ... Dad?" he stuttered.

"Yes. Dad," I said slowly.

"I'm going to be a dad?" He spoke the words just as slowly as I had.

"Yes," I repeated. I searched his face for his emotions. Was he bewildered, happy, upset, scared … or something in between?

His gaze went from my eyes down to my belly. "You're pregnant?" His hand cupped over his mouth and he stared at me for a moment.

Inside, my heart began to pound again. I wanted to know how he felt.

Suddenly he took my hands and guided me back to the sofa. His gaze had gone from crazed to concerned. "Are you okay?"

"Yes," I replied. "But are you okay?" I was still filled with trepidation. He hadn't yet voiced what he was feeling.

It took him a moment to answer as if he were trying to measure his words. Finally, he said, "I'm more than okay. I'm so happy."

It wasn't until that moment that I realized I'd been holding my breath.

Gently, he touched my belly. "Are you sure there's really a baby in there? *Our* baby in there?"

I nodded. "I'm pretty sure," I said. "I missed my period, which is always regular, and so I took two pregnancy tests. And they were both positive. But I'm going to the doctor on Monday to be 100 percent sure."

He just stared at me, trying to take in all of my words. His eyes never left me as he said again, "You're pregnant." This time, however, he said it with conviction: "You. Are. Pregnant." After a couple of moments of silence, he nodded. "I know for sure that you are." He picked up my hands and kissed my fingers.

"I know this isn't what we planned to have happen right now," I said as emotion welled up in my eyes, "and we aren't even married yet!"

"I know," he said quickly, apparently sensing what I felt. "But don't worry. It's not good for the baby. We'll be married soon and I couldn't be happier about this. Everything will be okay." His tone was soothing and his words reassuring.

Even though Samson tried, I was caught up in the moment with all kinds of emotions (and probably hormones) raging through me. The dam broke and the waterworks gushed. "I'm so scared!" I wailed. "We're not married, we're moving, and I may not even have a job! And then … and then, what about insurance?" I had to pause between a fit of sobs. "Maybe I should just take the promotion and the position in Tampa."

"Angela! Angela!" Sam had to raise his voice over my cries. "Stop it! Stop it. You have to calm down." With the tips of his fingers, he lifted my chin so we were looking eye to eye. With his other hand, he pulled tissues from the box on the end table next to us and then dabbed at my eyes.

"Listen to me." His tone was filled with certainty and authority. "God is not surprised by any of this. I don't know how or why, but I do know that *he* knows. Things are going to be okay. Calm down and trust that."

I tried to stop my tears, but they kept coming. "I want our baby to be here with our families when she's born, but maybe with this I should take the promotion."

Our baby was new news to Samson, but I'd had more time to turn this over in my mind. I thought about everything: my job, my promotion, our wedding, our baby. So every concern I'd had I poured out on Sam. I flooded him with all of my emotions.

"Angela!" he said again with assurance in his voice. "We are going to be okay." He paused, giving me time to gather myself as he kept dabbing my eyes.

It was because of his calm that I was able to calm down. Once I was able to stop my tears, he whispered, "We're going to be okay. And this is a promotion you will take."

Forget about crying; now I was shocked. *He wanted me to take the promotion? He wanted our family to live in Tampa?*

"This is the most important promotion you have ever gotten and will ever get," he continued.

Even though he was trying to be positive, his words weighed me down. I said I would take the promotion, but I didn't really want it. I wanted him to talk me out of it.

Instead, he said, "You've just been promoted to your most important role ever—Mom!"

I inhaled sharply, realizing what he was saying before he continued:

"This is the role you've been working toward and preparing for. This is the promotion that you will accept. And after that, everything else will be okay."

He spoke with such confidence that all I could do was have peace. My own confidence returned and my fears subsided. Samson was right and I knew we would get through this together. We were going to be a family, which meant that with each other we could get through anything.

20

Someday

(From Angela)

It was easy to have faith, but it was so hard to wait! I had faith that with all that was happening, and even with all that I had done wrong, God would somehow work it all together for my (and my baby's) good. What I was having trouble with was the waiting part! Anxieties and nerves had me jittery through the weekend as I awaited my appointment with Dr. Berman.

Having a child had been in my dreams and in my prayers, even as I was taking a break from men. This was one of the reasons I'd pushed so hard in my job these past few years. I had aspirations of rising up the corporate ladder and even building my own business one day, but it was always with a broader purpose.

What good was my position if I couldn't use it to benefit someone else? My hard work was for more than me—I worked hard, laying the foundation for the family I dreamed I'd have someday. Managing employees and being a leader at my company was great, but the leadership role I longed to fulfill was standing next to my husband and being a role model for our children.

These thoughts filled my mind as I stood right outside Dr. Berman's office. All of my waiting, working, planning, praying, and believing had come together. My someday was now at hand. With a deep breath, I stepped into the doctor's office, knowing that when I stepped back outside my life would be changed. I was pregnant; this was just a formality. But this formality meant everything. I wanted to hear the doctor say those words, "You're pregnant."

"Good morning, sunshine!" Diana greeted me as I walked up to the reception desk. As always, her cheeriness helped calm the butterflies that swirled in my stomach.

"Morning!" I replied with a grin so big I was sure all thirty-two of my teeth were showing.

"You know you got our first appointment, so you won't be waiting long," Diana told me as I turned to sit down.

"Great," was what I said, but what I was thinking was, *The sooner the better!*

Just moments after I sat down, the doctor's office door chimed, and Samson rushed in as if he'd missed something. I was glad Samson was in town. He'd dropped me off at the front door, insisting I didn't need to walk as he found a place to park. We didn't have the doctor's confirmation, but Samson was treating me as if I were already nine months pregnant.

Before he sat, he asked, "Did they call you yet? Are they ready for you?"

I guessed I wasn't the only one who'd been anxious.

"No. Not yet," I replied. "The nurse said it will only be a few minutes, though."

After a few minutes Diana opened the door that led to the examining rooms. "We're ready for you."

Samson and I nearly leapt to our feet.

Once we were behind the door, Diana said, "We're going into room number three. But first, Angela, you're going into room number two."

Why would Samson and I be put in separate rooms?

The look on my face must have made her explain, "Number two is our bathroom. You can change into a gown in there, as well as give us a urine sample."

I'd drank a whole bottle of water in the car anticipating this. Samson and I waved to each other as we headed into the separate rooms. Inside the bathroom, I moved as fast as I could, changing and providing the urine sample before I joined Samson.

I'd barely made my way to the examining table before Diana came in. "From the looks on your faces," she said, "I would say that you're pretty excited about the idea of becoming parents."

We smiled.

"Or maybe you're scared stiff!" she joked.

After we laughed with her, I said, "I think it's a bit of both!"

Samson nodded.

"Okay then. We'll have the results in no time and then Dr. Berman will be in to chat with you. But first, let's get your vitals and a few questions out of the way."

I sat as still as I could as she took my pulse.

"Good," she told me before she reached for the blood pressure sleeve. She wrapped it around my arm, and after checking the reading she said, "Good," once again. "One ten over seventy-five."

"That's good?" I asked, even though she had just said that it was.

"Perfectly fine," she assured me. "Now let's listen to your heart." Pressing the stethoscope against my chest, she said, "Deep breath in"—I did as I was told—"and deep breath out."

Again I followed the instructions.

After a few moments, she said, "I hear your murmur."

"Yes," I replied. I'd had a long-term condition: mitro valve prolapse, or what is commonly known as a heart murmur. Thankfully I'd never been affected by the condition, and the only thing I had to do was take antibiotics whenever I'd been scheduled for a dentist appointment from the time I was a child. Thankfully, that requirement had stopped the year before.

"Okay," Diana said as she dropped the stethoscope, and then jotted notes on my chart. "When was the date of your last period?" she asked.

I glanced at Samson, who'd been sitting silently but so attentively. It was as if he were taking notes in his mind. Turning back to Diana, I said, "Well, I missed my last one, so the period before that was around September fifteenth."

"Okay, the doctor will be in in a moment and he'll have the results of your urine test."

She had just gotten the last word out when the tall doctor bounded into the room. "Are these the new parents?" he asked, his jovial persona on display through his smile and his tone. But it wasn't his countenance that had my attention. I was focused on his words.

"New parents?" Sam and I said together.

"Yes," he said. "The test shows you're pregnant!"

Those were the words I had been waiting to hear for my entire life. I had said those words to myself a thousand times before, but hearing it from the doctor made it completely real.

You're pregnant. I let his words replay a few times in my mind before I squealed with delight. I squealed and Samson sighed, as if relieved, and then he laughed.

Dr. Berman turned his smile to Samson. "You've done it now!"

"It looks like I have!" Samson said through his own laughter.

"Well," the doctor continued, "get ready because life as you know it is about to change."

I was pretty sure Dr. Berman had said those words thousands of times to his patients through the years. It was just that Samson and I had no idea how true his words were going to be.

He still wore a smile, but Dr. Berman's tone turned back to professional. "From what you've shared with us, you're probably about seven to eight weeks along, young lady." The joy was gone from his voice when he continued, "I know Diana told you that I'm no longer delivering babies."

Even though I knew this, somewhere inside I'd been hoping that either Dr. Berman had changed his mind or that he'd make an exception for me. So I felt sad and anxious all over again.

"You're going to have to find an OB, taking into account your age, your race, and any risk factors that go along with it."

"Risk factors?" I asked.

He shook his head. "I'm sure everything will be fine, but unfortunately, African Americans have a higher mortality rate. And then your age …"

My age? What was he talking about? I was only thirty-five.

He continued, "Like I said, I'm sure everything will be fine. We just need to get you going with your prenatal care. Diana will give you the list we compiled as a resource of OBs in the area."

"You know, I thought you were going to be joking with me throughout my labor," I told him. "I thought you would be the one catching this Logan baby!"

He knew I was kidding but serious at the same time. "I'm sorry, my dear. I would've loved to have been your doctor, but with the malpractice insurance rates so high, it's a wonder that doctors are even able to stay in business. It shouldn't be that way, but because of the high costs I didn't have a choice. I had to stop our obstetrics care."

"I had no idea this kind of thing was going on," I said.

"Unfortunately, it is." As he approached the table, he motioned for me to lean back. "Okay, let me check everything out. Put your feet on Bessie and Jessie here."

Even though he always said this and I always had to rest my feet in the stirrups that he had covered with oven mitts with faces of two comical-looking roosters, I still giggled.

As I scooted up and he rolled his stool toward the end of the table, he kept talking. "I'm sure you know the basics, but to be sure, I want you eating well and getting plenty of rest."

"I will," I told him as he examined me. I kept my eyes on the ceiling.

"Okay," he said. "Everything so far is looking good. Looks like you will probably have a June baby."

"Perfect!" I said as he rolled back, completing my exam.

He snapped his gloves off. "You'll probably gain somewhere between twenty-five to thirty-five pounds. If you start gaining more than that, check in with your doctor."

"I will."

"Now again, I want to ensure that you continue to kick this pregnancy off in a healthy way, so find that doctor."

I nodded, and when I glanced at Samson, he was nodding too.

The doctor continued: "Your doctor will send you for some tests, again to be on the safe side. But in the meantime if you notice any spotting or experience any cramping, let us know right away."

"I will definitely do that," I assured him.

"I think I already had you on prenatal vitamins in preparation for this, but I'll make sure that's refilled and it's important now that you take those vitamins daily."

"Excuse me, Doctor," Samson chimed in. "Why do women take prenatal vitamins? I mean, I know it's healthy, but is there something she should be doing differently with her diet?"

"Just what I told her: eat a healthy, well-balanced diet with fruit, vegetables, grains, dairy, and meat. But even with that, most women don't get enough of some of the important nutrients like folic acid and iron that their body requires during pregnancy. And the prenatal vitamins are important for the baby too. They help with the development of the baby's neural tube, spinal cord, and brain development, along with preventing some birth defects." Dr. Berman quickly added, "So it's really important for the baby in these first few weeks especially. That means you have to make sure she's taking them."

"Got it," Samson replied.

"Good. And I've got another job for you, Mr. Samson."

At first I was concerned, but the big smile on Dr. Berman's face let me know he was going to say something that was typical for him.

"Take care of her! Listen to her and help her out. This will be a great time for both of you. Can you do that?"

"Well," Samson began with a sigh, "I'll try."

And then we all laughed.

Dr. Berman turned his attention back to me. "Okay, get dressed, and Diana and I will see you at the desk outside." He offered me a hand, helping me step down from the examination table.

The doctor left us alone and I dressed in silence. I guess we were both lost in our thoughts about this new part of our lives. Samson took my hand as we exited the room.

Outside at the front desk, Dr. Berman handed me my checkout materials. "Here's the list," he said. "I'm going to order some blood work for you so that it will be helpful with your new doctor and we'll make sure it gets to whomever you choose. And when you have the baby, make sure you send us a picture for our wall."

Samson and I followed his glance to the left where the wall was decorated with newborns that Dr. Berman had delivered. I wished things could be different, but I trusted the names he had given me.

"Thank you so much, Doctor," I said before Samson shook his hand.

We were silent on the walk from the office to the car, and even once inside, we sat there in stunned silence. We had entered the doctor's office knowing I was pregnant. But hearing him say it brought new meaning to both of us. A couple of minutes went by before we slowly turned to each other and then exploded into an excited mixture of talking and laughing.

"We're parents!"

"I'm going to be a mom!"

"You're having a baby!"

"You're going to be a dad!"

"This is really happening!"

We'd been driving for a while and we were still chatting, and I had not even noticed that Samson had stopped the car.

"Where are we?" I asked as I peeked out the window. He had stopped in front of Babies 'R' Us. "What are we doing here?"

"You know this baby is going to be good-looking, right?" Samson asked.

My eyes rolled up a bit, trying to make fun of his silliness. But his words, and this act, warmed my heart. He loved our baby already—just like I did.

"Yes," I replied, "I'm sure the baby will be a beautiful baby."

"He's going to look like me, so there's no other choice!" he asserted as only he could.

I laughed. "He? *She's* going to be adorable."

He pondered that for a moment. "He or she, I'll be happy with either," he said. "I just pray that we have a healthy child."

I grew serious.

But Samson went right back to joking. "You might be right."

"Me? Right? About what?" I asked. Samson hardly ever gave me credit when I was right about anything, so his words were a surprise.

"Yes, you may be right ... *this time*," he clarified. He paused for a moment. "A girl?" He looked at me with squinted eyes that studied me, then his glance shifted upward. "My little girl."

I wasn't sure if he was talking to me or having a conversation with himself.

"A little me without a goatee!"

He seemed to be settling into the idea.

All I could do was shake my head. "Excuse me, Daddy, why are we at Babies 'R' Us?" I was teasing him, but I sure did like calling him by his new title. The way his grin spread across his face let me know he liked it too.

"I would think the answer is obvious, Momma," he said. "We're going to need some things. With all that we have going on, there's no time like the present to look."

Samson jumped from the car, came to the passenger side and took my hand. We headed into the store as expecting parents and we probably looked like it too because we touched *everything*. We sat in every rocking chair, examined all of the cribs, and cooed at just about every outfit for infants in the store.

We were having such a great time preparing for this new chapter in our lives. Samson and I were definitely on the same page.

He gave me a peck on my cheek as he left me to look at the bouncers while he walked over to the stroller section. Just a few minutes later, I heard him all the way on the other side of the store. When I peeked over to where he was, I saw him race-walking different strollers up and down the aisles.

I stood in shock for a moment, especially when another man (maybe a new dad too?) joined him and the two of them raced strollers throughout the store. As I watched in horror (okay, not real horror), the workers in the store laughed, obviously enjoying the show and the competition between the two men.

Trying to get Samson out of the store, I motioned for him to come over to the checkout where I was standing with a few items. When he saw me, he raised his arms triumphantly and turned to the other man with a look of victory before he headed my way.

Shaking my head, I lowered my voice when I explained to the cashier, "We just found out we're going to be parents."

"Don't worry about it," the young lady said, waving her hand. "We see this all the time."

Samson rushed over. "We can't go home without *this*!" He pointed to the stroller that had brought him his victory. He seemed to be asking me, rather than telling me, we had to buy it, so I glanced at the saleslady.

She smiled and shrugged. "Well, *this is* a special day."

That was the best combination of showing genuine happiness and upselling I'd ever seen. When I turned to Samson and saw the smile that could light up the world, all I could do was say, "We'll take it."

Samson kissed my cheek. "Yes! We're taking our baby's stroller home."

I felt so right. Again, I had the thought that I was finally living my someday.

21

Change

(From Angela)

Samson stepped back from the car, looking at the trunk full of baby items. "Things are really going to change, Ang'."

"I know," I said. "We're used to getting up and going. We don't check in with anyone, we don't need any sitters, time is not a concern for us—we just get up and go."

"You're right," he said with a bit of a sigh.

We'd been feeling so good, so happy, and just a few minutes ago Samson had been running up and down the aisles in the baby store. Now Samson's change of tone worried me. Had the euphoria already worn off? Was the reality of all of this settling in and now he wasn't so sure?

"I know," he began, "but it's more than that."

His words felt heavy. My heart sank. I wanted—I needed—Samson to feel joy on this journey. Of course, this wasn't the timing we'd planned, but the timing for our family was here nonetheless.

Samson guided me to the passenger's door and helped me get inside. His expression was pensive as he walked around the car and got in the driver's side. He sat down but didn't turn on the ignition. His voice was low when he began. "This is definitely going to be a new chapter for us." He started the car. "We've got to stay on the same page."

I didn't tell him I'd been thinking the same thing. I paused to give him the space to share more. Something was obviously on his heart. "If you're blessed enough," he said with his eyes on me, "you will meet someone who changes everything. You and this baby are my family. My life is about to change. And this is a change that I've been preparing for, for so many years. And now it's here."

I reached for his hand, my heart bursting with gratitude for having him in my life.

"This baby is going to need both of us," he said. "He or"—he raised one eyebrow—"*she* needs to grow up in a home with both parents. We have to put the best of both of us into this baby."

There was so much I wanted to say, so many words I wanted to share to let him know he was right. We were on the same page, but I remained quiet—this was his moment.

"Our marriage is going to be the best example we can set for our child," he continued. "We have to do this right. We can't afford any more mistakes, you know?"

I wanted to hold onto these last few minutes forever. All his sharing touched me deeply. My eyes were already filled with water. It was my turn to pour out my heart, but then my cell phone rang.

Looking down at the screen, I picked up the phone and showed it to Samson. It was our Realtor. We'd been looking for homes for so long that everyone in our families thought we were serial lookers. We included them in our search for our perfect home, taking our parents to see whichever homes we were serious about.

Clearly it had taken us some time to land the one house that was right for us. Not that we hadn't tried. We'd found a couple of homes that were so perfect that not only did we put in bids, but we'd taken the whole family to see the houses. Each time, though, we'd lost out on the bid. It happened three times, so this last time, several weeks ago, when we'd found another home we loved, we decided not to include our families. Not until we knew for sure we had a home.

We were hopeful for this house—in the city of Williamsville and town of Clarence, an area Samson and I adored. We had actually seen it months prior, but it was so high-priced that we passed on it. Changing market conditions, however, along with a life change for the homeowners, had brought the price down. We had put a bid in several weeks prior and had gone back and forth with the homeowner on some details of the contract but hadn't heard back. So when I saw her name on my phone, I was thinking she'd found something new for us.

"Hello, Chelsea," I answered, putting the call on speaker.

"Hello, Angela," she said.

"Have you found some new homes for us to look at?" I asked. "Samson and I are actually together and out and about right now. We could drive by a listing if you have one."

"Actually I'm calling with some bad news and good news," she said.

I sighed. "Let's get the bad news out of the way. Give that to me first." I put the phone closer to Samson so we could both hear clearly.

"The bad news is that I won't be able to show you any more houses," she said. Both Samson's and my eyes rolled with frustration at the same time.

"Huh?" I questioned. *Why not? Was she leaving the business? Were we going to have to find a new doctor and a new Realtor?*

"The good news is," she continued through my thoughts, "I won't have to because the seller accepted your offer."

Both Samson and I were quiet for a moment as it took a couple of seconds for the good news to make sense to us. Then I shouted, "Really?" as Samson pumped his fist in the air.

She laughed. "Really. But one thing: This is a tough seller. They want to be done with the property so the closing has to be in thirty days or less. If you can't meet that, the deal is off."

"Meet thirty days? Can we move in tomorrow?" I laughed.

"Well, he's signed the contract, so it's official. Congratulations!" I could hear the happiness in her voice, but it didn't match what Samson and I were feeling.

"Thank you!" we told Chelsea together.

"I'll e-mail everything over to your lawyer so that she can move things along for you as quickly as possible," she said.

"Perfect!" I said. "Thanks again."

The moment I hung up, Samson grabbed his phone and plugged it into the car, pulling up his playlist and putting some music on. We laughed and thanked God at the same time. We laughed even harder when people passing by looked at us as if we were crazy.

After we settled down, Samson was finally able to move the car from the curb and drive us to my house. As I got out of the car, I said, "You were right, Samson."

Looking over at him, he was practically sweating from how much he had been clapping and shaking his hands in praise. "Of course I was right," he said. "This is me we are talking about, so me being right is natural. Hello …" But then it must've dawned on him that he didn't know what I was talking about, because he asked, "Right about what exactly?"

"Things are changing!"

"You got that right," he said. "We're in store for quite a month!"

"Can you believe all that's happened? We're starting our family in the home I hope that our child will grow up in. God's timing is perfect!"

"Let's drive by *our* home."

It was a fifteen-minute drive from my house. When we arrived at our new place, Samson pulled the car right in front of the house and we sat there, gazing at the home where we would begin our lives together.

"I can't wait to move in," he said, putting his arm around me and pulling me as close as he could in the car. "We'll have to have a housewarming right away."

"Yes," I confirmed, "and we have to do it while the weather is warm so you can barbecue in the backyard."

We sat there talking, making plans for the house: what colors we'd paint the rooms, the new furniture we'd have to buy.

Then Samson couldn't take it anymore. "I can't just sit here." He opened his car door. "Come on, let's walk around."

"We don't have the keys!" I exclaimed.

He shrugged. "So? That doesn't make it any less *ours*. Come on, we'll make it quick."

We knew the house was empty—the homeowners had already moved out—so I figured it was okay. After Samson helped me from the car, we opened the gate to the backyard and walked around, peering inside the windows, continuing our planning.

When we'd completed our private tour, Samson said, "We've got to get a quick prayer in after this day."

So we walked up to the house and as we laid hands on the brick, Samson prayed, "Father, we thank you for making us a family and making this our home. Lord, we ask you to bless this home and us as we start our life together. We pray your protection over this home and over us as we reside here. We ask for happiness, joy, and good memories to be upon us. We thank you for enlarging our territory and for this bountiful blessing. In Jesus' name. Amen."

I realized just how exhausted I was when we finished our prayer. I'd only taken one day off and that meant I'd have to be right back at work the following day. Even though I worked from home, I still put in my eight, nine, or ten hours every single day. So I needed to get to my (now temporary) home and rest up for the remainder of the day.

"I'm exhausted," I said to Samson. "Just so tired."

"Yeah." Samson nodded. "We've had a big day and the baby is probably wearing you out."

It was my turn to nod.

"Okay, let's get you back to your *old* house so that you can rest tonight, because starting tomorrow we've got a serious to-do list to tackle."

"You can say that again!" I said.

As we headed toward the car, I began to check off the points on that list. "At the top, I have to get to work on getting an OB. The second thing, we'll need a moving company."

Samson jumped in. "And the third thing is that we have to check in with the wedding planner to make sure everything is set."

Those were three huge items, and I was feeling overwhelmed. However, I was thinking that maybe, with some rest, the list wouldn't seem so daunting.

At my door, Samson kissed me goodbye, and I was grateful I'd be able to just go inside and rest. I changed clothes and relaxed for a bit, flipping through some of the home magazines I'd been collecting. It was still rather early when I headed off to bed, but it felt as if my head had barely hit the pillow when the alarm clock went off.

I had set the alarm for an hour earlier than normal; I figured I could go through the list from Dr. Berman and find a doctor before I began my workday. Even though I still felt tired, I dragged myself out of bed, showered, and dressed. As I ate breakfast, I went through the list of the obstetricians.

Looking at all the names for the first time, I was surprised the list was so extensive—over forty doctors. I was able to eliminate ten right away because they were too far away from where we'd be living. Plus, I had to consider the hospital; I wanted to deliver at Millard Fillmore Suburban Hospital. They had just done some upgrades to the building and completely renovated the labor and delivery wing. Not only was it close to where we'd be living, but there were a range of specialists at the hospital. The hospital had received glowing reviews from patients and the community about their care, so I wanted to find a doctor who had admitting privileges there.

I narrowed my selection down to ten doctors who would work geographically, and then I began doing my online research. I checked every resource I could from Health Grades, Rate MDs, Yelp, and Doximity, as well as the doctors' personal websites, to learn more about each of them, their specialties, and their patient reviews. From this I eliminated four more. Checking the time, I realized some of the offices might already be open, so I decided to call some of them.

I dialed the first number. When someone answered, I explained who I was and how I'd been referred by Dr. Berman. But the moment I said that, the receptionist said, "Dr. Clark isn't accepting new patients right now." I thanked her, hung up the phone, then tried the next number.

I went through the same routine before the receptionist said, "Dr. James isn't accepting any new patients right now."

I got the same from all of the rest of my calls. By the time I hung up with the last one, I became worried. It hadn't occurred to me it would be this difficult to find a doctor. With a baby on board, I couldn't afford to wait, but I had to get to work.

The next morning, I began the process again, this time calling a few of my friends and getting recommendations from them. The results were exactly the same, though: glowing reviews and good online ratings, but once I made the calls, none of them were accepting new patients. I began to think that the pressure of finding a doctor was wearing on me. Throughout the day, fatigue had taken over my body. By the time I was ready to be done with work, I was so tired I couldn't have picked up a pencil!

That night, as I talked to Samson, I relaxed and told him I was doing my best not to be concerned.

"That's right," he told me. "You have to pace yourself."

I agreed and again went to sleep as early as I could.

Change

The next day I decided to start with work, thinking I'd make more calls during the middle of the afternoon. But by the time lunchtime came around, I was too tired to do anything more. "It must be nap time," I said as I rubbed my belly.

If there was one calming thing through this process, it was that I loved talking to my little one. I kept talking to her as I lay down for a quick power nap. But my power nap turned into a power sleep and the next thing I knew it was six o'clock. That was in the morning, not the evening! I couldn't remember a time when I'd slept that many hours straight through. It had to be a pregnancy thing, which was all the more reason to find an obstetrician.

I hit the list once again, selecting eight other doctors from Dr. Berman's list, but this time I decided I needed a different approach. So I called Dr. Berman's office and asked for Diana.

She sounded surprised when she came on the line. "You're calling so soon," she said. "I hope you're not having any cramping or spotting." I heard the concern in her voice.

"No. I think I'm all right," I told her. "I'm really fatigued, though. I wasn't expecting the exhaustion to hit me like a tidal wave, but it has! But I'm calling for a favor."

"Okay. It depends on the favor, though." She laughed.

"I'm hoping that you can call a few doctors for me and request that they take me as a new patient," I told her. "I've been working on your list and even got some referrals from friends, but so far all of my choices aren't taking new patients. I'm running out of options and time!" I continued to plead my case: "I really could use some help, especially since I've been so tired."

"Well, tiredness is to be expected in your first trimester," she said, "because your body is working overtime producing hormones and the placenta. But of course you want to monitor yourself. We definitely don't want you to wait much longer to see anyone. Give me a few names of the doctors you've selected and I'll see what I can do. No promises, but I can try."

"Thank you," I said with relief in my voice. I gave her the names and she told me she would call me with news either way by the end of the day.

Taking that off of my plate, at least for the moment, gave me the chance to tackle some of the other items on my list. I called around and got a moving company for a great price. Check! At least one thing was done. Next up, I called my wedding planner.

"Hello, Mrs. Logan," Rebecca said as she answered the phone.

"I like the sound of that!" All I could do was smile, then I chuckled. "And what I would like just about as much is if you tell me that everything is on track with our wedding and it will be spectacular." I prayed she would tell me all was going well and I didn't have to add anything to our plans because, with the way I was feeling, the only energy I had was to plan to meet Samson at the chapel.

"I can assure you, Mrs. Logan, you will be pleased. We received the wedding dress you shipped and will have it steamed and ready. All of the other details are set, from the flowers to the music. The only thing you have to do is get your marriage license when you arrive in Las Vegas, then show up and we'll do the rest."

"Thank you so much," I told her as I mentally erased that second item from my list. As I sat down at my desk and went to work, I hoped for a trifecta. It would definitely depend on what Diana had to say. Around five the phone rang, and when I saw that it was Dr. Berman's office, I said a quick prayer before I answered.

"Hey, Diana. Do you have good news for me?"

"Well, I have some good news and some bad news."

At least she had something good to say; that gave me hope.

"The bad news is that two of the doctors simply said no, they can't accommodate anyone new right now. It took a little doing, but two of the doctors said yes."

"That's great!" I exclaimed.

"Dr. Bavarro is located in Buffalo and delivers at Sisters Hospital, and Dr. Walters is located in Williamsville and delivers at

Millard Fillmore Suburban Hospital. Both are pretty good doctors, so you can choose."

The moment she said Millard Fillmore, my decision was made. "Let's go with Dr. Walters," I said.

"Great! I'll note your chart. All you have to do is call Cheryl in Dr. Walters' office to set your appointment. Just remind her that she spoke to me. You should also call your insurance company to have your new doctor listed, and with that you're all set."

"Thanks, Diana! You're the best."

Hanging up, I wanted to dance, and I would have if I weren't so tired. But that was okay—I was happy. Trifecta achieved.

I called Samson and he barely had his hello out before I said, "We're on a roll. Our to-do list is now our to-did list. I got everything done!"

"Really?" he replied. "You did all of that today?"

"Yep!" I answered.

"You got a doctor?"

"Yes."

"Did you check him out? Are you going to be comfortable going to him?"

"I think it'll be okay," I told him. "He was on Dr. Berman's referral list and I did quite a bit of research online. He seems like he'll be good."

"Well, if you're happy, I'm happy," he replied. "So that means … are you ready to meet me in Vegas?"

I laughed. "I'm ready!"

22

War and Peace

(From Angela)

I was on my knees, praying. I felt the cold ceramic tile beneath me as my hands rested on the porcelain toilet. I had been in that position for so long that I had actually dozed off. That little bit of rest had been a relief because the previous few hours of the night had been horrible.

Now that I was awake again, the nausea that had taken over me before was back, pulsating through my body like rough tidal water. My tears were my only release and they streamed down my face. If I could just get rid of this feeling, get this nausea out of my system, this would all be better. Right?

Praying to throw up was something I'd never done. But as I sat hunched over the toilet, that's exactly what I prayed for. I'd been there for too long, and when nothing happened, I decided to call Samson. At least I could let him know what was going on.

I glanced over to the sink where I had left my phone, though it was just beyond my reach. Still I stretched, trying to grab it. I was going to have to get up if I wanted it. "Pregnancy rule number one," I said to myself. "If you can't reach, you don't need it." True to those words, I didn't move.

I was tired and only wanted to lie down for a little while.

Glancing around the bathroom, my eyes settled on the Egyptian cotton bath towels on the rack right above me, and for a moment an old memory made me smile.

Don't you lay a hand on those, my mother said of the fancy towels that hung in our bathroom. *They're for looking, not touching.* As I child, I had never quite understood that tradition that was handed down by my mother. Why would you have towels in a bathroom and not use them?

I grabbed both towels, then slid onto the floor before I laid my head on the soft cotton. Sighing with relief, I patted my stomach. "Don't worry, baby," I said. "I'll let you touch the towels—all of them. Oh, and there will be no off-limits rooms either," I assured her. "You can play in every room in the house!"

Settling in even more, I curled into a ball and wondered why no one had ever mentioned that being nauseated during pregnancy would feel like you were dying. My mother hadn't told me, my future mother-in-law hadn't told me, none of the dozens of pregnancy books I read ever said anything about it. And then I began to wonder: *Maybe this wasn't nausea. Maybe this was something else, something far worse.*

Just as I had that thought, a wicked pain shot through my abdomen. "Ugh!" I cried out. As the pain tore through me, I thought about my baby and how strong she was. I could feel her fighting with me; although deep inside, I had the feeling that her fight wasn't the same as mine. I felt as if my baby were fighting, but she didn't know if she was fighting to stay or fighting to go. Inside, a battle waged: should she stay so she could meet me and her daddy outside of my womb, or should she return to the one who had loved her even before I did?

"Stay with me, baby," I whispered. I was filled with fear. I couldn't lose my baby. Not only because I already loved her so much, but because she alone was *my* reason for fighting. Then my spirit turned to the Lord. "God, please let my baby stay with me," I cried out.

As I prayed aloud to God, inside I tried to communicate with my baby—I gave her a list for living. "There are snowflakes, sprinkles, hugs, bedtime stories, books, dogs, toys, sand between your toes, cuddling, ice cream, laughter, and there is Daddy and there is me … all waiting for you."

At that moment, another cramp strangled my stomach into a knot. I held my breath until the pain released me for a moment, and then I wondered if that was my baby's way of communicating with me.

I'd heard about all the pregnancy symptoms, including pregnancy brain and raging hormones, but in the last few days it seemed like every symptom had descended on me all at once. I'd developed a ravenous appetite. I lived in Buffalo but felt as if I could eat one every day, even though sometimes even thinking about food made me dry-heave. This was one of those moments.

I had to pee all the time, and then there were the mood swings—I cried a few days before when I opened the refrigerator and saw that Samson had left just a swallow of orange juice in the container. Then the final and most serious symptom: the fatigue. I'd been feeling like a slow-moving storm cloud blanketed me and zapped all my energy.

With all of that, what was happening to me and my baby now at this moment was different. It would have been a miscarriage of my faith to believe anything else, because I knew something was wrong.

People often think pregnant women are driven to be irrational and emotional by their hormones. To sum it up in one word, pregnant women are often thought to be crazy. But perhaps it wasn't pregnant women but the rest of the world that had been crazy all of this time. Crazy to let the world make us believe something that wasn't true. Crazy to let the world get in the way of what we authentically felt, what we authentically believed, and what we authentically knew from our experiences with God.

Yes, hormones like HCG, progesterone, and estrogen are likely the cause of some real mood swings and other symptoms, but hormones from heaven are messages from God. Every cell in our bodies knows when *he* is communicating with us, and I knew with every fiber inside of me that the tiny miracle God had placed inside me was calling out to me *and* God.

I knew he was listening, so I joined with her. "God, please forgive me for my sins. I ask you to bless this child. Protect her as she grows in my womb. Holy Spirit, comfort her. Perfect the work that you have begun in her. Bless me that I may be a good steward over her. Strengthen me in my weaknesses. God, please help us."

I rubbed my stomach, trying to soothe my baby and the cramps that were gripping both of us. And finally, I felt the urge to release it all. I pushed myself up to my knees, then crawled the few inches to the toilet. Raising my head over the bowl, I released the turmoil overflowing inside of me. Never in my life had I been so relieved to vomit.

I felt drained afterward but grateful. I thanked God profusely. Sitting there, I felt strength slowly returning to me. I garnered enough energy to crawl to the sink, lift myself up, and grab the phone before staggering back to my bed.

The new day's sunlight brought light into my bedroom. A quick glance at the clock on the nightstand told me it was 7:26—I'd been in the bathroom for about two hours. I dialed Samson's number, wanting to let him know what was going on. His phone just rang, which wasn't surprising given the time. The odds of him picking up this early were slim, but I didn't want to leave him a message. What would I say? That I was dying before, but I'm better now? That would cause my fiancé unnecessary panic because I did feel much better. Still I wanted to talk to him; I wanted him to know what was happening. So I called two more times before texting him: *Call me.*

The cramping had stopped and the nausea that had minutes before felt like an angry raging stream was now only a trickle. What I wanted to do was sleep, but for some reason my eyes seemed set on staying open. I lay there, still sick, but so grateful. I sensed in my soul that whatever had gripped me had passed, and this morning I felt joy, believing that whatever it was, whatever had happened, would not return.

There was no way I could say I felt completely well, but I was able to be still in the quiet. About an hour passed when my phone rang. Reaching out my hand, I lifted the phone to my ear.

"What's going on, Ang'?" Samson asked before I even said hello. I could hear the anxiety in his voice.

"I guess what they say is true," I told him. "Pregnancy is a happy reason to feel like crap!" I did my best to sound upbeat, but my tone did not seem to assure him.

"Why do you say that?" he asked. "Is everything okay?"

"It wasn't, but I think it is now." My words must have been too cryptic for him.

"What do you mean?" He sounded impatient, like he wanted to know specifically what was happening.

So I told him. "I've never felt anything like it," I said. "I was so nauseated, my stomach was cramping. I didn't even have the energy to call you when it was actually happening. I know it's too early to really feel anything, but I did feel like our baby was in trouble and the both of us were in the middle of a war." Quickly I added, "But we're still here, and thank God that has passed."

There was so much more that happened, so much more I wanted to explain, but I didn't have the right words to explain it to myself. Then I called out, "Sam?" He hadn't said a word and I wondered if he was still there or if he'd been disconnected. There was nothing, and I called out to him again. "Samson?" I heard some noise, a bit of shuffling and scuffling.

Finally, he said, "I'm getting dressed and will be right there."

The phone went dead and I lay back down. I'd been feeling better before, but I felt even more better now. Samson was on his way.

23

Gestation

(From Angela)

I had barely hung up the phone when I heard keys in the door. This was the first time Samson was using the emergency keys I had given him. Nothing on me moved as his footsteps approached my bedroom. Well, that's not completely true—my lips curled into a smile.

Samson peered into my bedroom, as if afraid to startle me or afraid of what he might find.

"Honey, you're home!" I said, only able to give him a faint smile.

He let out a sigh of relief. He rushed over, kneeling at the side of my bed. "Are you okay?"

"I think I'm okay now." I hoped my words would calm him. More relief came out of him when he exhaled. "I'm glad you let yourself in."

"I'm glad I had a key."

"'Cause if there is one thing I definitely don't feel like doing right now," I said with a light laugh, "it's moving!"

He knew I meant it even though I was trying to lighten the mood. "Sorry, Ang'," he said, "but you're going to have to. You need to get to a doctor if you're feeling this bad."

"I'm feeling much better," I assured him, "but you do remember that I have an appointment with Dr. Walters at four today, right?"

Together, we glanced at the clock: 8:59. He shook his head. "That's too long to wait."

"Okay, I'll call to see if they can take me earlier."

Before I could move to reach for the phone, Samson grabbed it, then scrolled through my contacts. "Dr. Walters, right?"

I nodded and watched until he located the name, then hit the dial button before he put the phone on speaker. When the receptionist answered, I said, "This is Angela Burgin *Logan*." I glanced at Sam with a smirk. "I have an appointment today at four. However, I've been experiencing some bad cramping and pain in my abdomen. Is it possible for Dr. Walters to see me sooner?"

"Let me see what we can do, Angela." She put me on hold for a moment and came back: "I can bring you in at ten thirty. Will that work?"

Although I was the only one talking, both Samson and I smiled. "Thank you," I said. "I'll be there."

Samson suddenly looked more angry than relieved when we hung up the phone.

"What's wrong?" I asked, knowing something was bothering him, more than just me being sick.

"I can't believe you didn't call me sooner!" he said, clearly exasperated. "What if something happened? What if something had happened to you and the baby?"

"I'm sorry," I said, genuinely apologizing because his voice was filled with such fear. "But last night wasn't like anything I've ever experienced. I was in so much pain!"

"That was all the more reason to call me." He shook his head.

"I wanted to get in touch with you," I explained, hoping he would understand. "I wanted to call you, and I tried to get to the phone, but honestly I could barely move. To tell you the truth, Sam, the whole thing last night made me realize that you can get to a place where the only one you can call on is God."

Samson softened, and he reached for my hand.

"What a difference a prayer makes!" I said. "Trust me, I'm feeling so much better than I did last night."

He squeezed my hand and I could see the gratitude on his face.

"I'll be happy, though, to get to Dr. Walters to ensure that all is well with the baby."

Samson held on to me as I slowly raised myself up. With his help, I showered, dressed, and got ready for the doctor. He chuckled when we made it to the doctor's office and signed in fifteen minutes early. "This has to be one for the record books," he whispered as the receptionist handed me the paperwork to fill out. "She's actually early! That never happens."

The receptionist smiled. "Well, maybe it's that little one inside. Perhaps she'll be an early baby too!" Now we all laughed, thinking that was a joke instead of the foreshadowing of things to come.

By the time I completed filling out the pages with my medical history, we were being called in to see the doctor. The nurse directed us to a room and began setting up the equipment and asked me to undress.

"Is that the ultrasound equipment?" I asked.

"Yes," she said. "Today you'll be getting the first photo of your baby!"

A photo? Of the baby?

Samson and I smiled again, though I was sure the nerves I felt he felt too. It was exciting to be getting our first picture of her, but there was still last night and what had happened. This ultrasound would let me see our baby and know she was okay.

"I'll be back in a moment," the nurse said. "I'll get more information from you and your vitals."

When she stepped out, I quickly changed into the gown she'd placed on the examination table. Just a few moments after that, she returned, handing me a cup. "We'll need a urine sample. When you're done, just place it in the small trapdoor. It's already been labeled with your name."

Heading to the bathroom, I knew peeing on command was not an issue. My baby girl's first bouncy house was my bladder! I was in and out of the bathroom and back in the examination room, where the nurse took my blood pressure. As she waited for the results, she asked, "Do you have any concerns before I go through your medical history?"

"I do." Giving Samson a quick glance, I continued, "I've been extremely fatigued."

She nodded with understanding.

"But things last night turned from fatigue to a really rough night. I had a terrible bout of nausea. Really, it was unbearable. And I had severe cramps and pain in my abdomen."

She asked, "Is the discomfort still there?"

I glanced at Samson again. There was concern all over his face. "It has gotten much better," I said to the nurse and to Samson. "And the nausea has started to subside."

"Well, the doctor will definitely want to take a look at the baby to ensure everything is okay."

"I'll feel much better when he does," I said.

"Have you ever suffered a miscarriage?" the nurse asked.

I knew before I came to the doctor's office that word would be mentioned. There was no way to avoid it, even though I didn't want to speak it out loud, I didn't even want to say it in my head. "No, never," I said, finally responding. "This is my first pregnancy."

"I'm sure everything will be fine," the nurse said, "but about one in four pregnancies end in a miscarriage."

She spoke with the tone of a technician, her words matter-of-fact. Her tone erased all the calmness I'd worked hard to have. Now I was once again filled with anxiety.

"From the look of things," the nurse said, "you're close to ten weeks along, so we will likely see a fetal heartbeat on the ultrasound and that will let us know that everything is okay with the baby." She must've seen that I was a ball of nerves, because she finished with, "Let's stop talking and get the doctor in here!"

Gestation

That was what I was thinking too.

When she left us alone, Samson stood and came over to me. "Relax," he said, taking my hand. I hadn't said a word, but, of course, he knew my thoughts. "Look around." He pointed to the doctor's accolades framed on the wall. "This doctor obviously knows what he's doing. We're in the right place. He'll guide us through this pregnancy. Everything will be okay."

His words were soothing, but I couldn't get the word *miscarriage* out of my mind.

A few more anxious minutes passed before the doctor came into the room carrying my chart. He extended his hand to Samson. "Mr. Logan, I assume?"

"Yes, you can also call me Sam. Hello, Doctor." Sam shook his hand.

"So this is the missus?" He spoke to Samson but looked at me.

"Yes, yes. Very soon to be." Samson smiled.

Finally, the doctor spoke to me. "Hello, Mrs. Logan." As Samson stepped aside, he extended his hand.

I greeted him and then watched as he looked down at the chart.

"We received your records from Dr. Berman and the tests that he ordered." He stopped and looked up. "There's just one thing that caught my attention in the tests."

His tone and his expression showed no concern, but that was okay because I was concerned enough for all of us.

"Yes, you're definitely pregnant, " he said, cracking a smile.

It was only when I let out a big sigh that I realized I'd been holding my breath. I tried to smile, wanting to show him I appreciated his bedside manner and that he had a sense of humor too. But I couldn't help it—all I could do was get straight to the point: "I was hoping that today would be a routine prenatal visit, but I'm worried about the baby." I touched my stomach for emphasis.

Dr. Walters walked to the small sink in the corner and washed his hands.

Then I said, "I had some cramping last night that took my breath away."

"Have you been spotting at all?" The doctor dried his hands as he came back to me.

"There was some. Not a large amount, but I did spot."

He placed the stethoscope that was hanging around his neck against my back. "Deep breath in."

To try and keep calm, I'd been taking long, slow breaths the whole time he was in the room, so this wasn't difficult.

He continued his exam while he talked: "Cramping is actually a common symptom of pregnancy. And it is usually nothing to worry about."

"Whew!" Samson exhaled from across the room. "See, Ang'? Just relax."

The doctor's exam had moved to my abdomen. "This is your first pregnancy, correct?"

"Yes."

"Relax," he said, repeating Samson's advice. "I'm sure everything is fine. We'll take a look at the baby on the ultrasound in a moment." He motioned for me to lie back, then examined my breasts as he explained, "The cramping is normal too. Cramping during pregnancy, especially at this stage, is a sign that the uterus is growing and there is increased blood flow to this area."

That was something I hadn't read, and I felt better about it already. I did want him to understand what had happened the previous night. "I had never experienced anything like that before," I told him. "It was so painful."

"Well, pregnancy is hard work and many new moms aren't prepared for how difficult it can be. But you'll get through it." He pulled out the exam table stirrups and sat on the stool. "We're going to do some cultures and a pap smear and send those out for testing. I'll also be ordering frequent blood testing on your visits and get ready to do a lot of peeing because we'll do a urine sample at each visit." He chuckled and then moved to the pelvic exam. As he pressed down on my stomach, he said, "Hmm."

I glanced at Samson and watched his eyebrows rise.

"You have a bit of a titled pelvis."

"What does that mean?" I asked.

"It's generally nothing to worry about," he said. "You may experience some back pain and some women can have back labor. But what usually happens is that as the uterus continues to grow, it will correct the tilt. There are rarely any issues or complications from it."

I released another huge sigh. "With all of these deep breaths I'm taking, you can tell I must be getting ready to have a baby!"

"We'll get you some help with that as well. During your last trimester, I'll send you to a childbirth class to help prepare you for labor and delivery. You'll learn some pain relief options like breathing techniques, massage, and relaxation. They'll talk to you about medication during delivery, the whole gamut."

"Let's not wait until the third trimester to talk about medication," I said. "Put that in your chart: I will want medication during my delivery! You can give me the epidural now if you want!" I laughed, but I wasn't kidding. Not after last night.

"Okay, hopefully you'll have time to get pain medication. Everyone's labor and delivery process is different, but generally most women will labor long enough to have pain meds administered." After another moment, the doctor announced, "All right. Let's see if the baby is a chip off the old block." He looked at Samson and pointed to a screen. "You'll be able to see the baby here."

Samson came to the side of the exam table, and we both stared at the screen as the doctor rolled the probe over my stomach.

After a few moments, the doctor asked, "Do you see that?"

I gasped. I saw my baby! She was so small, no bigger than an olive, but I could see her head and developing limbs.

"These are your fallopian tubes," the doctor said, pointing. "And this is your uterus. The baby is implanted properly, so even though you had some cramping, you don't have an ectopic or tubal pregnancy. In other words, the fetus is right where it should be."

Samson cupped his hand over his mouth.

The doctor continued his explanation. "And you have an active little baby. Can you see the movement?"

"I see it!" I nearly shouted as a tear rolled from my eye. I grabbed Samson's hand, wanting to be even closer to him in this moment. He seemed frozen at the sight of our baby growing inside of me.

"Oh, and do you hear that?" the doctor asked. "That is your baby's heartbeat."

My mind danced to the steady swooshing sound that seemed to be accompanied by a fast drumbeat. Samson was the musician in the family, but this sound was music to my ears.

"Whoa!" Samson finally thawed from his frozen state and gripped my hand tighter.

"That flicker on the screen is the baby's heart. What I'm listening for is the baby's heart rate and rhythm … and all is well."

"It just got so real," Samson said. "That's my baby right there." He spoke, but his words weren't for us. He was talking to himself. Then he became more conscious and asked, "So everything is okay. Right, Doctor?"

"So far, so good, Sam."

"You've got to take care of them, Doctor. This is my family," he said, as if Dr. Walters didn't know.

"Will do. I'm sure they'll both be fine." But then the doctor paused before he added, "There are a few things we have to watch for and consider."

Both Samson and I snapped out of our joyful trance and gave the doctor our full attention.

He continued, "With the nausea you said you've been feeling, drink plenty of water and stay hydrated. In your medical history, I saw that both of your parents are diabetics, Angela."

I nodded.

"That doesn't mean that you'll develop gestational diabetes, but considering your parents' history and your race, this is certainly something we'll have to watch for."

"Okay," Samson and I both said simultaneously.

"You also need to consider having an amniocentesis."

"Aren't there risks associated with that?" I asked.

This time he nodded. "Yes. There is a risk of miscarriage, but women over thirty-five are offered that test."

I looked at Samson, and in my eyes he already knew my answer.

Samson asked, "What exactly is it and why should we consider it?"

With patience, the doctor began his explanation. "A long, thin needle is inserted into the abdomen and we draw out a bit of the amniotic fluid that is around the baby. This is tested to determine if there are chromosomal abnormalities." He paused as if to give me and Samson a bit of time to digest this information. "If there are any abnormalities, this gives you time to decide whether to terminate the pregnancy."

Terminate the pregnancy? was what my mind said while my mouth told the doctor no. Shaking my head, I repeated it again, this time a little louder, "No!"

Even as loudly as I spoke, the doctor said, "You don't have to make up your mind today. The test isn't done until around sixteen weeks, so you have plenty of time to decide."

Samson chimed in, "I don't think that will be for us, but we'll let you know if we reconsider."

"Okay," the doctor said, sounding like he finally understood our position. "What I will do is send you for a nuchal translucency screening."

"I've heard of that, but don't really know what it means," I said.

"The NT screening measures fluid at the base of the baby's neck and can be helpful in determining whether the baby has an extra chromosome indicating Down's syndrome, congenital heart problems, or any other genetic issues. It's done just like the ultra-sound, but we send you to a different lab to have it completed."

Looking at Samson, I nodded. "Okay, that won't be a problem."

"All right, we're done here." The doctor pulled the probe away. "I'll have a few photos to take with you."

"Question, Doctor," I began as he removed his gloves. "Do I have any restrictions on flying? I travel a lot for work."

"No. You can keep up your routine during these first couple of months. Just walk around during the flight and remember to stay hydrated."

"This fatigue has been tough," I told him. "Is there anything I should do or can do about that?"

"Sleep! Remember, your body is working hard so you will be tired. It's normal," he reassured me.

"What do I do if the cramping returns?" I asked.

"Just try to rest. If it goes on for a prolonged time, or if it's accompanied by some substantial bleeding, then call me." His advice seemed simple, like there was nothing wrong. He shook Samson's hand as he prepared to leave.

Samson told him, "I travel a lot too, so I may not be here for some of this. Please take care of her, Doc!"

"She'll be fine. Doris will set up the NT screening and let us know what you decide on the amniocentesis. You'll get the day and time for your next appointment when you check out."

Slowly I sat up and my head was spinning. Last night, I'd had an experience with my baby in the spirit, and now I got to see her in the natural. Each time I saw her heartbeat flicker on the ultrasound, my own heart felt like it grew a few more chambers, opening up to make room for all of the love I felt for her.

I dressed, and outside the nurse gave us each a picture of our baby. We walked to the car not speaking a word, just staring at the pictures we held. As we buckled ourselves in, Samson asked, "You feel better now that you've seen the doctor?"

"Much."

"Well, not me," he said, "I actually feel kind of nauseated."

My eyes widened. "You do?" Then I realized he was putting me on.

"I'm sick over here." He contorted his face as if he were in great pain.

"You having sympathy pains already?" I asked with a smile on my face.

"I'm going to be a dad." He pointed to my stomach. "That's my baby in there."

We laughed as he pulled the car onto the street. With one hand he drove, and the other he rested on my belly. We'd only been in the car for a few minutes when Samson began to softly sing "Go to Sleep My Baby."

I was sure his voice soothed our baby because Samson certainly soothed me. I sat silently, listening, imagining our baby's smile as she heard her daddy sing. When he finished, I said, "That was beautiful. I'm sure the baby loved it."

"That's good. I hope she did," he said. "But the song was for you." He held my glance for a long moment before his eyes turned back to the road. "Me and the baby are cool." He winked, and just like that my heart expanded a few more chambers, this time for Samson.

24

Touched by an Angel

(From Angela)

Dear me: Nothing will go as planned.
Dear me: It's okay because God's plans are greater than yours.

I hadn't planned on starting my pregnancy journal out that way, but when I put pen to paper, that's what came out.

When I got the idea to create a belly book, my plan was to document my pregnancy journey. I thought my first entries would be about seeing my baby on the ultrasound for the first time, the names we were considering, how far along I was, the usual pregnancy fare. So when I wrote those words, they surprised me. I guess they came from this feeling I had, a feeling deep in my spirit I could not describe, a feeling that kept seeping into my mind.

Something's wrong.

As happy as I was about being pregnant, this feeling was getting to me. I understood that feeling of imminent death when I was suffering from that ferocious nausea and cramping attack. But that had pretty much ended. So why, when those symptoms had subsided, did that feeling remain?

Something's wrong.

"You are so much better, Ang, aren't you?" I said aloud, which was my way of battling those words that were trying to rise inside of me.

Looking back, that feeling was real, that feeling was right. But you don't know what that *something* is until you actually know what that *something* is. At that time, I chalked up the words I'd written as my opening pregnancy entry and this "something" feeling to all of the changes happening with me.

There was still so much going on. Not only was I pregnant, not only was I about to get married, but my job was still up in the air *and* I was getting ready for the move into our new home. There was a lot going on while having a baby. I had longed to be married, move into a house with Samson, and have a baby. I just didn't expect for all three to be happening around the same time, not to mention what was happening with my job.

I was moving up to mommy in chief. It was a joke, but I really liked the idea of approaching my life and pregnancy like a business. Business was what I knew best, and I had previously managed my life as I were the CEO of self. Now I was moving from being a sole proprietor to a partnership, and our baby … well, she was a start-up.

The choices I now made in life would no longer be only for myself. They would be for my husband and for my baby. There was nothing I could think of that I would enjoy more than the business of running my family. That's why I was keeping a journal; it was my business plan. And, as mommy in chief, my first responsibility was to deliver a healthy baby.

I had my title, my business plan, and we had our investors—our friends and relatives who would pour into us. We were so grateful to have the kind of families who would allocate time, money, and resources into growing our family. They were our village and I knew it would take one to help raise our child. I needed them.

My village was in place, but they were not yet in the know.

Samson and I had decided we would wait on meeting with our elders to tell them all that was going on. This was a lot to spring on people (our destination wedding by ourselves, being pregnant, and moving), so we needed time to get settled with all that was going on ourselves, then we'd be able to present it in the best possible light to all those around us.

To be honest, I was relishing this last bit of quiet time where it was our little family—just me, Samson, and our yet-to-be-born baby. I was really looking forward to telling everyone and sharing in the excitement of the news. The talk would soon turn toward baby showers, bonnets, and bows. There would be lots of belly patting and name-guessing games. For now, however, I loved that it was just us.

I just didn't know how much longer we were really going to have this time. My life looked totally different, and although it had been easy enough to explain my lack of holiday decorations and the packed-up boxes that were all around the house (I told everyone I was planning to redecorate for the New Year, leaving off the part that I'd be redecorating a new house!), it was much more difficult to explain my expanding waistline. I looked pregnant.

That surprised me. I thought I would have been well into the second trimester before my body began making major changes. But a little bit of weight started to sneak up on me. My breasts were filling out and most of my clothes were more than a little snug.

Then there was the look. It must be true that pregnant women glow, because at a holiday party Samson and I attended, everyone kept telling me I was glowing. I tried my best not to be startled, but it was hard to keep a straight face and not burst out with the news. Instead, I worked on my Academy Award–worthy performance, only saying, "It must be the season."

Our friends accepted my explanation, but my family ... they were totally different. I thought the jig was up at a huge family holiday gathering. Both of our families were there, and the moment Samson and I walked through the door, someone actually shouted, "Ang', you finally got hips!" Suddenly it felt as if the record scratched, the music stopped, and all eyes were on me.

It must've been my deer-in-the-headlights look that made Samson jump to my rescue. "She looks great, doesn't she?"

The conversation should have ended there, but it didn't. Several others joined in with:

"Yes, you look great with a few extra pounds, Angela!"

"I never thought you'd pick up any weight, but you look good!"

"You are filling out those jeans!"

From the moment Sam and I began to make plans about getting married in Vegas, I'd toyed with the idea of after we said I do, I'd walk into a family gathering and have a *Color Purple* moment. How much fun would it be if I walked in, held up my ring, and triumphantly said, "I's married now!" But if this was how it was going to be, I'd never have that moment because, with the way everyone was acting, this was much more like the color red.

Their words made me blush, but not from being proud. I was melting inside. Everyone wanted to talk about my hips and my weight—really? I never expected to walk into any place where my family would be and have them talk about how fat I'd become. After the fat moments, they told me I also looked great, and I knew that every word they said was meant as a compliment. But all my ears could discern was:

"Extra pounds!"

"You picked up weight!"

I was afraid I was going to burst into tears right then and there.

Was this one of those mood swings that came with pregnancy? Was that why I was feeling supersensitive? I was already a little concerned about the weight I was picking up so quickly, especially since it wasn't totally in my belly. My family was right. My legs, hips, and thighs had gotten bigger. I had gained ten pounds and I wasn't even in my second trimester.

It could have been because I had a huge appetite, but the nausea had fixed that. Now the smell of most foods turned me off. The only cravings I had were for fruit, especially pineapples, which was fine with me because I wanted to do my pregnancy right. I was trying to eat healthy and keep track of everything I ate.

Even with all of the books I was reading, and all the journaling I was doing, I feared I was missing the mark. What I was doing wasn't enough. My family's comments made me realize it was true, and their words made me wonder if I was eating more than I realized. The moment I had that thought, I tossed it aside. I wasn't over-eating—my journal showed me that.

It is really amazing what your mind can process in a few moments. All of those thoughts flooded my mind, all of those insecurities rolled through me as I stood there in front of our families, blinking excessively and not saying a single word while everyone else spoke and gawked.

Just as my "first of all" finger started to rise into the air, Samson swooped in, grabbed my hand, and kissed that finger. "There's just more of her to love!" He winked at me and I stared at him. Then he looked around and shouted, "Hey, is there any eggnog?"

From there, every woman in the family wanted to show Samson the dishes they'd prepared, taking the attention off of me. I appreciated his efforts to distract everyone as the talk turned to food. Even though they were no longer gawking at me, their words had stayed and still hurt. I sat down on the sofa and watched everyone showing off their delectable dishes. But I couldn't find the joy to join in.

There had to be something that I was doing wrong because I knew two things: My family's hearts were in the right place, and sometimes family members could see much more than one is willing to see. So I decided I was going to have to be more diligent about journaling every single thing I ate and keep track of my weight daily.

Once I made that decision, I was able to join in the festivities, smiling once again, chatting and laughing with everyone. I made it through the party without spilling the beans about the baby, and I didn't get any kind of pregnancy nausea. Those were two big accomplishments for which I was grateful. I'd made it home that night with our secret still intact.

As more days passed, I began to question how much longer I would be able to keep my pregnancy just between Samson and me. It was because of something that kept happening that filled me with so much wonder and delight.

I'd been shopping more than usual since there were so many things coming up. My wedding was now only days away, and we needed so much for the new house, and then, of course, the baby. It seemed like I was always in the stores.

One day, when I was in one of the children's clothing stores, I walked up and down the aisles, admiring all the adorable baby clothes. I stopped to pick up a cute little dress. As I held it up to admire it, I was suddenly pushed forward a bit; before I could get my bearings and figure out what was happening, I felt something "attach" to my leg. I looked down and the most adorable pair of little dimples (part of an equally adorable face) smiled at me.

Taking a quick glance around, I saw a woman, whom I presumed to be the toddler's mother, going through the clothing rack in the next aisle. Her back was turned to us so she had no idea that her precious and precocious daughter was holding on to me.

Returning to the little girl, I said, "You are a doll!"

Her smile got wider and her dimples became deeper. She patted my belly. "Ba-be."

Her words startled me! Yes, I'd picked up weight—my family reminded me of that at the holiday gathering—but even though everything was larger on me, my stomach wasn't yet protruding.

Then she did it again—she patted my belly and said, "Ba-be."

My pregnancy hormone meter went off the rails. The corners of my lips rose, spreading my mouth into the widest smile, and I was sure that my heart was going to burst wide open with delight.

"Gabriella! Gabriella!" her mother called.

I heard the panic in her mother's voice and raised my hand to wave at her. "She's over here." I hadn't yet had a baby, but I shared the mother's anxiety.

The young mother hurried over and glanced down. Gabriella was still holding on to my leg. "I'm so sorry!" she said, trying to pry the little girl away.

But no matter how much she tugged, Gabriella would not let go. "She loves people!" the mother said to me. Looking down at her daughter, she admonished her, "Gabriella, let the nice lady go."

"No worries," I said. "She's an adorable child."

Gabriella finally released me, but when she did she once again pointed to my stomach. This time, she looked at her mom when she said, "Ba-be."

Her mother smiled. "Oh, are you having a baby?"

I paused for a moment. I hadn't yet said this to anyone who knew me, but to Gabriella's mother, I said, "Yes! Yes, I am."

"Congratulations!" she said. "You can't even tell. How far along are you?"

"I'm just about twelve weeks."

"Well, congrats again," Gabriella's mother said. "Life as you know it is about to change!" She picked up her daughter, who squeezed her neck in a cute embrace, then added, "But it's worth it."

All I could do was smile as she walked away.

I didn't move from where I was standing. I stayed there, holding my belly in shock. Within her spirit, that sweet, innocent child recognized the sweet, innocent child within me. She sensed the little miracle from God that was growing inside of me.

Elation was the only way to describe what I felt, and this mood swing had nothing to do with my pregnancy. These were hormones from heaven. I was overjoyed. And there was something else I felt. I felt closer to God, closer than I'd ever felt to him before. This new little soul in the seat of my belly was stirring something inside of mine. My pregnancy was like a spiritual awakening, and I felt blessed and favored and filled with his grace.

Then it happened again. Three more times in that same week, kids I didn't know, whom I had never seen before, spontaneously came up to me and hugged me. Each time I walked away from one of these encounters feeling the presence of God more than the last time.

I always shared these experiences with Samson, of course, but I could never fully describe what it truly felt like. How do you explain being touched by an angel? That's what it had to be—little angels connecting with me, because, surely, the four encounters were no coincidences. This was all divine, a message from God. Perhaps he had sent them to prepare me for what was to come. Maybe he wanted me to have that hug now, in advance, to show me that the love of God was around me and his hand was on me. Maybe he just wanted me to believe that it happened.

Whatever his reasons, each time I felt uplifted and inspired. Each time I was filled with wonder and delight. And each time I felt closer to him.

25

The Tight Squeeze

(From Angela)

A nd just like that, my wait was over. Long before we hit thirty thousand feet, my head was in the clouds. I looked out at the expanse of blue sky and billowy clouds that surrounded the plane flying us to Las Vegas. I took a long, deep breath, wanting to live in the moment of this season I'd prayed so long for.

I am ready to jump that broom and he is ready to be my groom! Inside, I chuckled at that thought—we were wedding bound! Leaning over, I rested my head on Samson's shoulder. "I'm going to rest my eyes a minute."

Without looking up, I knew he was smiling. "I know what that means," he said. "I'll wake you when we get to Vegas!"

I laughed, but his words sounded good. The nausea may have been subsiding, but the fatigue was growing as each day passed. Today was one of the worst days, but I attributed it to all I'd been doing over the past week preparing for our wedding and our move.

Before closing my eyes, I looked at Samson. "Are you sure you're good with this?" Even though he told me he was, I wanted to be sure he was going to be happy getting hitched without all of the normal hoopla.

"One thousand percent," he said. "I'm so happy we decided to do it this way." After a slight pause, he then asked, "Are you happy? That is the question."

I sighed with contentment. "We aren't even there yet and everything's perfect," I whispered. "This is exactly what I want."

He didn't say anything for a moment. "Well," he then said, "I have to be honest. There is one thing I would change."

Lifting up my head, I said, "Really?"

"Well, I was talking to my boy, Chris Poole, about everything, and he wants to stand up with me."

My mouth dropped wide open. "Samson Logan! We said we weren't telling anyone about this until it was over!" I pouted. "I knew you couldn't hold it!"

"Did I say that?" he asked. "Did I say I wasn't telling anyone?"

"You did." I rolled my eyes, my pout still in place.

"Okay, okay," he said. "But I realized it would be a good idea to have some of our own witnesses."

I rolled my eyes again, but this time I was listening and thinking about what he said.

He continued, "And what if you need something? I want someone there for you."

I leaned back and frowned. "Me?"

Again he nodded. "Chris is bringing his wife, Natasha."

I was incredulous. "You already arranged this?"

"Well, sort of," he said. "Chris is in LA, so he and Natasha are just going to drive to Vegas to be there for us."

I wanted to protest, but I only had to think about it for a moment to know it was a good idea. Plus, Chris and Natasha were a great couple. Chris was one of Samson's best friends and it would be comforting for Sam to have him there. On the other hand, it would be good to have a girlfriend there if I needed anything too.

My head was turned away as I let his news sink in, and I didn't turn back to face him until he gently nudged me in my side. His smile was huge as he nodded. "Now you know that is a good idea, right?"

I could do nothing but crack a smile. "Well, it is a good idea," I said slowly, not wanting to totally give in.

"I know, that's why I did it!" Samson said. "Plus, that's my boy! I'm going to be happy to have him there. Not to mention, I may have him bless us with a song."

This time I perked up. Chris had become an ordained minister at his church. But before that, he was a member of the gospel singing group Commissioned and had a heavenly voice.

Softly Samson said, "When you look back on our wedding day, I know it's going to be about us exchanging our vows. But I also want you to feel that you had everything you needed." He raised one eyebrow and then added, "Besides me, of course!"

Any residual annoyance I felt about him sharing our plans faded completely away as I smiled.

"Now get some rest," he said. "You look tired."

Once I returned my head to his shoulder, it only took a few minutes for the hum of the jet's engines to lull me to sleep. It seemed like only moments had passed before I awakened to his soft voice and gentle nudging.

"Wake up, Ang'."

I blinked. "We're there already?" Easing up slowly, I rubbed my eyes.

"No, but remember the doctor said you need to walk around and drink water."

Samson was absolutely right, especially since this was a cross-country flight. I got up slowly, surprised at how sluggish I still felt. It wasn't until I stood up that I realized I needed to make a beeline to the bathroom. When I returned to my seat, Samson had a bottle of water waiting for me.

I took a sip. "I'm exhausted."

"We've got another three hours, so go back to sleep."

What I wanted to do was stay up and chat with him about our plans for the next few days, but my body would not cooperate. Sleep was what I needed. After what felt like only five minutes, Samson was nudging me again.

"Wake up, Ang'!" he said excitedly.

It took effort to pry my eyes open. "I'm up. My eyes aren't, but I am," I said gruffly.

"Open your eyes. Something awesome is about to happen."

I shook my head a few times, partly to wake up and partly to stop the dizziness I was feeling. But after a few moments, my eyes finally opened.

Samson said, "Something crazy cool is right outside your window."

As I was turning to see what had Sam so excited, the captain's voice came through the loudspeaker: "Ladies and gentlemen, we are now passing the Grand Canyon!" I peered out the window with Samson hunched by my side, and together we took in the sights as we flew over the towering rock formations and broken cliffs. The oranges and reds from the soft setting sun were the perfect complement to the geological colors that decorated the canyon. The majesty of it all was … grand!

We saw people (they looked like ants) walking along what I thought was the North Rim, which filled me with a sense of peace. As small as the people looked, and as grand as that canyon looked, I knew the people weren't insignificant in God's eyes. In his eyes, those people were greater than this magnificent canyon.

My own life had been like this canyon, filled with plateaus and chasms much like the ones at which we were gazing. And like those people, I was small in the grand scheme of things. Yet God still cared about me, he still cared for me, and he was running through me like the living water that was still forming the mighty canyon.

We turned away from the window and snuggled together as close as we could in our separate seats.

The flight attendant walked by and paused. "Going to Vegas to get married by chance?"

I didn't bother to ask her how she knew. Instead, Samson and I laughed and simultaneously said, "Yes!"

After seeing the Grand Canyon, in no time at all we began to see the lights from the Las Vegas Strip appear in the now pitch-black desert. We landed, and as we gathered our bags, Samson excitedly talked about checking in and taking in the sights, even that night. When he didn't sense any enthusiasm on my part, he said, "You can't be tired with as much as you slept on that flight!"

I wanted to share his enthusiasm because I really did feel as excited as he was. But I couldn't shake my overwhelming fatigue. While Samson was ready to go (he hadn't slept at all on the flight, but that's how he was—four good hours a night was enough for him), I was already dreaming about taking a spa bath and then slipping onto some luxurious sheets. That would be the perfect night.

Then I remembered that things were changing. This couldn't be all about me anymore. I was about to get married and I had to think about Sam's wishes too. So I smiled through my tiredness and said sure with as much oomph as I could muster.

The fatigue remained with me, but my spirits rose as we drove down the Strip in the town car that had picked us up. How could I not perk up as the car zipped by all the landmark hotels and brilliant displays of glowing lights that made the night almost seem like day.

I was excited and surprised to see I wasn't going to miss the New Year. We'd traded in the Buffalo New Year's Eve ball drop for the Bellagio, and I thought that it would be all about Las Vegas without a hint of the holiday. But it seemed I was wrong—Vegas did the holidays big.

We pulled past the fountains of the Bellagio and watched as the interwoven water danced against the lavender Las Vegas sky. When we stepped into the hotel, we were hit with the fragrant smells of jasmine, gardenias, lilies, pine wreaths, and then the thousands of poinsettias that decorated the lobby and the Bellagio's conservatory and botanical gardens.

Our wedding planner had made sure our check-in would be smooth and our suite would be ready. It only took minutes to get our keys and make our way to the elevators. We were mesmerized by the forty-two-foot-tall fir trees, twelve-foot-tall snow globes, and so many twinkling lights, we were sure not even management knew exactly how many bulbs were on display.

When we finally opened the door to the expansive two-bedroom penthouse suite, Samson dropped our bags, ran through the living room into one of the bedrooms, and jumped on the bed. "This is amazing!" he said while laughing.

The two of us took a tour of the lavish suite that featured an open living room and dining area, and each bedroom had a full bathroom with a steam shower and a soaking whirlpool tub. The suite was plush and perfect. He pulled me over to ceiling windows that overlooked the fountains, and together we gazed at the sights below.

"I know that when people come to Vegas, they want to hit those tables," he said, "but right now the only table I want to hit is the dining table!" He grinned. "I'm starved and I made plans for us to have dinner at Nove Italiano at The Palms. So get showered and dressed!"

I was excited that Samson had thought all of this out and made dinner plans for our first night in Vegas. But this exhaustion …

He made his way to his room and I went to mine, hoping that a shower would snap me out of this being-tired funk. I knew pregnancy made a woman tired, but this was ridiculous, bordering on almost debilitating. Frankly, I was getting a little upset with myself. This was our wedding! I needed some energy. Then that feeling arose inside of me.

Something's wrong.

I pushed it down and gave myself a diagnosis. "I must be anemic."

I headed for the shower, though I longed for the bed. As the shower's water pelted me, I prayed for energy. As I dried myself off,

I prayed for energy. As I dressed, I prayed for energy. The bodycon dress I'd packed felt extra snug and every curve that I had was working overtime. I slipped on my stilettos, and by then even they felt tight. I glanced at myself in the nine-foot mirror.

Okay. My curves were on full display, but I still looked respectable. Until I turned to the side. "Oh my goodness," I said aloud. "Did my belly pop?" There was a bulge there, a bulge that hadn't been there yesterday it seemed. My belly had grown a bit overnight.

I pressed my hands against my belly, staring at my reflection in the mirror. In that moment, it was just my baby and me. I didn't know it was possible, but I loved her even more in that moment.

The soft tap on the door made me twirl around. I wished I hadn't because the room began to spin. Samson walked in and took my hands, not noticing that I was dizzy. Giving me a once-over, he said, "You look great!"

I'd been happy to see my pooch but was seriously thinking I needed a wardrobe change! "You sure?" I asked. "Does it look too tight?" I knew some of my questions were my own insecurities.

"It looks perfect," he reassured me as he dropped my hands and admired his reflection in my mirror. "You look almost as good as me!"

"I think you may have me beat." I laughed. "You look awfully fine, Mr. Logan."

"Thanks! Now let's go. I have a car waiting for us downstairs because I know you aren't about to walk far in those heels!" He laughed as he grabbed my hand and headed toward the door.

All of those prayers had been answered as I made it through dinner, all the while enjoying the wonderful company of my soon-to-be husband. We laughed so much, then afterward we strolled around The Palms, enjoying each other and the ambiance before we made our way back to catch the midnight grand finale show of the fountains at the Bellagio. It was the perfect romantic evening, but I was so ready to get into bed.

Just as we were about to get on the elevator to head to our room, someone grabbed Samson from behind and hoisted him off the ground. Samson was as startled as I was, but a second after he turned around he was fist-bumping. "Hey, LaVan Davis!" Samson said with his bright smile.

"Samson Logan!" LaVan replied. "What are you doing here, man? Just ringing in the New Year?"

"That and I'm getting married!" he said as they both turned and looked at me.

"Whoa! What happens in Vegas—" LaVan began.

Samson jumped in laughing. "No, it's not like that, man. We planned this and thought this would be the perfect time of year to get married here."

He turned to me and did a formal introduction. "Angie, this is my man, LaVan Davis. We go way back. We worked together on some of my first shows. He's doing his thing right now with *Tyler Perry's House of Payne*."

"Nice to meet you!" I offered him my hand, but LaVan wasn't having it.

"No handshakes, young lady," he said. "You're part of the family now!" He grabbed me and gave me a big hug.

"Now this is as close as I am going to get!" LaVan said when he stepped back from me. "I definitely don't want to catch that marriage bug yet."

Samson laughed. "You will when the time is right, man!"

He shook his head and then changed the subject. "You lovebirds turning in already?" he said looking at his watch. "The night is just getting started!"

"We've got a big couple of days ahead, so we're going to chill the rest of the night," Samson said.

LaVan looked at me. "You got him sprung! He's definitely got that marriage bug." Even I joined in with their laughter. "It's time for me to go," he said, "'cause I can't catch it yet. But I will see you good people later. Congrats!"

His smile was warm when he hugged me again. To Samson he said, "Call me, man!"

We were quiet as we got into the elevator, and even when we stepped off, I didn't say a word until Samson slipped the key in our door.

"You're sprung!" I said.

"I am not sprung!" he protested. "I may have a slow leak, but I'm not exactly sprung."

I didn't budge. I stood there in the hallway with my hands on my hips, giving him the eye. I was playing and he knew it, and he was playing and I knew it, but he also sensed this was a comeback he better get right.

He stepped into the suite and said, "I am not sprung." His tone was defiant.

I stood there, not moving, waiting for more.

He explained, "Sprung is something you can fix. What I have for you is definitely not going to stop. It can never be fixed." He moved closer to me, then put his hands on my hips and guided me into the suite. "Tomorrow, I'll be carrying you over that threshold."

"I hope you can pick me up!" I laughed as he embraced me. He held me tight, but I pulled away and sighed. "Just one more night!"

He knew what that meant as I headed to my room while he watched until I closed the door.

Inside my room I sighed, but not only because I'd had to leave Samson out there. I sighed because I couldn't wait to pull my strappy stilettos off my feet! I kicked them off, tossed them to the side, then looked at the imprints on my skin that the straps had left. "The agony of da feet!" I chuckled to myself.

My plan was to change out of my clothes, then wash the makeup off my face. But first I wanted to test out the bed. I fell forward, face-planting into the bed.

The next thing I knew Samson was shaking me awake.

"Ang'! Ang'!" At first he sounded far away.

But as his voice got closer, I roused from my sleep.

"You scared me! I was knocking forever." He paused. "And you didn't even change clothes last night."

Last night? I'd just lain down for a moment. I heard his words but wasn't quite sure what he was talking about since it was taking me more than a few moments to come out of my groggy state.

"Are you okay?" he asked.

I blinked and blinked, trying to get my eyes to focus against their will.

"Ang', are you okay?" he asked again.

"I … am … okay," I said, as if I had just finished running a race. The confusion was deep on his face. "You don't sound like it."

I tried to nod, but it took too much effort. "I'm just a little out of breath."

"Why don't we get you up, get your face washed, and then I'll run you a bath before we have to leave for the courthouse."

I could tell he wanted to do anything to help me feel better.

"Sounds good," I said.

He helped me from the bed, which was good because my legs felt like weights had been attached to them. I felt stiff, achy, and sluggish. When I glanced at my reflection in the mirror, I was surprised at how disheveled I looked.

Another realization hit me: *This is your wedding day!* I couldn't help it. I began to cry and the tears left tracks through my already smeared-from-sleep makeup.

"Hey, hey," Samson said. "What's this all about? You aren't supposed to cry until later today."

"You're not supposed to see me looking like this on our wedding day!" I blubbered.

"I'd marry you looking just like this," he said, sounding as if he wanted to keep me calm. "You'll be fine. You just need to get into a relaxing bath for a few minutes." With a washcloth, he wiped my tears away.

We had the entire morning planned out: We'd get the license and then return to the hotel where I'd have the works—a facial, manicure, hairstyling, and bridal makeup—and then we'd meet each other at the chapel. But for some reason I felt like I'd ruined a part of this with Samson seeing me so messed up on the morning of our wedding.

"I'll run you a bath," he said, heading to the whirlpool tub.

"Okay." I stood over the sink and tried to pull myself together.

As the water filled the tub, Samson said, "I've got some surprises that will make you feel better."

I tried to perk up at the word *surprises*.

"Change into your robe and I'll be right back."

He dashed out of the room, and I turned off the water, which was at the perfect level. Changing into the sumptuous robe hanging near the tub, I sat on the edge of the tub and waited for Sam to return.

A few moments later, I heard clanging and then saw Samson pushing a cart into my bedroom. I couldn't even see all the food, but it looked like a lavish breakfast. Stepping out of the bathroom, I got closer to check out the mouthwatering scones, muffins, two Western omelets, bacon, eggs, and a bowl that seemed to contain every variety of fruit: watermelon, kiwi, cantaloupe, strawberries, blueberries, and more.

From beneath that huge cart, Samson raised another tray filled with nothing but pineapple. "Rebecca obviously got the memo about your pineapple craze."

"She did all of this?" I asked.

He nodded and handed me a handwritten note from the cart: *Your happily ever after has started. Enjoy this breakfast and I'll see you later in the chapel. You're going to get married!*

"That was so sweet!" I sighed while looking at the card.

"And there's more!" Samson announced. Before I could ask him what it was, he ran from the room again and this time he came back carrying the most exquisite floral bouquet of cascading orchids, roses, and Swarovski crystals.

"Oh! How beautiful," I exclaimed.

"Outside looks like a florist shop," Samson told me. "Our wedding flowers have arrived."

Just a little while ago I'd been so tired, but my body was filling with energy now. "I am definitely feeling like it is my wedding day!"

"I knew that you would." He pushed the breakfast cart through the bathroom door and over to the tub. "Get in and enjoy! We've got an hour before we have to leave."

An hour of soaking in the tub and eating seemed heavenly. "Perfect!" I said. "Oh, and before you go, leave your suit, the flowers, and anything you want to go to the chapel dressing room by the luggage rack. Rebecca said she would have everything transported down for us. All we have to do is show up!"

"Great!" he said. "I'll handle all of that, but there are two more things I need to do. First, I need a plate!" He grabbed one of the pieces of china and loaded the plate with everything he could from the cart. Then as he balanced the plate in one hand, he said, "And second, my dear, I'm going to need your ring."

I gave him a what-are-you-talking-about look.

He said, "I promise I'll give it back to you later today at just the right moment."

With a smile, I held out my hand so he could remove the dazzling princess-cut diamond ring he'd given me.

He tried to pull it off suavely, but after a couple of tugs, he couldn't.

I could tell he was trying not to grunt as he tugged a bit harder. The ring did not want to budge. Taking my hand away from him, I tried to tug it off myself. It took some effort and three tries, but I was finally able to slide it off. It had left quite an imprint on my finger. As I handed him the ring, I said, "Wherever it stops when you put it on later today is fine!"

He smiled and nodded as he took the ring and stuffed bacon in his mouth at the same time. He was still eating as he left me alone in the bathroom.

I eased into the tub and sighed, feeling content. Lying my head back, I closed my eyes and stayed that way, only lifting my head a few times to nibble on some pineapple. My morning may not have started off as planned, but this bath was helping things turn around nicely.

I was so happy because I wanted time with God to meditate and thank him for every one of the blessings he'd given me. I prayed, asking for more of his blessings for Samson and me. And I prayed for strength.

Just thinking about what he'd done and what I knew he would continue to do refreshed and renewed me. It was because of God that I'd made it to this day. I'd sought him and at times I had fought him, pleading for him to stay true to his promises. I had cried out to him and celebrated with him. And although many times I had faltered terribly, I still waited on him and trusted in him. All of the joy and all of the pain had brought me closer to him and to this moment.

I got out of the tub with enough time to dress without feeling rushed. By the time Samson and I left for the courthouse, I was almost feeling myself again. Almost. I was happy for sure, but I was hoping that my body would catch up.

The courthouse paperwork went smoothly and a couple of hours later I kissed Samson goodbye for the last time as Angela Burgin and then headed to the spa. Talk about getting pampered. This was my first time getting the works at a spa, and all I could think was, *This is the life.* I laid back slightly in a chair as one woman worked on my hands, another applied my makeup, one curled my hair, and still another worked on my feet. The best part was the pedicure, because the foot massage made me want to stay there all day long. It was heaven for my aching feet.

As I sat there, I felt like Esther, sitting in a Persian palace, preparing to meet her king. It was so soothing, so comfortable, that I closed my eyes. I guess I'd fallen asleep because not long after I heard a gentle voice. "Mrs. Logan. Mrs. Logan, we have something for you."

My eyes opened slowly, but this time it wasn't because I was tired. This time it was from the lashes that had been applied. I was already smiling.

Mrs. Logan. I loved that name already.

One of the attendants of the spa rolled a cart in front of me, adorned with flowers and filled with fruit and juices. "Thank you!" I said simply, filled with the joy of being catered to in this way. I picked up a glass of juice.

The attendant said, "There's more." She pointed to a small jewelry box sitting discretely amongst the food.

My eyes widened as I picked it up. The women surrounded me, making me feel as if I had my own bridal party in the spa. They'd all stopped, as eager as I was to see what was inside the box. Just as I was about to lift the cover, one of the ladies shouted, "Wait," then she grabbed my hand. "There's a note." She handed me an envelope from the tray.

Tearing it open, I read it aloud: "For my bride. Love, Samson." A chorus of ohs rang out, and I held the note to my heart for a moment before I picked up the box again. Even I had to gasp when I opened it to see the sparkling diamond tennis bracelet. Another chorus of ohs went up as the women peered over my shoulders.

I was so busy admiring the bracelet that I didn't notice another envelope inside the box. As one of the women hooked the bracelet onto my wrist, I read the note aloud: "Here's something blue. A 'Ribbon in the Sky' for you." Underneath those words were the opening lyrics from our special song:

> Oh, so long for this night I prayed,
> That a star would guide you my way ...

And just like that the waterworks began, ruining my makeup. Samson's gift and note made my gift to him seem unsatisfactory now. The team of women hurried to put me back together and finish me up since I had less than an hour to get to the chapel.

Just as they were finishing, Rebecca walked through the door. "I'm here to escort the bride!" she announced, and I had to fight to hold back more tears. From the spa, we walked through the large hotel that felt like a city. All that was left to do was to put on my gown and exchange our I dos! We arrived at the dressing area and I smiled at the sign on the door.

"Mrs. Logan," Rebecca said out loud, reading the sign. Once we stepped inside, she told me, "By the way, you have some guests who checked into the hotel—a Mr. Christopher Poole and Natasha Poole. They're on their way down now." After I filled her in, she asked me, "Do you want to get a quick sneak peak of the chapel?"

"Sure," I said, feeling like a giddy about-to-be-married bride.

She peeked out the door first, making sure neither Samson nor our guests were around. Then she grabbed my hand and we dashed into the chapel.

The minister was already there wearing a splendid cream clergy robe adorned with gold trim and crosses. The chapel was breathtaking, but the extra embellishments we added took it over the top: From the monogrammed aisle runner covered in white roses, to the ornate pew markers and the stunning floral arch. It was everything I had imagined.

"It's amazing!" I squealed.

"Great!" Rebecca grabbed my hand and we dashed back to the dressing room. "The best looking thing in that chapel will be you if we can get you dressed! Times a ticking!" she said, laughing.

Inside the dressing room, I noticed how Rebecca had perfectly laid out everything: my gown, veil, and shoes. "Get started with the gown," she said, "and I will be back in to zip and clip whatever is needed."

When she stepped out of the room, I began to get undressed, but only moments after I started, I heard a man laughing. *Samson.* He had to be heading to his own dressing room, which made me hurry because knowing him, he'd be dressed in no time.

I stepped into my undergarments, then I clipped on my earrings, and finally I turned to my dress. I placed the gown on the plush carpet so I could step into it. I began to pull it up when something weird happened. It stopped at my hips. *That's odd,* I thought. There had to be something wrong with the way I was putting it on. So I pulled it down and started all over again. Same result. It wouldn't budge past my hips.

Oh! It has to be the zipper. But when I stepped out of it again, I saw that the zipper was all the way down. Then the most horrible thought crept into my mind. *You can't fit in this anymore.* Panic invaded every part of me.

"Rebecca!" I shouted.

There must have been something in my tone, because the way Rebecca came flying into the room and the look on her face told me she knew there was trouble. "What's wrong, Mrs. Logan?"

"I can't get into the dress!" My eyes welled with tears.

The concern that had been on her face seemed to ease, as if she'd dealt with this kind of problem before. "Not to worry," she said. "I'm sure we can get you into it together. This happens to brides all of the time. Putting on gowns is really a two-person job."

With a confidence I was glad she had, but that I didn't share, she took the gown from my hand and stretched the dress so I could step into it. "Okay, let's do this! Step in." She smiled even though I didn't, but I followed her instructions. She pulled the dress up, and then it stopped … right at my hips. Even though I was squirming and twisting, trying to do everything I could to get into that dress, it stopped in the same place.

I could almost hear my mother saying, *You're trying to squeeze South Carolina into Davis Station.* That's what she used to say to me and my sister when we tried to put on clothes that were too tight.

"Okay, let's try something else," Rebecca said. Her voice was still calm, though I didn't hear the same confidence she'd had just a couple of minutes before. She brought over a chair for me to hold on to while she tugged and pulled for about five minutes. She huffed and pulled and began to break out in a sweat. In all of that time, with all of that effort, all she could do was get the dress to move up a couple of centimeters. She was out of breath when she looked at me sullenly and said, "We may have a problem here."

"What am I going to do?" I whined as tears already made their way down my cheeks. I couldn't imagine how I was going to solve this. I'd worn a sweat suit to the chapel and didn't have enough time to make it back to my hotel room to try to find something else. Rebecca had made it clear we had to be on time—we didn't have the chapel for long.

As I dropped onto the chair, Rebecca got on her walkie-talkie. She gave orders for someone from her office to join us, and then she contacted the spa for the makeup artist. When she was done, she returned her attention back to me. After handing me a glass of water, she said, "I would let you wear what I have on, but I don't think it would work."

Then it hit me! "Natasha! Are my guests here yet?"

She didn't know why I asked, but Rebecca peeked outside and returned with news that they hadn't arrived. I'd been thinking that maybe I could wear whatever Natasha had on.

As I paced back and forth trying to come up with another idea, there was a knock on the door. Two women from Rebecca's office came in, and then the three of them went to work. I paced, breaking into a full-on stress sweat as they pulled my wedding dress apart. They got to the corset and began snipping away. As they worked, the makeup artist came in, watching them with wonder in her eyes.

I walked over to the mirror and took a good look at myself. Standing only in my undergarments, I could see how much bigger

I'd gotten, especially in my thighs, legs, and stomach. Could I really have gained that much weight in just the last few days?

I still hadn't been eating much. Yes, Samson and I had a lavish dinner last night, but besides that for the last few weeks I'd hardly eaten to keep the nausea at bay. And still, the only craving I had was for pineapple.

I heard the material ripping as the women continued to pull and snip and tuck. Then I heard the soft chime—the alarm Rebecca had set to let us know when it was time for me to make my way into the chapel. All I could do was lower my head and say, "Oh, God! Please help."

Right after that, Rebecca shouted, "Okay. Let's try it again!" She waved me over.

"If this doesn't work," I said as a joke, "I'll just wear my sweat suit. This is Vegas, right?"

No one laughed.

Rebecca looked at me determinedly: "We are going to make this work! Now get in!"

I stepped in and held my breath as the three women pulled the dress up. One tugged with all of her might and the other two stretched the material as far as it would go. "Keep tugging!" Rebecca grunted. I grabbed on to the chair so I wouldn't topple over. And with a couple of squirms and turns, the dress made its way over my hips!

"Quick," Rebecca ordered the makeup artist. The woman dabbed the sweat that felt like it flooded my brow, then went to work on touching me up as the other women worked on getting me zipped up.

Then … music. And Chris Poole's voice! The women worked furiously and I sucked in everything I had. The zipper made it to the top. There was no time for a celebration, though. Rebecca grabbed my veil, adjusted it on my head as one of the other women helped me into my shoes. They were tight, but I was able to squeeze into them.

Rebecca flung open the double doors of the dressing room that led to the vestibule right beside the chapel just as the wedding march began to play. With a deep breath, Rebecca quickly adjusted her own suit and handed me my flowers before walking behind me to air out my train.

I wanted to cry—we'd done it. But there was no time for tears. I was getting married.

26

Altar Call

(From Angela)

When I saw my groom standing at the altar, all of the drama of the last half hour was forgotten. I beamed. I could tell Samson was a little surprised—he figured I'd be a weepy mess. I was so glad to be here, in this dress, though if we hadn't made it work I was going to walk down the aisle in my sweat suit. I didn't really care what I was wearing; I was getting married.

My smile was contagious because Samson's lips began to rise and the chaplain actually let out a chuckle. There was so much behind my smile. Not just the gratefulness I felt from all that had transpired, but thankfulness for this moment. I was filled with the hope God had for our future even as I continued to suck in my breath so my dress wouldn't explode at the seams.

I was filled with wonder that no matter how many times I went to God with all of my little issues and mess-ups, he cared enough to meet me in the middle of those situations. And now he was here, with Samson and me, in the middle of the vows we were about to take, in the presence of the minister and our few guests.

The ceremony was simple but felt so powerful. When the minister pronounced us husband and wife, Samson looked at me. But he wasn't wearing the mischievous grin he always had; he was smiling, but all I saw on his face was love.

Our lips met in our first kiss as husband and wife and a cheer arose. When I looked into the small sanctuary, Chris and Natasha were smiling and clapping, but it was the girls in the back who had nearly busted their backs trying to get me into my dress who had erupted in applause. I was thrilled they'd stayed to witness our wedding since they'd played such a big part in it.

The next few hours were a whirlwind of toasts with sparkling apple juice, hors d'oeuvres, a light meal, photos, and finally a stroll through the Bellagio's Mediterranean Courtyard and the pool. The high I'd been on from the wedding began to wear off and I leaned into Samson. Whispering, I said, "I've got to get out of this dress!"

His eyes widened and he immediately said, "Uh, Chris and Natasha, good night!"

They laughed and said good night as Samson and I made our way to our suite. There was no way for Samson to know the real reason behind my words. I'd never had the chance to tell him about the ordeal I'd experienced. But even if I'd wanted to share that with him now, I couldn't. I had waited too long to go back to our suite. I felt lightheaded and dizzy and those aches had returned. Each step became more difficult to take, and Samson had to catch me as I stumbled toward the elevator.

"You okay, Angela?" he asked.

I nodded and I knew that my voice sounded weak when I said, "Yes, just get me back to the room, please."

At the suite's door, Samson slipped the key into the lock, but then, before I could move, he hoisted me off my feet and carried me across the threshold. "A husband has to keep his word," he said. "I told you I would be carrying you over the threshold."

I laughed through the pain as Samson carried me inside. He was about to set me on the bed when he paused. Red rose petals were laid out on the bed in the shape of a heart, and candlelight flickered all around the room. On a sterling tray next to the bed were straw-berries, chocolate, and bottles of sparkling juice.

"Oh, Angela, this is so sweet," Samson said, moving me over to the nearby couch as if he didn't want to disturb the bed. "I didn't know that you planned this!"

"I didn't do this!"

We looked at each other for just a moment. "Rebecca!" we said together.

Our wedding planner had executed every detail I asked for and then some. I wanted to join in with Samson as he glanced around the room and took in everything Rebecca had done, but I was too busy trying to catch my breath. It had to be the tight dress, the long walk, and the hours since the wedding that had me feeling this way.

"Sam," I called out to him as he walked around the bedroom. "I really need help getting out of this dress."

He grinned. "Oh yeah!" He dashed over.

I leaned forward a bit, and when he unzipped me, I let out a deep sigh of relief. "Can you help me with my shoes?" I asked, knowing I couldn't bend down.

He pulled off the lace pumps I was wearing, then paused. "Whoa! Your feet are so swollen."

I looked down and saw the shoes had left a deep imprint in my feet.

"Good thing you swept me off my feet," I said. "I couldn't make it another step."

He chuckled, then stood up, taking off his tuxedo jacket and walking toward the bathroom. He closed the door, humming a tune, the way he always did.

Whatever fuel had been in my gas tank was completely gone, especially now that I'd sat down and had come out of the dress and my shoes. I laid my head back on the couch, thinking I would simply take in the beauty of the room and the fragrance of the flowers that seemed to be floating in the air, but what I took in were a few z's.

Samson came out of the bathroom to find his new bride practically passed out on the couch. Gently he shook my arm. "Ang', why don't you get more comfortable," he said. "You're still half in your wedding gown."

"Oh! Oh sure!" I shook my head a bit to snap out of it. I needed to get some energy, even if I had to fake it.

Samson helped me up and I wobbled to the bathroom, holding the back of the dress so that it wouldn't fall down. Behind me, I closed the door, thankful I had a few private moments to pull myself together. I glanced at the white satin and lace nightgown I'd hung on the back of the bathroom door, knowing that Samson had surely seen it. This was the special night we had longed for, the night when we could be with each other with no guilt and no regrets.

I was so tired. "Come on, Ang," I whispered to my reflection in the mirror. "Summon up some energy! This is your honeymoon."

What I needed was a shower; surely, that would pep me up. I tried moving quickly, but my feet had concrete blocks attached to them. I felt some relief when I shimmied out of the dress and my undergarments and felt the warm water from the shower massage my skin. I stayed there enjoying the solitude, and it gave me time to talk to my baby, something I did every day but hadn't done because of how crazed the day had been.

I caressed my stomach. "Please forgive me, sweetheart. For having you squished in my belly all day." I spent those quiet moments with her, then got out of the shower. The airy satin gown felt good against my skin. I took a deep breath, praying I could inhale some energy as I made my way back into the bedroom, *our* bedroom. It was obvious I had been gone a while because Samson was lounging in the bed as if he had been there all night.

When I got to the bed, he began snoring loudly, pretending to be asleep. I crawled in next to him, laid my head on his chest, and rubbed it softly. Little did he know how much I wanted to join him in that snore!

"Mr. Logan, why are you doing that?" I asked.

"What? What?" he said, opening his eyes, then shaking his head like he was trying to snap out of it. "Mrs. Logan, I'm just acting like you! You haven't been able to keep your eyes open for days!" He laughed.

The rubbing I was doing on his chest turned into a slap. "What!" I said in protest, even though his words were true. He was playing, but he'd actually hit a soft spot in me because I was trying: I wanted to be fun and full of life, but I just couldn't do any of that.

"I'm just playing!" he said. Then his voice got softer when he said, "I know you're tired. You've been carrying a lot." He rubbed my belly.

With that, I rested my head on his chest. "I'm so sorry, Sam," I said softly. "I have never felt this kind of tired in my life. And I'm so achy. My shoulder's been hurting, my feet ache. I've just been a mess!" As I spoke, I felt even worse. All I wanted to do was shower my husband with attention.

"Stop, Ang'. It's fine." He massaged my shoulders. "Seriously, let's just relax a minute."

The massage felt wonderful and sensual as the candlelight flickered around us. After a few minutes, he lifted my chin and kissed me. "Today was perfect and I love you," he whispered.

"I love you too," I replied softly and laid my head back onto his chest. I snuggled as close to him as I could get and closed my eyes.

When I opened them what seemed like a few minutes later, there was a soft light coming through the curtains. I couldn't imagine what it was.

I glanced at the clock on the nightstand. The numbers read 9:32. It was confusing at first: *It couldn't be morning, could it? Did I sleep through my wedding night?* My movement caused Samson to awaken too.

"What's wrong?" he asked, though still groggy.

"I. Fell. Asleep."

"Oh." I could tell from the way that he said that, he still didn't get it.

"On our wedding night!" I said, completely exasperated.

As upset as I was, Samson was calm. He took my arm and guided me back so I was once again lying on his chest. "It's fine, Ang'. It was still a good night."

"It was?" I didn't know if he was being sincere or trying to make me feel better.

"Yes," he continued. "I'm here with you, you're here with me, so it's all good."

A rush of relief came over me. One of the things I'd been looking forward to the most after being married was waking up to Samson every day. And this proved that waking up with him was going to be a gift.

"That's one of the sweetest things you've ever said to me," I said. Then I kissed him, first his lips and then his face, over and over again.

He laughed when I wouldn't stop. "Really, Ang'?" he asked.

I knew he was the one who was tired now, but I had energy. And since I didn't know how long that was going to last …

We celebrated our first New Year's Eve as husband and wife watching Robbie Knievel do a fifty-foot freefall at the Mirage as fireworks lit up the Las Vegas sky. We were catching the tail end of Usher's performance at the Bellagio's nightclub, The Bank, when I turned to Samson and said, "You ready to turn in?"

"Turn in?" He had to raise his voice over the din in the club. "Most people are just starting to turn up."

"I know," I said. "I'm just exhausted." This time I could tell that Samson was a bit disappointed. Usher was one of his favs. But he escorted me from the club.

On the walk back to our room, I told him, "I'm going to check in with my doctor when we get back about this exhaustion."

"You've got to," he said, sounding more serious than usual. "I know you're pregnant, but you're tired *all* of the time. Let's just make sure that's normal."

"I will," I promised.

The rest of our honeymoon was a whirlwind of sights and sounds and sleep. We did manage to get in some shopping as well. The Forum Shops at Caesars Palace was a shoe girl's dream, but my passion for pumps had faded fast on this trip. I finally located the store I was looking for ... UGGs! Comfort was king and some UGG boots were exactly what I wanted. After just about every pair of eights in the store wouldn't fit, the saleslady asked if I wanted her to measure me.

"Sure," I said, even though I knew I was an eight. I'd been an eight since eighth grade.

The saleslady checked both feet. "I know what the problem is," she said. "First, your right foot is a bit bigger than your left. Second, you're definitely a size nine."

"Come again?" I said, confused.

"See." She pointed to the foot measure.

With my own eyes I saw I was definitely a size nine! "Oh my goodness!" I said, a little bit shocked. I pointed over to the stack of size-eight boots she had brought out for me. "Okay, can I try those in a nine?"

She returned with the boots, and the first pair slipped onto my feet with no problem at all.

"My feet must have gone up a size. I'm pregnant," I told her.

"Well, these will be perfect," she said. "They stretch a bit over time and they are super comfortable." She reached down to help me take the boots off, but I stopped her.

"Oh no," I said, "I'm wearing these out of here!"

The next day, when our trip came to an end, I was a little sad;

this time would always would hold a special place in my memory. But on the other hand, I was excited about getting back home and starting our life together. We chatted happily in between my naps on the red-eye to Buffalo, until we started talking about my pregnancy woes.

One of the first things I wanted to do was get in to see my doctor. "Maybe all of this tiredness means I'm just one of those women who will have a difficult pregnancy," I told Samson. "I've heard of women who needed bed rest for weeks."

"Yes," he said. "But I never heard of a woman having bed rest this early. You're not having twins or anything."

Samson was right; I was barely out of the first trimester. "Well," I said, "the doctor said that my body is working overtime right now. Hopefully he'll tell me it'll get better as the weeks progress."

"Hopefully."

"To be honest," I said, opening up to Samson for the first time about more of my concerns, "I am little worried about the weight I'm gaining."

"You look good, but I will say that you've gained a little more weight than I thought you would at this point," Samson confirmed. "Your belly isn't really sticking out yet either."

I was glad he was noticing the things I was. "I can't figure it out," I said. "I've been watching what I eat. I mean, I did indulge a few times in Vegas when I wasn't feeling nauseated, but it was nothing over the top. Just a bit richer than I would normally cook at home. And can you believe that my feet went up a size? That really took me by surprise." I'd taken off my boots, and I raised my foot up so Samson could see. When I pressed my finger against my skin, it left an impression.

He leaned forward as if trying to give my feet a good inspection. "We did walk around a lot in Vegas. Maybe that's it. Maybe it was too much for you."

"Maybe." I looked at my feet.

Something's wrong.

"I guess I won't know until I talk with the doctor," I said, then I paused. "There is one pregnancy thing I'm looking forward to."

"Just one?" Samson said.

"One for this week!" I smiled.

While we were in Vegas, Samson and I had cooked up the big reveal for all of our news. I had enjoyed our alone time bonding with our baby, but now I needed the support, guidance, and prayers of a whole team to get behind me and this pregnancy.

"I'm looking forward to telling everyone … kind of." I grimaced, thinking about their reactions. This could be very good or it could be very bad. "I hope everyone will be accepting and forgiving."

"I think they will be," Samson said, trying to reassure me.

I slept for the rest of the plane ride back home. We arrived back in Buffalo early in the morning, and by the time I got settled at home, the doctor's office was open. When I called, the nurse answered, and I said, "Hi, Doris. This is Angela Burgin Logan. I was hoping to make an appointment to see Dr. Walters or to speak with him."

"What seems to be the problem, Angela?" She'd said *problem*, in the singular.

But I began to break down all of my problems to her. "I've had some debilitating fatigue, a lot of achiness, and there are times when I'm a bit dizzy," I said, giving her a litany of my symptoms. "I've also been putting on weight a little faster than I thought I would."

"Hmm, any spotting or cramping?" Doris asked.

"No, just difficulty getting anything done as the tiredness and achiness wipes me out most of the time. It feels out of the norm, even for pregnancy."

There was a pause, then she said, "I see you're scheduled for your NT screening next week and an office visit. Perhaps the doctor can speak with you, and if he wants to see you in the office, we'll bring you in. Otherwise, you'll have your screening and office visit next week."

"Okay," I said, not sure I should wait that long.

Doris added, "We'll be seeing you soon. Oh, this might make you feel better: you'll probably be able to find out the sex of the baby."

She was right. That news did make me feel better.

"Isn't that exciting?" she asked, but she didn't pause long enough for me to answer before adding, "So let me have Dr. Walters get back to you on his next break, and we'll go from there."

"Sounds good," I said. We exchanged goodbyes, and I hung up.

Looking around, I told myself there was no need to unpack. Samson and I were scheduled to get the keys to our new home the following day. I had plenty to do to get ready, but I decided that the best thing to do for now was to rest up.

Samson had gone out to pick up a couple of baby items, so it was the perfect time for me to relax and recover from our trip. I was beginning to close my eyes when Dr. Walters called. After the normal greetings, he got right to the point: "I understand that you're feeling some discomfort," he said. "What is going on exactly?"

Just as I'd done with Doris, I gave him a list of all of my symptoms, from the fatigue to the weight gain. "I went away this week and gained four more pounds! None of this is normal, is it?"

"So let me get this right," he said. "You're tired, achy, and gaining weight, correct?"

"Yes. That about sums it up," I answered, waiting with anticipation for the doctor to explain to me why I was going through all of this.

"Mrs. Logan," he began. "You're pregnant." His tone was filled with so much sarcasm that I figured this was his attempt at humor. He couldn't be serious. That couldn't be his answer.

When he didn't say anything else, I said, "Umm ... yes, I know I'm pregnant, but is this normal?" I'd asked him that question again because I wanted him to think about it. What I was going through couldn't be the symptoms of a normal pregnancy. "I was thinking that maybe my iron levels are low."

He sighed a little. "Mrs. Logan, I thought I told you when we met that pregnancy is hard work. Your body is going through a lot of hormonal changes that can leave you feeling fatigued. Aches and pains are common during pregnancy and you can get lightheaded from blood shifts in your body if you stand up or change positions too quickly, so be mindful of that.

"Now, there are things that you can do, like getting prenatal massages and taking warm baths. And about your iron levels, I'm looking at your blood work and everything is in the acceptable range, so I'm not too concerned about an iron problem. You're getting a bit more iron in the prenatal vitamins you're taking so you should be okay with that."

He must have heard my sigh, maybe that's why he kept on.

"Now about your weight. The old adage that you're eating for two when you're pregnant is a myth. So you have to watch what you're eating." He paused for a moment. "Have you experienced any spotting or have you noticed a rash?"

"No, no spotting or rash," I assured him. I felt a little hopeful because at least that wasn't happening.

"Good, then I would suggest that you rest when you're tired and do what I suggested. And remember that pregnancy can be tough, so you just have to toughen up a little bit."

I inhaled, trying to take in all of his words.

"These are normal pregnancy symptoms," he added. "A lot of women actually start to feel better in the second trimester, so hopefully within the next few weeks you'll feel some relief."

"Okay," I said, really hoping he was right.

"There's no need to come into the office. Just get your NT screening and we'll see you next week as planned."

When I hung up the phone, I felt a little better. After all, he was the doctor. But there was still an uneasiness in my spirit. It wasn't that I ever thought having a baby would be easy. I'd seen enough episodes of *A Baby Story* on TLC. I was physically and emotionally tough. I was prepared and I tried to constantly gain more knowledge by reading everything I could find … so what was the problem?

"Toughen up," I said to myself, following the doctor's orders. "This is new to you, Angela." But there was still that quiet voice: *Something's wrong.*

Samson bounded through the door full of laughter and bags, taking my attention away from the doctor for the moment. Just seeing how happy Samson was made me smile.

"I know you gave me a list," he said, "but I picked up a few more things!"

"Any excuse to shop!" I said, putting my hands on my now-ample hips.

He shook his head. "No, these were all necessities. Plus, I'll be heading out of town in a week or so, and I don't want you to have to worry about picking stuff up. I did it for you, being the good husband that I am." He laughed and pulled item after item from the bag. "See? Diapers, necessities. Baby bottles, necessities." He kept going through the list of onesies and other items. "I left the bassinet in the car, but it was an incredible sale, like you said. And I got one more thing."

I watched, stunned, as he pulled out a baby-sized basketball. "Samson! What if it's a girl!"

He looked at me as if that weren't the smartest question. "What if it's a girl?" he repeated my question. "Then I'll teach *her* to shoot!" He pretended to pump fake and dunk.

Shaking my head, I told him, "Well, you'll be happy to know we'll find out for sure if we're having a boy or a girl before you leave town."

He stopped moving. "We will? You spoke to the doctor?" He couldn't hide the excitement in his voice.

"Yes. He just called me back about all my 'nesses.'"

He looked confused. "'Nesses?'"

I nodded. "My tiredness, dizziness, achiness …" I began going through the list.

While I was making a joke, Samson took it seriously. "What did he say?"

"He told me to toughen up!" I paused for a moment, thinking about what the doctor had actually said. "Can you believe that?" Having thought about it now, I was ready to go in, because I was really irritated by the doctor's tone with me. Of course, I was going to do what he told me, but still …

"Wait. Wait. Wait!" Samson didn't let me go off. "Before you get hot about it, maybe he's right. What else did he say?" he asked, trying to get me to focus on the message, not the messenger.

"He said these are some normal pregnancy symptoms," I replied. And then, I went through the list of all Dr. Walters had told me to do.

"Well," Samson began when I finished, "this is good news then. Basically, he told you that everything's going to be fine."

I twisted my lips, letting Sam know I wasn't sure.

He continued, "Ang', maybe it's just that you don't have a high threshold for pain. Remember you told me that growing up you didn't even break a fingernail? Maybe all of these aches and pains are to be expected. They're just new for you." He was trying to get me to think about what Dr. Walters said. "This doctor has delivered hundreds of babies and this will be our first, so since his ratio is better than ours, let's just take his word for it."

The equation of one baby for me and hundreds of babies for him made me think that maybe the doctor's assessment of what was going on was correct. After a moment, I said, "All right!" though I said it reluctantly. What Samson said made sense. Reading books and watching shows about having a baby and then *actually* having a baby are two different experiences. Dr. Walters had come to me highly recommended, and, like Samson said, he had delivered tons of babies. Maybe it really was a case of me needing to toughen up.

"Let's go grab something to eat," Samson said, his way of ending this part of the conversation. "We can stop by our parents' to let them know we're back and invite them out for dinner on Sunday to complete our plan. Oh, and we have to show them your new car. No one has even seen it."

"Okay," I said, even though I didn't have much of an appetite. But I wanted to see our parents, and I wanted to show off the cream Land Rover I'd bought. This was the first time I'd had my own car in years, since I'd been driving a company car from the time I began working. The Land Rover was perfect for me and for Samson, who's a major car lover. I paused at that thought: *This isn't just my car; it's our car.*

As he reached down to help me up from the couch, he said, "Remember to get up slowly. No sudden movements." When I stood straight, he added, "I'll grab your winter coat. We definitely traded palm trees for pine cones. We are back in Buffalo for sure!"

I nodded as I looked out the window at the frosty lawn.

When we got outside, Samson said, "Doesn't it look good?" He pointed to the SUV. "I had it washed and the wheels shined, so it's the perfect time to show it off."

We grabbed a quick lunch and then drove to his parents' house first. On the ride over, I was thinking, *Hard to believe that just yesterday we were in tropical temperatures. But here we are now, back in Buffalo in January.* At least the sun was shining brightly, and no snow had fallen.

When we pulled up to Samson's parents' home, his mother and father were outside, removing their holiday decorations from the windows and the doors.

Samson's father came over to us first. "Good to see you two!" Then his attention turned to the new vehicle. "Ooww-whee!"

His mother joined us and gave her own approval in between the hugs she had for us. "That's mighty sharp there. I like this car, Angela," she complimented.

"I might need to trade in my van for this!" his dad laughed as he walked around the SUV.

Eager to show off the car, Samson said, "Let me show you the lift gate!" He was all smiles when he pressed the button on the car key, lifting the back door of the Land Rover.

Everything began moving in slow motion. I heard myself saying, "Noo," but it was too late. The trunk was going up, and the huge baby bassinet Samson had forgotten he'd left in the car was on full display.

Frowns were on both of his parents' faces when his mother said, "What's that?" and his father answered, "A baby bassinet?" The two of them looked at each other, then slowly turned to us.

I tried to look everywhere else, doing everything I could to avoid their eyes. Grabbing Samson's hand, I held on to him for comfort, though I squeezed him, letting him know he'd blown it. This was not how we were supposed to reveal the news to his parents.

"Oh my!" his dad said.

"Angela, you're pregnant?" his mother asked, shock filling her tone.

"Yeess." I released that word slowly. But then I quickly added, "And married!" I figured since they knew the first part, I definitely needed to tell them the second part.

His mother walked over to me and pulled open the oversized coat I was wearing. "I knew something was up!" she said. "Now it makes sense!"

Samson and I stood there in unsure silence, smiling through clenched teeth. We certainly didn't want to let our parents down, and my hope was that after the shock of this news wore off, they'd be understanding and happy.

His father said, "We kind of figured you both going to Las Vegas at the same time was a strange coincidence. Plus, as parents, you kind of just know these things. But we didn't know all of this!" He shook his head. "Oh my goodness! Well," he said, pausing to look at both of us, "there's a lot to talk about, but we're happy that your union is covered by God now."

His mom added, "And I'm not happy that I didn't get my big

wedding, but come on"—she flashed a wide smile—"give me a hug now, *daughter*."

My hug was tentative, only because I was concerned about Samson's dad. He finally let out a chuckle, and as his mother hugged me, Samson's father held him in his own embrace. I could tell Samson was as relived as I was.

They walked us inside, we sat down together on the sofa, and Samson and I spent the next hour sharing all that had been going on. Once we told them, his father went into counseling mode, making sure we remembered that God had to always be at the center of our marriage.

After his father led us in prayer, Samson said, "Well, it's time for us to go."

"Where are we going now?" I asked. I wanted to stay with his parents for a little longer. While our news had taken them by surprise, once the intial shock had worn off, it felt good to speak to them and to get their counsel.

"We've got to tell a few more people," Samson said.

He was right—I knew that. We definitely had to tell my mom and dad, but Samson had said a *few* people. "Well, after my parents, who else are we going to tell?"

He looked at me as if I didn't know anything. "Who else are we going to tell?" he repeated. "*Everyone!*" he replied. "We've got to tell *everyone!*"

27

Model Home

(From Angela)

*S*am and I were not afraid of what our folks would say; we only wanted to make our parents proud. They would never be pleased with everything we did—we'd had enough punishments as kids to know that! But having them be proud of the adults we had become was a small payment in return for all the deposits they had made into our lives. What would make them the proudest was being all we could be in God's sight.

Living right and setting the right example was what Sam and I wanted to do because we were a show business family. Eyes were on us. People were watching what we did and how we lived our lives. Our roles as leaders in our families and careers made people look up to us. When people looked at me, I wanted them to see all I was—a woman who had made it by grace and who lived fearlessly by faith—and I wanted people to see the hope I have in my life.

This caused us to be concerned about what others thought of our choices (our marriage and our pregnancy), and so we were happy and relieved that everyone was thrilled about our news. Of course, we did have to hear it some too.

Kris and April were not too thrilled they weren't the first to know. But as sisters do, they forgave me. Their short-lived disappointment quickly turned into giddy excitement. Just as I had imagined, the guessing games began:

My mom said, "I think it's a boy."

Samson's mom said, "I don't think it's a girl. I *know* it is. Samson's daughter is on the way!"

April, who was by then the mother of twins, said, "Angie definitely can't handle twins, so let's just hope it's one or the other, not one of each!"

We all laughed knowing she was probably right.

Over the next few days, as more and more people found out about the news, the barrage of questions was steady. But one finally popped up that set the stage for our last reveal. "Where are you guys going to live?" Kris asked.

Once she asked that, everyone wanted to know. No one knew this was a question and a topic that had been heavily weighing on me. My job was still uncertain, and the offer for me to move to Tampa was still there. I wasn't going to take it, but I was prayerful that I was making the right decision by remaining in Buffalo.

"We have a few houses that look like good prospects," Sam answered.

Then I tag-teamed with, "Would you guys like to come with us to see one on Sunday after church?"

Everyone said they were on board, and our plan was set in motion.

The closing for the house had gone smoothly, we already had the keys, and all we had time to do before Sunday was to clean the place, hang some of our clothing inside the closets, and stock the kitchen.

We gave everyone the address and said we would meet them there at four o'clock. Since my dad was always prompt, Samson and I made sure we were sitting outside fifteen minutes early. As expected, my dad was there five minutes early, which was late for him.

While we waited for everyone else to show up, we stood outside and admired the house and talked about the development. As each person arrived, they talked about the look of the house and how they couldn't wait to see inside.

"This seems like it is going to be one of the best homes you've seen," my dad said.

Samson's mother added, "This really looks like you and Sam! I think this one is it!"

As a few others added their comments, Samson and I looked at each other. Then together we said, "We agree! That's why we bought it!" I pulled out the garage door opener I'd hidden in my pocket and hit the switch. The hooping and the hollering began as the garage door lifted and my car was already parked inside.

"What!"

"You guys!"

"You really got us!"

That was the chorus of comments in between the laughter and the hugs.

"Come on in," Samson said with one of those ear-to-ear grins. He led the way and the eager group followed, anxious for the tour.

Sam and I wanted our home to be a gathering place for our families—for barbecues and Christmases, Sunday dinners and football game parties. It seemed as if our families agreed. Their excitement and approval only added to our joy. And on that day we had our first family gathering, even without furniture! That didn't matter—we had each other and we had a blast. It was dark by the time everyone finally said their goodbyes, leaving Sam and me alone.

Even though the house was empty, it felt full. The day had made us so happy and had left me feeling exhausted. "This is where our baby will call home," I said while patting my stomach as we sat on the floor in her bedroom.

"You're going to love your room!" Samson said, leaning down so he could talk to our baby.

Samson and I sat there for a while. I relished the time since it was my last day before returning to work after the long vacation I had taken for our honeymoon. I didn't know that by the next day, the honeymoon really would be over.

28

Good News and Bad News

(From Angela)

I need a vacation from my vacation. That was my thought as I sat in one of my coworker's home offices. I was dragging, especially as I typed. When I worked, I was used to hearing the clicking sound on my keyboard moving at sixty words per minute. But now it was more like one word every sixty seconds.

I was trying to keep up with Pete so we could get these customer plans done. But I was so tired. And I ached everywhere. My feet felt tight, my legs were stiff, and I had a nagging pain in my shoulder.

The fatigue made me want to go home, and I could have done that since I still had plenty of vacation days to use up. But I figured I should push through even though I felt lousy. Plus, I was still waiting to find out about my job. My hope was that my years of dedication and hard work would help them find a way to retain me in my home market.

While I worked, Samson was busy with the movers getting all of our big items to our new home. He would be leaving in just a few days, and this time he'd be gone for six weeks. On top of my other aches and pains, my heart hurt because he was going to be gone for so long. Of course, I was used to him traveling, but I wasn't used to him traveling *and* us being married.

I knew I had no right to complain when there were many others who had to live this way and under circumstances that weren't as kind as ours. I'd watched news reports on TV of military newlyweds having to say goodbye in moments that seemed like "until deployment do us part." Those families had to spend months, even years, apart. So what were a few weeks here and there in the grand scheme of things? Especially since he wasn't going into harm's way.

That's what my head was saying, but my heart still wanted Samson with me, especially with all that was going on. We may not have been a military family, but I was battling fatigue, nausea, aches, and that something-is-wrong feeling. My mind was telling me to hold on, and in a matter of months the victory would be sweet. My baby would be here! But somewhere inside, I knew it would not be that easy.

In many ways, the concerns I had didn't seem logical. *It's biology. Pregnant women get fatigued and nauseated, right? It's all normal.* That's what I told myself because that's what my doctor kept telling me. Yet no matter how many times I repeated those words, that feeling in my gut wouldn't go away, and it was growing inside, just like my baby.

I wished I could Google this gut feeling. I wanted to click on a link and discover what was truly going on with my body. But the only place where I could search for the answers was within me, and I simply didn't have the answer yet.

The NT scan was scheduled for after work at five thirty. Maybe with the news of whether we were having a boy or a girl, some of these feelings would dissipate. I desperately wanted everything to be okay with my baby, and so I just needed to toughen up, like the doctor said.

With those thoughts, I was able to focus my mind a little bit more on work, finishing up with Pete. When we'd completed the last plan, I said, "We got a lot of work done!"

"Yep, ten plans in one day isn't too bad," he said. "We typed so much, it looks like your fingers got swollen!" He pointed to my hands.

Looking down, I noticed for the first time that my hands were puffy. They were even more swollen than they were in the morning when I tried to put my wedding ring on and it wouldn't even think about going over my knuckle. "Wow. They are really swollen!" I said. "I guess that means its quitting time for sure! I better run to the restroom before I head out."

I stood up, but my body wasn't interested in following my commands. I tried to walk but stumbled back to my seat, feeling dazed and seeing stars.

"Whoa! You okay?" Pete asked while rushing over.

"I feel a bit dizzy!"

"Let me get you some water." Pete left after he helped me settle securely in the chair. He returned quickly, and by the time I took a few deep breaths and drank half of the water, I had regained control.

"Thank you," I said. "I feel much better now."

"Good! Because I have a rule: no one passes out in my office!" Pete said, trying to bring a smile to my face.

Even though I wasn't as dizzy, I knew jumping into my car and driving probably wouldn't be the smartest thing to do. "I think it would be best to have my husband pick me up," I told Pete. "Do you mind if I stay here a few minutes until he arrives?"

"No worries," Pete said. "Stay here as long as you like."

Samson arrived in no time, and we were both happy I had the appointment for the NT scan. Maybe someone would be able to explain what had just happened.

"Maybe I got up too fast," I said to Samson on the way to the appointment. "But I told you that I've been feeling terrible. I don't know. I feel like something is wrong."

"Don't worry, Ang'," Samson said. "The doctor said that getting up too quickly could do this to you. This is probably normal for pregnant women." He was trying to assure himself as much as he was trying to reassure me. I needed that assurance, however; I wanted to know our baby was okay.

Within minutes of arriving at the clinic, I was settled on a table in the hi-tech lab on Maple Road. It felt good to simply relax after that dizzy spell. The female sonographer came in wearing a smile. "You two are a gorgeous couple!" she said. "Are you ready to see your little one?"

"Yes!" we said simultaneously.

As she dimmed the lights and prepared the room, I asked, "What are you going to be doing exactly?"

She was already working, applying gel to my abdomen. "We're going to see things like the size of the baby and the baby's heart rate. But one of the main reasons for the nuchal fold scan is to measure the small fluid collection within the skin at the base of the baby's neck."

She slid the transducer back and forth across my belly. She pointed to large fifty-inch screen saying, "There's your baby." And just like that, some of the worries I had just minutes before began to subside. I saw my baby moving in three dimensions!

Samson squeezed my hand at the sight. "See, I told you the baby is okay!" he said as we watched our baby moving around in my belly.

I nodded at Samson's words. This was a miracle, seeing the little soul I spoke to each day.

"I understand that you want to know the baby's sex." The sonographer looked over at us.

"We definitely do!" I said enthusiastically.

"We should be able to tell without an issue today," she said.

"All right!" Samson was as eager and as excited as I was.

"Will we also be able to tell if everything is okay with the baby?" I asked, needing reassurance.

"I should be able to get a good idea," she replied. "But of course we will want you to follow up with your doctor to get the complete report."

I took another deep breath. "How do things look?"

"So far, so good. The baby's weight, length, and heart rate all look good."

"How big is the baby?" I asked.

"The baby looks to be about 3.4 inches long and 1.5 ounces," the sonographer told us.

"Wow. That's great, but that's it?" I asked. "I've gained over twenty pounds already! Do you think that's unusual?"

"Twenty pounds already?" she asked. "That is unusual. But I'm kind of like a photographer. I produce images of the baby so that we can assess things and diagnose conditions. I'm no doctor, but I have seen a lot of pregnant women and I would say that much weight at this stage is a bit high. It's not totally unheard of, though. You could have something else going on. Be sure to consult with your doctor about it."

She continued to take her measurements while Samson and I marveled at the baby. "Can you feel that?" Samson said, seeing the baby moving and even stretching out her leg.

"No!" I said, then laughed as the baby seemed to wave to us on the screen.

"Okay, now I'm measuring the translucent skin at the base of the baby's neck and the normal range is usually between 2.5 millimeters and 3.0 millimeters. And I can tell you that this baby is well within the normal range."

Samson and I both let out a huge sigh.

"Thank you!" I said, more to God than the woman.

While I was still thanking God, she added, "I can also tell you that it's a girl!"

"Yes!" I screamed, and both my arms shot up in the air as if we'd made a touchdown.

Samson's hands covered his mouth, and then he pointed at the screen. "That's my little girl?" he asked the sonographer.

"That's your little girl," she replied.

"Are you sure?" he asked. It was obvious he believed it, but he was still trying to fully absorb the news.

"Oh, I'm sure," she said. "She's also a good little girl. She's been very cooperative today. Here, gently push down on Mom's belly." She motioned to Samson.

He placed his hands on my belly as the sonographer helped him to press down a bit. On cue, the baby stuck out her leg again. Samson jumped back and nearly knocked over a table of supplies. "Oh my goodness!"

I couldn't do anything but laugh, smile, and cry at the same time.

"She gave us the perfect view between her legs. It's definitely a girl." The sonographer smiled. "I'll print out some pictures for you to take and will send the full report to your doctor." She turned off the machine.

Pure joy and thankfulness invaded my heart! I was thankful for the good news about the baby's development, and I was thankful because I had always dreamed of a girl!

Samson and I knew we had done enough dramatic reveals in the last few weeks. So our gender reveal consisted of some excited phone calls to our families. I wasn't in the car before I was on my cell phone with my sister. "It's a girl!" I told her. We exchanged squeals of delight before I went on calling everyone else.

By my fourth phone call, I must have sounded out of breath because Samson said, "Angela, you are wearing yourself out. Listen to how you sound."

Though I was panting a bit, I just chalked it up to the enthusiasm of the moment. But Samson was right. After all that had happened, I needed to slow it down a bit.

"You're right," I said. "Trying to call everyone is probably not a great idea. That's why they created e-mail!" I smiled after my light-bulb moment. A group e-mail to our friends would be a great way to share our baby news. "You know, I am definitely going to start a blog. That would be so much better than e-mail in the future. Plus, it would be great for ladies to come together in a community around the topic of motherhood and everything in between. There is so much we can learn from each other." I turned my head to the side while thinking aloud. "Hmm, LadiesLiveandLearn.com sounds perfect."

"There you go. Always creating," Samson said with a smile. "I think it's a great idea. You should go for it."

Inside the house, there were boxes everywhere, but our bed-room, my office, and our family room were pretty much set up. "You head up and settle in the bed," Sam said. "I'll run out in a minute and get us some dinner. We couldn't cook if we wanted to. I have no idea where the pots and pans are!" Samson laughed looking at the boxes stacked in the kitchen.

"Perfect. That will give me time to get my e-mail out." I took my time heading up the stairs, then settled into bed. I typed up the baby news e-mail excitedly and hit send. As I waited for the replies I knew were coming, I checked my work e-mail. I logged in and my eyes landed on an e-mail with the words *Severance Package* in the subject line. My stomach did a couple of somersaults that had noth-ing to do with my baby.

I had officially declined the offer to move to Tampa, so this news shouldn't have sent shock waves through me. I had learned from my boss that even his position in Chicago was being consoli-dated. The company's cuts were running deep. They had given me two options: I could either take the Tampa job or lose the one I had.

Even though I had made my decision, the questions still haunted me. Should I take the position and then leave if it didn't work out? If I did that, where would that leave me? I'd get uprooted *and* lose my severance because I would've quit. Where would that scenario leave my baby? Tampa was a long way from Buffalo and the village I was counting on to help raise my daughter.

I'd invested a lot into the company, but I knew the job hadn't made me and the loss of it wouldn't break me. I had to do exactly what the company was doing—I had to do what was best for my family's bottom line. Plus, Samson and I had prayed about this, and my hope was that somehow this change would be for our good. I took a deep breath and finally clicked on the e-mail. A quick glance was enough for me to gather that I had four more weeks.

29

Don't Worry, Be Happy

(From Samson)

L ook at it like this," I said, still talking about Angie's severance offer on our way to her prenatal visit the following day. "You've got paid maternity leave."

"I guess that's one way to look at it." She sighed and cradled her belly with one hand and her head with the other. She'd awakened not feeling well again. I wanted her to feel good about this; I wanted her to feel good about her decision to leave her job. "Hey, you're not Ms. Independent anymore," I said. "We've got each other, *Mrs. Logan.*" I was the performer in the family, but my words were no act.

My entertainment career was like many others in the field—it had as many highs and lows as my vocal range. But my career was on the rise and I was sure we would be okay, even without Angie working.

"It's going to have to be a short maternity leave," she said. "I found out the cost to continue our health insurance coverage with Cobra is going to be almost eight hundred dollars per month and that is only for me and the baby. It will be over twelve hundred to add you. Plus, we'll have to pay 50 percent of the cost of any medications."

There was a lot of concern in her voice, and I understood why. "Whoa! That's crazy," I said to Angie while what she'd just told me sunk in. Even though I was acting or singing almost every day, my career was inherently freelance in nature; I was an independent contractor. I loved what I did for a living, and it came with a lot of perks. But those perks were usually about and around adoring fans, not 401(k) plans and health benefits. This did worry me a bit, but I was hopeful.

"You need time to heal, bond with the baby, and adjust to motherhood," I assured her. "But after that, I still think you should pursue *you* full time for a while. Building your own brand the same way you have for so many others. This LadiesLiveandLearn.com thing will be bigger than you think when you put your know-how behind it."

Then I added, "Plus, you've had headhunters calling you like crazy. If you wanted, you could test the waters and go on a few interviews. Maybe you could manage your blog while you're helping to build another brand." The more I talked as we drove, the more convinced I was that this setback was more like a setup for something great.

"What do you think?" I asked, taking my eyes off the road for no more than a split-second. I gave her a quick glance, then turned my focus back to driving.

"Well, I did have two great phone interviews with a really good company and they requested that I come in for a full day of interviews with their executive team."

"That's great! But you don't sound excited."

"I'm just worried that when I test the waters," she said, "I'll start a tidal wave! You see how big I'm getting, plus in another month when the interview is scheduled, there will be no hiding this belly!" She pointed to her stomach with a smirk.

"Well, if that happens, just smile and ride the wave!" I patted her belly, and she finally laughed. When we both settled down, I said, "I wish you would do that more with this pregnancy, Ang'. You're carrying the dream—*our* dream—and we're living it. These are the days we prayed for. We're married, living in a great home, and you're having our baby. I know you haven't been feeling great and this job thing threw you for a loop, but I never thought any of that would faze the confident woman I knew in the past."

After a moment, I decided to open up to her all the way. I wanted her to understand that I was frustrated—just a little. "You don't seem as happy as I thought you would be," I said. "I thought I'd hear you laughing and joking all of the time."

Her head whipped around and she shot me a look that was a cross between confusion and anger. And then her tears came. That was not what I had intended. "Ang'! Where is this coming from?" I asked, surprised by her sudden emotion.

"I. Am. Happy," she said between sobs as she lowered her head.

"I. Can't. Tell," I said, once again trying to get her to smile and lift her head at the same time. I made a mental note to file this under things not to say to a pregnant woman in the future, at least not to *this* pregnant woman.

"You and this baby are the best part of my everything," she said. "But I haven't been just feeling bad during this pregnancy. I have a bad feeling." She raised her head and looked at me, and the concern I saw on her face melted away all of my frustration.

"Baby, I understand that you're scared," I said, "but you don't have to be. This is a new experience for you. I don't know what it's like to carry a life, but I would bet my life that you'll do and already are doing everything you can for this baby."

I was silent for a moment, wanting my words to settle inside of her. I wanted her to know I believed in her; I wanted her to stop being concerned. "Dr. Walters said that pregnancy is difficult, and from what I've seen, you're doing a great job. Ask Dr. Walters all of the questions that you want today and then some. I'm sure that you'll see everything is going to be okay."

When we pulled into Dr. Walters' parking lot, I turned off the ignition, then handed her a tissue for her tear-stained face. "Here, wipe some of that happy off your face," I said with a big smile. She grabbed the tissue from my hand and managed a laugh. That was what I wanted.

Our wait to see the doctor was long enough for Angie to compose herself, and the examination went quickly. I was glad because I wanted Angie to have time to open up and really talk to the doctor. "So how do things look, Doctor?" I asked. "She's been worried."

"Everything looks fine," Dr. Walters said matter-of-factly. "I don't know what she's so worried about. I got the results from the NT scan and they were perfect. The baby is doing well and your wife is also."

While the doctor sounded a bit nonchalant, Angela's tone was not. "I'm worried because I feel like there's something more going on with me," she said. "I almost passed out at work. I'm gaining so much weight, I'm exhausted, incredibly achy in my belly, and my shoulder hurts. My hands are so swollen I can't fit my wedding ring on and my ankles have turned into cankles already. It seems really early for all of these things to be happening."

Dr. Walters was not fazed, neither by her tone nor her words. "As I've said before, a lot of women think that pregnancy is going to be easy, but it can be a difficult process. Aches and pains come with a healthy pregnancy. These are all normal signs that your body is adjusting to your growing baby. There's no reason to be concerned," he reassured us.

Angie shook her head, not giving in. "But my discomfort in my belly and shoulder has been persistent. Plus, I've put on over twenty pounds already. That can't be normal this early."

"You're going to have some ligament pain as your womb grows and even some cramping as your uterus expands. It's all *normal*. You're going to have to adjust the way you sleep a bit and that should help with other discomforts. And your weight? Well, you'll have to watch what you eat to control that."

The doctor's answers seemed perfectly fine, perfectly logical to me. But when I looked at Angie, I could tell she didn't feel the same way.

"I haven't even been eating that much," she said. "I can't figure it out."

"Try not to consume foods high in fat and lay off fried foods. Enjoy being pregnant, Mrs. Logan. Everything is fine," he said, getting up as if he were ready to move on to the next patient.

Angie persisted. "It's hard for me to enjoy it when I feel like there's something wrong."

Wanting to help my wife, I jumped in. "Look, Dr. Walters, are there any tests we can take or anything more we can do to calm her concerns?"

The doctor glanced down at his chart, then looked up. "The tests we did today and her blood work are in the acceptable range. Her blood pressure is a bit elevated over the last visit, but first-time moms often experience an increase in their blood pressure. The NT test came back fine, so she's good."

"Are you sure?" I asked. "Because I'm going out of town for a while and I want to ensure that there is nothing to worry about and that she's okay," I said firmly.

As Angie looked on, Dr. Walters pulled me to the side. Lowering his voice, he said, "This is your wife's first baby. I'm not sure what she was expecting, but all of these symptoms are normal. I've delivered lots of babies and this is nothing new."

His words made sense to me. "So what do you recommend?"

This time he turned so he was facing both of us, and he spoke so Angie could hear him too: "Watch your diet, try to relax, and remember that your body and hormones are going through lots of changes. Everything is going as it should. You'll be fine." He opened the door to the examination room. "I have to see my next patient now," he said. "On your way out, we'll have the day and time for your next appointment, which will be in four weeks."

243

"Okay. Thank you, Doctor," I said as he exited. His words had made me feel better. After all, while I was used to delivering hit records and Angie was used to delivering sales for her company, this doctor was used to delivering babies. I hoped this news would help her get her happy back.

We left the examination room in silence and remained silent for most of the ride home. But once we were inside our house, I said, "Samantha's doing great! And so are you."

She gave me a quizzical look. "Samantha?"

"Yeah, Samantha," I said and looked away.

"Ah, that's a cute name," she said, "but who said we're naming our baby Samantha?" Then looking down, she said to her belly, "Angelique, don't worry about it. Daddy just got confused."

"Angelique?" I said. "That's a cute middle name. But this baby is going to be named after me."

"What!" She pouted and put her hands on her hips.

"I told you, this baby is going to be a little me without the goatee. You saw her on the sonogram yesterday. She looks just like me. She has to be named after me."

I grabbed her and pulled her close. She wiggled from my embrace and reached for her purse on the table, where she pulled out a sonogram photo she had tucked inside.

"You made her sonogram photo into wallet-sized pictures?" I laughed.

"Duh, yeah. This is my baby." She laughed and studied the picture.

We were both looking at our little nugget, only the size of a plum, and debated who she looked like, knowing we couldn't tell a thing.

"You're lucky she's a cutie pie and probably *will* look like you. I might consider Samantha." She rolled her eyes playfully. "But I really want her name to mean something special. I want it to embody her."

"You know we agreed that my boy, Tip Gilchrist, and his wife, Angie, could be one set of godparents, right?" I asked.

She nodded.

I continued, "Well, I guess they're taking their roles seriously because they left me like five messages telling me that they came up with the perfect name."

"Really?" she said. "Why didn't you tell me before? Call them!" She grabbed my phone.

"All right, all right," I said. "But I don't know what's going to be better than the name I chose."

Tip answered on the first ring. "It's about time, man!" he said, knowing it was me on the line. "Me and Angie have been waiting for you to call us."

"I'm sorry," I said. "Me and the wife have been crazy busy, but she couldn't wait to hear this name." I put my phone on speaker. Both of the Angies jumped into the conversation for the big name reveal.

"I can't wait anymore," Angie said. "We haven't found the perfect name yet. What did you come up with?"

Our friends counted down. "Three, two, one ... Samia," they said together.

Angie stopped and looked at me. Then she turned her eyes up as if studying the name, and finally she looked down at her belly. She didn't say anything; she didn't have to. I liked the sound of it—more than the sound of it, my baby would be named after me.

"What are you thinking?" I asked Angie after giving her a minute to ponder it.

"Sa-mi-a." She said the name slowly. "I love it!" she finally exclaimed. "I think this is it. I have to go and look up the meaning. Love you guys!" She didn't even wait to hear anything else they had to say. She took off toward her office, leaving me on the phone.

I heard the printer in the office running while I was still talking to Tip, but I paid no mind. A few minutes later, when I hung up, I joined her in the office.

"What are you doing?" I asked, taking a look at all the papers she had on the desk.

She turned over one; it was an eight-by-ten of the baby's sonogram with her name, Samia Angelique Logan, printed in a gorgeous font above the picture. In just the few minutes it had taken me to wrap up the call, Angie had created this.

Picking up one of the other sheets, she read, "Samia: Arabic and Aramaic, meaning 'high, exalted.' Angelique: Latin, meaning 'messenger of God.' And Logan is Scottish or Gaelic, meaning 'out of the hollow.' This is it," she said excitedly. "This is our baby's name. Samia Angelique Logan is our high, exalted messenger of God out of the hollow." She beamed and held out the documents to me.

I couldn't believe it. That quickly, she had done all of this. I was taken aback by how touched I was with *hearing* her name and *seeing* her name with her picture. I actually got a little misty-eyed as I held the print.

Angie grabbed some tissues from the box on her desk and came over to me. She kissed my cheek and said, "Here, wipe some of that happy off your face."

30

A Mother's Intuition

(From Angela)

I can do hard things.

That's how I started and stopped the latest entry of my pregnancy journal. I was prepared to leave it there, but after a few minutes I added the words *with God*. Then, as I pondered the words I'd written, I thought, *This journal doesn't feel maternal.* I couldn't help but groan. I wanted to write about a milestone, but in reality each week I made it through my pregnancy felt like a major achievement.

I was trying to do all I could to convince myself I could overcome this "hardness." That was the word that stuck in my mind after every doctor's visit—pregnancy is hard. I kept telling myself I knew it would be, and I thought I was prepared to endure the pain of pregnancy for the gain of my little angel. But the hardest thing wasn't dealing with the swelling, nausea, aches, and pains—it was dealing with not being able to sleep lying down. I had to sit up, propped up with pillows, because if I lay flat on my back, I couldn't breathe.

The most difficult thing was knowing something greater was wrong … and not finding anyone who believed me.

Part of that may have been my own fault. Even though I'd tried to Google my symptoms, I couldn't solve the mystery by myself. And then I began to wonder, *Is my mind playing tricks on me?* But I answered that quickly enough. The knowing didn't come from my mind; it came from my soul. It was my soul that was telling me, it was my soul that sensed ... death.

Every week that passed, this intuition grew stronger, just like my symptoms. I'd gone to the doctor so many times that he didn't want to hear it anymore. In fact, I felt as if he were becoming annoyed. I'd overheard him refer to me as "a regular" to one of the nurses. And his prescription to me was always the same: a dose of "toughen up" because pregnancy is hard. He never gave me an answer to what was ailing me.

Then there was Samson. We were miles apart in more ways than one. Not only was he physically away for work, but there was distance between us because Dr. Walters had convinced him this was all in my mind. Whenever I complained, Samson would say to me, "Angie, you're not a doctor. If the doctor says you're fine, then you must be."

What he didn't understand, however, was that I wanted to agree with him, but how could I when my feet and legs were so swollen and tight that it was difficult to get around? How could I when I ached and was so tired that the fatigue was debilitating?

One of the blessings in this was that I only had one more week of work. I'd canceled my final trips, knowing that with the way I was feeling, getting on an airplane would have been too grueling. So I worked from home, preparing all of the transition documents for my company.

As I was sitting at my desk, trying to work through all of my aches, the doorbell rang. It was the middle of the day and I wasn't expecting anyone. Making my way down the stairs was an effort, but when I peeked through the window and saw my sister's smiling face, I felt a million times better.

"Hey, what are you doing here?" I asked her when I opened the door.

"I came to see how you and my niece are doing over here," Kristy said. "Instead of calling, I went for the pop-up!"

I laughed and led her from the foyer into the kitchen. She was right; she usually called me every day to check in, but it was good to see her in person. I needed someone to talk to.

"Would you like something to eat or drink?" I opened the refrigerator.

"No, I'm fine," she said. With concern in her voice, she then asked, "But the question is, how are you? You sound out of breath, like you just ran a race!"

I was panting after coming downstairs and taking the extra steps into the kitchen. "I've been out of breath a lot lately!"

"Well, come on, let's sit down then." She led me into my family room and when we sat, she propped up some throw pillows behind me. "How are you feeling … really?" she asked again.

"Good!" I answered, making sure I had a smile on my face.

It didn't take my sister a second to say, "Uh, Angie, I know you and I know that *good* you just gave me is as fake as they come. What's going on?" she persisted.

Kris wasn't only a great confidant, she was someone I could turn to for advice. When I thought about it, she was partly responsible for my condition. After all, it was her wedding to Pete that God used to bring Samson and me together. So I opened up to her, sharing with her as I'd done in the past. "I just feel like something is wrong!"

"You're still feeling bad?"

"Yes. Like I told you before, everything hurts. And the new thing is that I can't even sleep right."

Confusion was written all over her face.

I went on to explain, "Whenever I lay flat, I feel like I can't catch my breath. You see how I get when I walk?" After she nodded, I continued, "Well, when I lie down, I feel like I'm choking."

She was shaking her head before I even finished. "This can't be right," she said. "What did your doctor say?"

"I talked to him about this on my last visit and he told me to go buy a body contour pillow. He said that pregnant women are often uncomfortable when they sleep, so I should just do that and deal with it as best as I could."

She made a face like that wasn't a good enough answer for her. "A body contour pillow will help, but that still doesn't sound right."

"Oh, and look at this." I pulled up my pant leg and showed her a large blister and scab on my leg.

"Eww!" she said. "How did you get that?"

"My legs have gotten so swollen that they've actually been cracking and bleeding."

"Angie, this doesn't seem right. I got some swelling with my pregnancies, but what's going on with you is extreme. Have you considered getting another doctor?"

"You know me—you know I have—but it hasn't worked out. The doctors I checked into aren't taking new patients and the ones who are have a long wait for a new patient's first visit. Plus, with the changes in my insurance, I was advised it might be best to just stick with the doctor I have." I sighed. "He's supposed to be a good doctor. He's gotten all kinds of awards and was highly recommended. But I feel like he's not listening to me. He treats me like I'm a hormonal nervous new mother." I shrugged, then said, "Who knows? Maybe I am."

"Listen, don't get me wrong," she said seriously. "I love doctors— we need them and couldn't make it without them. But what a doctor thinks he knows and what a mother feels are two different things. You have to trust what you feel."

She was right. This was exactly what I'd been thinking.

All of a sudden, my sister cleared her voice, put her thumb and her pinky to her ear like she was talking on a phone, and said, "This is Dr. Kristy Tasca and I'm calling in a prescription for my patient, Angela Logan."

That made me smile. I looked her up and down. "Where did you get your medical degree?"

"From Mom University," she said as if I should have known that. "I graduated cum laude with a degree in 'I have two kids.'" She put down her hands. "What I'm prescribing for you is bed rest, at least until the fab baby shower that we're planning."

"Okay, Dr. Tasca," I said, and we both busted out laughing. I was grateful for the lighter moment, and so grateful for my sister.

"So you're going to rest more?" my sister asked, back to being serious once again.

"My last day is next week anyway," I said as she stood up, "so bed rest here I come."

I tried to push myself to get up with her so I could walk her to the door, but she held up her hand. "No, you stay put and elevate your feet. I'll show myself out. But remember my doctor's orders!" she said before she gave me a hug and then left.

Taking my sister's suggestion, I stayed in place and tried to relax. I thought about going upstairs, but taking the stairs was getting more difficult because of the tightness and swelling in my feet and legs.

Finally, I went up about nine. Not that I was sleepy, but I wanted to be in place for Samson's call. He had been gone on tour for a few weeks now, and we had established a nightly routine where he called me right after his show ended. The time varied, of course, but the call usually came in about ten fifteen.

I looked forward to Sam's calls. Our talks were about everything and nothing at the same time. They reminded me of how we would talk when we fell in love, and now this was playing a role in us staying in love. Sometimes the most intimate thing a person can share with someone is a great conversation.

By the time I had the pillows propped behind me, on cue, Samson called. We were both breathing slightly hard when I answered the phone.

"What are you doing?" I asked.

"I'm backstage at the theater walking back to my dressing room," he told me. "What are you doing? You sound like you're out of breath."

"The baby is keeping me winded!" I told him. "I've been getting really short of breath lately."

"You know," Sam said, "I'm kind of glad you aren't going to be working for a while. The way this pregnancy is going it seems like it would've been hard on you to travel as much as you did with your job. I want you and my baby to be okay."

"I have to agree with you. I would have just been getting back from a meeting tonight, and with the way I felt today, that would've been so hard." I paused. "Hold on, I think the baby is trying to hear your voice—she just moved! Say hello to her. I'm putting the phone to my belly."

I hit the speaker button and Sam said, "Hi, princess!" Right as he said that, a roar filled the house. It was shocking, especially when the bed shook and the windows rattled.

"Oh my goodness!" I yelled. "Did you hear that?"

"No!" Samson said with alarm in his voice. "What's going on?"

"I think we just had an earthquake!" I said, breathless at this point. I sat silently for a moment. "Whew! It seems like it's over. The house literally shook."

"Wow," Samson said. "I can't ever remember having an earthquake in Buffalo."

"Well, whatever that was, it made the house shake," I told him, still struggling for breath. "I'll turn on the news in a few minutes to see if they say anything about it."

Once I calmed down, Samson and I went on talking as we usually did, but just a few minutes later I heard the sirens and blaring horns of fire trucks and police cars. It sounded as if there were dozens of them.

"Hold on, Sam. I'm turning on the TV." I flipped through the channels as we talked, but I didn't see anything. There was still a little time before the local news, so I decided to check out CNN. That's when I saw the breaking news in the news crawl at the bottom of the screen: *CNN has confirmed that a plane has crashed in Clarence, New York.*

"Oh no!" I yelled out. I got up as quickly as I could and went to my bedroom window, pulling up the shades. In the distance, I saw a faint red glow.

"What's going on?" Samson asked.

"That wasn't an earthquake," I told him. "That was a plane crash! It's on CNN!"

Samson and I talked longer than normal that night, but even after we hung up, I stayed up long into the night, flipping the channel from CNN to my local news station. As I watched, I prayed for the people on the flight and their families.

It wasn't until the next day that my heart sank even further about the plane crash. The reason I'd felt the shaking and the roar was because the plane, Flight 3407, had stalled right above our home and then crashed less than a mile away. But what had me most shaken was that I could have been on that plane. A coworker who had remained with the company was on that flight, returning home from a company business meeting.

My head spun as I processed that I could have been coming home from that same meeting! I began to wonder: *Was this where the bad feeling came from that I'd been having? Was this why I felt like death was so close to me?* The foreboding I had came when I'd found out that I was pregnant *and* that I was losing my job. Maybe that feeling had been connected to my job this whole time and not to my baby and pregnancy.

As bad as this feeling had been—and as bad as this news was—what would be worse would be forgetting to give praise to God, even in these circumstances. I was often quick to praise God for the good news, but I had to remember he was still God, even in the bad news. His will and his purpose may have been a mystery to me, but he was far greater than all the good and all the bad. I had to remember to trust him in all things. And so that's what I was going to do: trust God.

In the weeks that followed, I tried to release that something's-wrong feeling, believing the bad thing had already passed. Even though I tried to release it, it never released me. My own bad news seemed to continue to mount, namely that my pregnancy was getting worse by the day. It had truly reached the point where I didn't know how much more I could bear, and I kept trying to tell my doctor about it. With each visit, our doctor-patient relationship got worse. He didn't understand I was a patient with a problem, not a problem patient, which is how I felt I was being treated.

Whenever I went in and complained of my symptoms, I would get an eye roll and the same ole "Pregnancy is hard" or "These are normal pregnancy symptoms" or "Toughen up" speeches. But never did my doctor give me an answer to the questions I had about my ailments, which I was absolutely convinced had nothing to do with a normal pregnancy. I wasn't looking for sympathy—not at all. I was looking for solutions.

That's why I asked him to test me for everything possible, which he declined to do. And that's why I asked him to send me to a specialist for an assessment of some of my pain, to which he finally said yes. He referred me back to my primary care doctor, who took a look at my shoulder but couldn't determine the cause because I couldn't have an X-ray while I was pregnant.

At the last appointment, I'd asked Dr. Walters if he could help me with the only solution I could determine. "Can you induce me a bit early or schedule a C-section?" I asked him.

Dr. Walters gave me that look he'd been giving me for the past few months, as if I were being overly dramatic. "The womb is the best place for the baby's development," he said.

"I'm not saying to do it now," I clarified. "I'm saying once the baby is developed enough." I was almost begging him because I was sure my symptoms would stop once I had my baby in my arms.

Dr. Walters sighed. "Mrs. Logan, I can't authorize an unwarranted cesarean section. All you have to do is remember that pregnancy is hard."

If he says that to me one more time …

Although I was suffering physically, in the midst of all of this there was something powerful happening. I knew something bad was going to happen, but at the same time I *knew* that God was with me. I *knew* his presence was around me. My pregnancy, even with all of its troubles, had birthed the closest connection to God's presence I had ever experienced.

So there I was, in between this bad feeling and God. And there, in that space, I gave it to him. There was nothing else I could do; I couldn't carry it since I didn't have the physical or spiritual strength to do so. My only choice was to give this burden to him, and while my body still felt horrible, both physically and spiritually, I felt some comfort in this closeness to Abba.

I was grateful for feeling as if I could release my overwhelming anxiety to him, but there was one facet that still burdened me: this sense of death that hung over me made me more than a little concerned for my baby. She was the reason I held onto this feeling—I was so scared for her. I wondered if something happened to me, who would love her? I had certainly planned for and counted on my village to help raise my child, but again I asked myself the question, who would love her?

Of course, there was more to my question than that. I knew that her father, our parents, families, and friends would certainly be there for my daughter; they would all love her. But the greater question was, who would give her a mother's love? Who would whisper into her spirit while she slept that she was wonderfully and fearfully made? Who would make it clear to her that she was the daughter of the King? Who would kiss her boo-boos, tickle her toes, and hug her endlessly? Who would be her confidant, mentor, teacher, and friend?

All I could do was pray: "God, please allow me to be here for my baby." That was what I asked for nightly. I felt like sometimes I was in a weird space, between bad and good. One of the good parts was that Samson was home for my upcoming baby shower and my next doctor's appointment. Over the last three months, his travel schedule had been heavy, but he made sure he was able to come home whenever he could.

I was always glad to see him and he was glad to see me, but each time he came home my appearance startled him. "Wow! You've gained some weight," he said the first time he came home after being away for a few weeks.

"I know," I said. "I've been trying to tell you that's one of the symptoms." I had long passed the typical one- to two-pound weekly weight gain for the last two trimesters of pregnancy—I'd gained sixty pounds.

The week of my baby shower, Samson was home the entire week, which gave him the chance to see the way I watched my diet and how I wasn't eating out of the norm. That didn't matter, though, for I gained fifteen pounds!

In. One. Week.

For those who didn't know me, I probably didn't even look pregnant. My baby bump was cute for about a week at the beginning of my second trimester, but then it disappeared as the rest of me exploded. My face, hands, legs, and feet had grown so large that I looked overweight instead of pregnant. My swelling was so extreme that I had trouble bending my legs and knees.

How was I going to give birth when I could barely bend my legs in the stirrups at the doctor's appointments? How was I going to push the baby out?

As with all of the previous doctor's appointments, I had a list of questions for Dr. Walters. But this time, with Samson there, I hoped to get more answers—something besides the usual toughen up speech.

Once again, I shared my litany of worries with Dr. Walters, especially the abnormal weight gain that he had to notice, but once again he gave me the same speech: "I don't know what you're worried about, Angela. All of the things you're complaining about are normal pregnancy symptoms."

Was he even hearing me? It was as if he had his speech prepared for me even before I said anything. "Normal?" I couldn't keep the anger out of my voice. "How can it be normal to gain fifteen pounds in one week?" I practically screamed.

While I was losing it, he sighed. "Nothing I say seems to satisfy you," he said, his voice monotone as he spoke. "This is all in your head."

I was dumbfounded and enraged by his response. I wanted to tell him to open his eyes. "Really? It's all in my head?" I screamed. "Is it in my head that my legs and feet literally cracked and bled as I walked in here today?" I lifted my legs so he could see them. "Is it in my head that I can't breathe when I lie flat? I have been sleeping upright for months now. Is it in my head that each time I come in here my blood pressure is steadily rising? I'll tell you what's in my head: *Something's wrong!* And I need you to use your head to figure it out." I was so furious I was shaking.

Samson jumped in. "Angela! Calm down." Then turning to the doctor, he said, "Dr. Walters, there has to be something that can be done. She's in a lot of pain." But Samson's interjection didn't move the doctor.

"I understand, Mr. Logan," the doctor said, "but she really just needs to toughen up. She'll be okay. This is what pregnant women go through."

"Can you just induce me?" I asked loudly, since the doctor wasn't even facing me as he addressed Samson.

Another sigh. "I told you before that isn't an option. That could hurt the baby."

"But what about me?" I asked. "What if I'm hurt or something happens to me? What will happen to the baby then?"

"You're going to be fine," he said once again. Then turning back to Samson, he asked, "Mr. Logan, can I speak with you?" The doctor motioned for my husband to follow him outside.

"No!" I jumped in. "Whatever you have to say to him, you can say to me."

"Fine." Dr. Walters grunted. Still he addressed Samson only. "Your wife needs to toughen up a bit. Her hormones are everywhere right now."

"But my wife is strong," Samson insisted, looking over at me.

The doctor shrugged a little. "Pregnancy can make even strong women act strange. But she's talking about inducing labor and seems a bit irrational. She'll be able to handle the delivery. Everything will be okay. She just needs to calm down."

"It's really not like her to complain like this," Samson said. He wouldn't let it go. "Are you *sure* this is normal?"

Now the doctor sighed at him. "I'm telling you that this is in her head. I have been doing this a long time, and these are normal pregnancy symptoms."

I didn't have any words left. I was just fed up and near tears. But my feelings of anger melted, and in their place was my desperate need for help. I wanted *someone* to help me. "Can you send me for some outside testing?" I'd asked him this before, and I hoped this time he'd actually hear me.

"Fine," he said, sounding equally fed up. "I'll send you to the lab at Suburban, where you'll be delivering. But I'm telling you now, they're going to tell you what I've been telling you. I'll get you an appointment with them as soon as possible."

Even though the doctor agreed to my request, I didn't feel any better. Especially as Samson tried to echo Dr. Walters' words over the next few days. "It's just normal pregnancy symptoms," he kept telling me.

I knew he was trying to get me to feel better, but he wasn't helping. The one thing Samson and I focused on was being on the same page. With this, we clearly were not. He couldn't comprehend the bad feeling I had wasn't in my head; it was in my gut. Words couldn't express this.

So I stopped trying to get him to understand. I just kept it to myself and God. I continued to pray because if there was anyone who would hear me, if there was anyone who would help me, it would be God. That was becoming clearer by the day.

31

Proxy

(From Angela)

Jam, I need you to take a look at this." I handed him some papers as he ate breakfast.

He squinted, looking down. "What is this?"

"It's my health-care proxy. It gives you the right to make medical decisions for me in the event I'm unable to do so myself."

He gave me a blank stare.

I continued, "The hospital I'll be delivering at requires this to be completed."

"Okay," he said after a moment. "I'll look at it, but we won't be needing it because you're going to be fine." He gave me a quick peck on my cheek, then took the papers from my hand.

"I wish that were true." I sighed. "But I have a bad feeling about this." I kept repeating that to myself, over and over. I'd said it at least a thousand times, but I didn't have any other words to describe what was going on.

Like always, Samson responded: "There's nothing to be worried about, Angie. You're going to be fine and the baby is going to be fine too."

When Samson would say this lately, I left it alone. But I just couldn't leave it alone this time. "You're obviously not the man who sleeps next to me," I said to him. "Oh wait, that's right, you aren't since you can't because I have to sleep upright in the chair." Frustration filled my voice. "I haven't even been able to lie down next to you, and you believe that everything is fine?"

"You're talking so negatively and you have to stop that," he said with frustration in his voice. "This isn't like you. Everything is fine. You're okay," he repeated. "And the baby is too."

"You're starting to sound more like the doctor and less like my husband."

"Where are all of these insecurities coming from?" he asked. His frustration had obviously gone up a couple of levels.

"These are not insecurities," I said. "This is intuition. I have so many things wrong and so many things hurting that I'm losing count. But what's hurting me most is you not listening to me." My frustration had turned to disappointment.

"I'm not trying to hurt you, Angela," he said, his frustration turning to anger, "but I've been listening to you for all of these months talk about symptoms that the doctor says are normal."

"So you believe the doctor over me?" I said incredulously.

"What do you expect me to do?" he asked. "Who should I believe, Angie? The doctor does this every day. This is what he does for a living. This is medical stuff we know nothing about. If he says it's going to be okay, why would I believe anything differently? If you were me, don't you think this is what you'd be saying?"

"If this was happening to you," I said as I looked into his eyes but tried to connect with his heart, "I would believe *you*. I would back *you* with everything within me and no one could tell me differently."

He shook his head. "That's not fair, Angie! This is medical stuff. We have to listen to the doctor. He's the one with the degree."

"Sometimes a mother's intuition can be more valuable than any degree," I yelled, almost in tears.

"Angie, stop it," he said, his voice much softer. "Calm down."

My volume now matched his. "I'm having trouble breathing, my legs are cracking and bleeding, I can't lie flat, and my doctor tells me that these symptoms are in my head. And now my husband is acting like he believes him over me." I started to cry. "You told me that we always needed to be on the same page, but right now I don't know what page you're on." I paused. "What page are you on, Sam? Are you on my page?"

"Angie, just relax," he said. "Getting worked up is not good for you or the baby." He reached for me and tried to pull me close to him, but I pulled back.

"I need to know what page you're on," I said again, adamantly. "I need to hear you say it. Are we on the same page?"

"Yes! We're on the same page," he said firmly, letting me know his response was much more than lip service—it was heartfelt.

I collapsed into his embrace. I needed his support, wanting and needing someone to believe me, to understand what I was going through. I had given the burden of the outcome of this bad feeling over to God, but I still had to go through the process, I still had to go through the trial. I was in a battle, and I needed the comfort of knowing I wasn't fighting alone.

I already knew God was with me, but now Samson was too. My husband and I were finally on the same page. That gave me the courage I needed to fight death, and it gave me something equally important, equally needed: Samson's belief in me gave me hope.

32

Testing

(From Angela)

I was relieved to be getting this independent testing done at Millard Fillmore Suburban Hospital. Dr. Walters had come through with at least this, and it had only taken a few days to get the appointment.

Although I was happy to be doing this, I was also anxious as I made my way into the maternal and fetal ward. The tests I would be given would take a few hours; they would be monitoring the baby's heart rate and my own vitals over a period of time. What I wasn't prepared for was actually meeting someone who heard me and who got it.

A female lab technician came out to greet me with a smile. "Hello, Mrs. Logan," she said, shaking my hand. But as she touched me, her smile faded away. She stopped shaking my hand and looked down at it. There was concern in her eyes when she looked up. "Come with me."

I followed her slowly, since moving quickly was not something I could do. Inside the examination room, she looked me up and down as she eased me onto the table. It was her expression that made me ask, "Is something wrong?"

"I think so." She nodded. "Would you mind if I looked at your legs?"

I was grateful as she lifted up each of my pant legs.

She gasped a bit when she saw how big my legs were and how bad they looked from the broken skin caused by the swelling. She pressed her hand down gently on my leg, shaking her head. Then she turned to me and said, "Let's get your blood pressure." She removed the stethoscope from around her neck and pushed up my sleeve. When she finally released the cuff from my arm, she said, "It's two hundred over a hundred." She took a deep breath. "I know I'm supposed to be doing some more testing, but I need to call your doctor about your blood pressure and all of this swelling."

Even though she was concerned, relief washed over me. "Please call him," I said. "I have been telling him for months that something is wrong, but he keeps telling me these are normal pregnancy symptoms."

She was shaking her head before I even finished speaking. "No. This is not normal. I test pregnant women every day, and I have not seen anyone as swollen as you. I'm even thinking that you should be admitted for some long-term monitoring." As she continued to examine my face, legs, and feet, she was talking to me, but it seemed as if she were talking to herself. She grabbed my chart. "Dr. Walters is your doctor, correct?"

"Yes," I replied.

When she walked over to the phone, I simply lifted up my eyes and thanked God that someone was seeing what I had known. After a few moments, I heard, "Yes, this is the lab at Millard Fillmore Suburban. We have your patient here, a Mrs. Logan. I'm concerned about this patient. She has a significant amount of edema and her blood pressure is two hundred over one hundred. I think she may need to be admitted for some long-term monitoring, much more than what I can do for her today."

She paused while listening to the doctor. Then she said, "Yes, but, Doctor, this patient doesn't seem well." There was another pause. Then again she spoke, "Her swelling is some of the most extreme I have ever seen." Another pause before it was her turn again. "And her blood pressure is high."

After a few minutes of this back-and-forth, the tech hung up and slowly turned toward me. "Your doctor seems to think you're fine," she told me. "He said that you're probably just worked up, which is why your blood pressure is high. He asked if I'd monitor you over the next hour to see if it goes down. He already said that he doesn't want you admitted." She sighed and shook her head. "If he says no, then there's nothing I can do. The doctors trump what us nurses and technicians say. We can't do anything without them."

My hope was sucked out of the room and my chin fell to my chest.

"Don't worry," she said. "You'll still be here for a while, so let's get a fetal monitor on you. Maybe some of these tests will tell me what's going on."

I stayed for several hours, going through a battery of tests to monitor the baby's health. The baby seemed to be doing well, thank God, but my blood pressure only went down to 190/90.

The technician called the doctor. I once again listened as she said, "Dr. Walters, we have completed the testing. Mrs. Logan is still hypertensive. Now her blood pressure is one ninety over ninety and—"

She stopped as if she were being interrupted on the other end. She said a few yes, buts, then she hung up and turned to me. "Your doctor seems to believe that the decrease in your blood pressure means that you were just worked up and that it will probably continue to decrease throughout the night." She was shaking her head. "I don't agree with him, but he thinks your swelling is normal. I asked him repeatedly to have you admitted. I don't understand why he won't at least do that. It wouldn't hurt anything. But he said no and insisted that you're fine and should go home."

With a sigh, she reached over and held my hand. "I don't want to send you home, but I don't have the authority to have you admitted." After I nodded, she smiled. "Just monitor yourself and take care, okay?"

"Okay," I said, forcing a smile to match hers.

I'd been told many times by Dr. Walters to just go home. But this time I was scared. The technician had seen what I saw. I was in trouble and she knew it. And this time I believed my baby and I were being sent home to die.

33

In the Flash of a Light

(From Angela)

I was drifting down, down, down, until my body settled at the bottom of a vast ocean. I felt heavy and weightless at the same time. And then I sensed the white light. I was moving through the light at a pace I had never before known.

Slowly and purposefully, my mind processed what was happening. Inside the white light, there were flashes—moments of my life. In between the flashes I heard, "Get a crash cart in here!"

From the bottom of the ocean, I could see the woman who was yelling. Her mocha-colored skin glowed and she wore a doctor's surgical cap. But my mind didn't stay with her. Instead I went back to the flashes—I saw myself and my sister at the ages of eight and five running toward an ice cream cart, both of us waving a dollar in our hands.

That beautiful moment faded to the voice of another woman with curly jet-black hair and kind eyes, flashing a light in my face. "Talk to me, beautiful." Her voice was filled with compassion.

"I. Can't. Breathe!" I managed to speak through what felt like rocks in my throat.

"Eyes appear exophthalmic," someone yelled out.

I wanted to go back to the light, especially the flashes, and so I did. I saw myself being handed a baton and then running before crossing the finish line ahead of everyone else. Everyone was cheering as I worked to catch my breath after running that four-hundred-yard relay in high school.

"Where's the anesthesiologist?" That was the voice of the first woman again. The kind one. She said to me, "We're going to help you." I wanted to go back to the light, but I felt her touch my leg. "She's got at least plus two pitting edema."

Then I felt a stethoscope pressed against my chest. "Bilateral crackling heard in the lungs."

"Please help me!" I struggled to lift my head.

Back to the light. I was throwing my cap up in the air. My college graduation.

Then I heard my husband's scream. "Ang'!"

The light was gone and I turned my head. I was moving in slow motion, though around me everything was happening at rapid-fire speed. My eyes finally set on my husband, but only for a moment. Two men were holding his arms, dragging him from the room.

Then the flash returned—me and Samson. In an instant, I lived through our entire relationship, from the first moment to the last. From our first meeting when he pulled up in his Mustang, through every challenge and every blessing, our wedding, our new home … it all played out in my mind. At the same time my natural eyes battled to focus. I wanted to see my father and I searched for him, but I couldn't find him. Maybe it was because of all the activity around me, so fast and furious. My thoughts were slow and clear.

I have to hold on. I have to hold on until my dad gets here.

That was one of my thoughts as everyone around me moved so fast. It was all a blur. Still, there were little things I could see. An Indian gentleman rushed into the room, pushing a cart. My eyes set on him and he stared back. Without words, we spoke. His eyes said,

I am here to help. He grabbed my arm, though I couldn't discern why. I didn't have enough energy to figure out what he was doing; I had to focus on just breathing. And on my baby.

I could feel my baby struggling inside me. *Mama loves you* is what I tried to communicate to her with every fiber of my being. I needed to breathe so I could give her some strength. What I really wanted to do was scream out, *Somebody help my baby!* But the energy was draining from me quickly.

This is it.

The end was coming and that meant I needed to use my last ounce of strength wisely. So I took my final breath, lifted my head, and said as loudly as I could, "Jesus, please help me!"

Suddenly I was drifting, drifting above my bed, before I began falling, like a freefall. From above, I saw myself collapse onto the hospital bed, then I heard the thud my body made when I fell back onto the bed. I was lying flat, in the position where I could never breathe.

Looking down, I saw the doctors working diligently, frantically trying to save me. Then I was fully inside the white light. I was out of my body.

34

Dying to Give Birth

(From Samson)

I grabbed my phone as I paced back and forth outside of Angie's hospital room. My hands were shaking as I dialed her father.

"Hey, Sam! How's it going?" he said when he answered.

I was sure he was expecting an update, just not one this unimaginable. "Mr. Burgin," I began, trying to keep my voice together and not fall apart, "there's an emergency. Can you get here right away?"

"What? I'll be right there," he said.

"Hurry, she asked for you." I hung up because I could feel it—I was about to lose it. I looked at the chairs against the hospital wall, but there was no way I could sit down. Instead, I paced and talked to myself. "No," I said over and over. "No! What is happening? What is happening to my wife, to my baby?"

These words came out of my mouth repeatedly as I paced in front of her hospital room. There was so much frenzied activity that finally all I could do was moan out loud and sink to the ground. I sat where I landed. I sat there and prayed, "God, please help my wife and our baby!"

This was a Sunday morning and ordinarily we would have been in church. But on this Sunday, I sat right on that hospital floor and had a church service, beseeching God to save Angela and our baby. I wasn't sure how much time passed. To me, it felt only like a few moments, but it had to be more because my father-in-law came running down the hall. It was only because of him that I managed to pull myself up.

"What's wrong, Sam?" The look on his face matched the fear in my heart.

"She's in trouble," I started, but before I could tell him, more Angie's doctor bounded out of the room and rushed straight toward me. We didn't give him time to get to us—we ran toward him. "What's wrong, Doctor?" I yelled out even before we got to him.

Complete fear was frozen on Dr. Walter's face as he took a deep breath. "Mr. Logan, I have to be honest with you." Another breath. "She's in critical condition."

"What!" I yelled, filled with rage and fear. "No! No! Dr. Walters, you said that she would be fine!"

"I know I did, Sam. But right now she's not, and we have very little time."

Angie's father gasped.

I cupped my mouth to keep from yelling at the doctor, who said, "I need your permission to perform an emergency C-section."

"Of course, of course, you have it," I said as quickly as I could. "Whatever you need."

"We will induce her into a coma," he explained. "She has to be placed on a ventilator in order for her to continue to breathe. I need your permission to give her a tracheotomy."

Inside, I thought:

A tracheotomy? What's going on? Why does he need to cut her like that? Angie wouldn't want that.

But all I could say was: "No, no, no!"

"Mr. Logan, please," Dr. Walters said. "We have to do this. It's her only chance."

I could not believe what I was hearing. "Her only chance?" I shook my head. "This can't be happening. Can't you do something besides cutting her throat?" I asked. All kinds of thoughts raced through my mind. Thoughts of what a tracheotomy would do to my wife. Thoughts of what she would want to do. Thoughts of all of the times she'd told me something was wrong.

"We can give her an endotracheal tube instead," Dr. Walters said. "But whatever we decide, we have to do something fast and I need your permission."

I made the split-second decision. "Give her the tube!" I yelled. "Give her the tube!"

At the same time, her father screamed, "Get in there and save my daughter!"

Dr. Walters nodded and then turned back and ran to Angie's room.

"She told me this was going to happen." I gripped my father-in-law's shoulder. "She tried to tell me something was wrong."

Her father shook his head as if denying my words. "No, my daughter is going to be all right. She has to be."

My head turned toward the sound of footsteps as Angie's mother, sister, and friend April rushed toward us. For a moment, I wondered how they knew, and then I realized her dad must have called everyone. As they approached, I knew they had no idea of the severity of what was going on and they were going to be crushed when they heard.

I told them what the doctor had told me, and they stood stunned until April pulled out her phone and called her husband. Tim was a minister at their church and she told him what was going on. A couple of minutes later, he called back to let us know the pastor had stopped the church service and asked the congregation to immediately pray.

We paced and prayed, the whole time waiting for someone to come out of that room. After what felt like forever, a doctor finally emerged and came straight toward me.

"Mr. Logan," she said.

I couldn't move to her fast enough, and everyone followed behind me. "Yes." My voice was shaking.

"Your baby is here and we finally got her breathing."

"Thank God," we all said together.

Then I asked, "And my wife?"

But before she could answer that, the doors of the hospital room where Angie was burst open and three doctors and a nurse rushed past us, pushing her hospital bed.

I moved as quickly as I could, trying to get over to her, but another doctor held me back. From where we stood, we could see her, and to me Angie was almost unrecognizable. There were tubes coming from what seemed like everywhere, and the nurse beside her bed was pumping a respirator to keep her breathing.

"My daughter!" Angie's mother yelled out. "My daughter!" Like me, she tried to get near Angie, but the team of doctors had wheeled her by in a hurry.

For a second, I stood there not knowing what to do until Dr. Walters came out of the room. "Where are you taking my wife?" I asked.

He answered, "We've got to get her to ICU and on mechanical ventilation." But he didn't stop moving; he spoke as he ran by. "I'll come back to give you an update as soon as I can." He then rushed into the elevator where they'd just wheeled Angela.

All I could do was watch as the door closed. As the elevator went down, my heart sank with it.

"Mr. Logan."

Someone was calling me. The voice sounded far away, but when I felt the tug on my arm, I realized a woman was standing right next to me.

"Mr. Logan," she repeated, softly. When I turned to her, she told me, "We're going to move your baby to the NICU temporarily to ensure her breathing stabilizes."

Our baby! I'd been thinking about Angie and now this nurse was telling me about our baby. My heart couldn't take much more.

She continued, "Would you like to meet her first?"

"Yes, yes, I would."

The nurse told everyone that only I would be able to go with her. She led me down the hallway, slightly holding me up because she could tell I needed it. When we arrived inside the room where doctors were still caring for the baby, she turned to me and said, "She's the most beautiful baby I've ever seen."

Then I saw her. The nurse was right: she was startlingly beautiful with a head full of black hair and skin that was the softest I'd ever felt and the lightest I'd ever seen. Her opened eyes were darker than any night sky.

The nurse put my newborn into my arms, and she simply looked at me. She was mine and I was hers. I was filled with such a mixture of emotions—happiness and fear at the same time. But it was happiness that I felt most while holding her. "It's Daddy," I said as I rocked her slightly. "It's Daddy," I said again and again.

Until the nurses finally started to pry her away from me.

"She's going to be okay, right?" I asked, not wanting to let her go, but giving her back to the nurse.

The nurse nodded. "She's a preemie, but we believe that she's going to do just fine. There was some meconium present, and we do need to monitor her to ensure no problems arise. But this baby's a fighter. I think she's going to be just fine, Dad."

Right before the nurse took her away, I told our little girl, "Mommy can't wait to meet you." My eyes were filled with tears as the nurse disappeared with my baby girl.

"There's just one thing, Mr. Logan," another nurse said.

I wasn't sure I wanted to hear what she had to say. I couldn't handle anything more. I was staring at the nurse blankly, when she said, "Her name. We just need her name."

First my thoughts went straight to how excited and enthusiastic

Angie had been about the name we'd chosen. Then I smiled and said proudly, "Her name is Samia Angelique Logan."

I asked the nurse to wheel Samia by the window so Angela's family could see her before she went to the NICU. When I stepped back outside, we agreed to split up. April, Kris, and Angie's mother headed down to the NICU to be with the baby. Angie's father and I headed up to the ICU to be with Angela.

All the way down in the elevator, I prayed, and when the doors opened, we saw a team of doctors, including Dr. Walters, standing just outside of her room. Through the open door, I could see Angie hooked up to tubes and being monitored by several nurses. I pushed past Dr. Walters and ran to my wife's side. I was waiting for one of the doctors or nurses to stop me, but none did.

Looking down at my wife, I couldn't believe we were in this place. The only good thing was that Angela didn't seem to be in pain; instead, she appeared to be asleep.

"Forgive me, Angie," I whispered as I held her hand. "I am so sorry. So sorry I didn't listen to you. But now please come back to me. We have a baby to raise. Samia needs her mother, and so do I."

Angela's father had been watching from the back of the room, and I felt him when he came and stood at the foot of her bed. "Hey, kid," he said softly. "Your dad is here. Come on and wake up." Gently he shook her foot.

"Mr. Logan and Mr. Burgin, correct?"

Both of us turned when one of the doctors peeked into the room. "Yes," we answered together.

"May we speak with you?" He motioned for us to step into the hallway.

Now that they'd let me into her room, I didn't want to leave Angela. But I needed to hear what the doctors had to say; I needed to hear their plan to make her well. I kissed her hand, then reluctantly stood up. The moment I stepped into the hallway, I asked, "What's going on with my wife?"

"Sir, we need to speak with you." That came from a different doctor, who motioned toward a small room across from Angie's.

I didn't want to go anywhere. All I wanted to do was run back into Angie's room, hold her, and beg her to wake up. But like I said, I had to get to the bottom of what was going on with my wife.

My father-in-law and I followed the trio of doctors into the room. It was the way they shut the door and the solemn looks on their faces that sent me into panic mode.

"Why are you bringing me in here?" I asked. I didn't give them a chance to answer before I said, "Don't bring me in here to tell me I'm going to lose my wife. This is *my* life," I shouted. Turning toward Dr. Walters, I moved toward him, about to charge him. I didn't get far, though.

Angie's dad restrained me. "Calm down, son," he kept whispering. "Calm down."

I knew he was right, but it was hard for me not to lose control. "What is happening to my wife?" I yelled, even as Angie's dad still held me.

One of the other doctors said, "There was obviously something missed in your wife's care."

"Missed?" Angie's dad said. That word made him release me and now it was his anger that was spilling out. "My baby is in there fighting for her life over something that was missed?" His eyes moved from one doctor to the others.

I joined my father-in-law, but I directed my anger toward the man who was supposed to be caring for Angela and our baby. "Dr. Walters, how could anything be missed?" I screamed. "She *told* you, she kept *telling* you that something was wrong. She told me the same thing and I took your word over my wife's!"

Dr. Walters simply cowered in the back of the room. He didn't part his lips to say a single word.

It was one of the other doctors who said, "Mr. Logan, please give us the chance to tell you what's going on." He paused, giving me and my father-in-law a chance to calm down. "Your wife is in critical condition. She has been categorized as the sickest person in the hospital right now."

"Oh no, no," her dad said, trying to fight back his emotions.

I was glad he said something because I couldn't speak.

My father-in-law asked, "What happened to my baby, Doc?" The way the words seemed to squeeze through his lips, I could tell he was fighting as hard as I was to stay in control.

Dr. Walters finally spoke. "She has what is called preeclampsia."

"What is that?" I asked.

"It's a disease that affects pregnant women. It's a hypertensive disorder that can happen during pregnancy or even afterward. When severe, it can be fatal." He paused before he added the worst part. "Angela's case is severe."

Before I could gather my thoughts about this revelation, before I could say anything, another doctor asked me, "Has she complained of headaches recently or had any problems with her blood pressure?"

"Yes!" I exclaimed, glaring at Dr. Walters as I spoke. "She's had everything. She's had headaches, her blood pressure was up, but Dr. Walters said it was going up because she got worked up." My eyes didn't leave him.

"Mr. Logan, I'm your wife's cardiologist," one of the doctors said. "How long has she had this extreme swelling?"

For months! I wanted to scream, but I only replied, "Dr. Walters said it was normal for her pregnancy." Then I paused. "Wait. Why does she need a cardiologist?"

Silence.

The doctors exchanged glances. "Your wife has also suffered congestive heart failure, peripartum cardiomyopathy, and cardiomegaly," one of them said. "This is all likely connected to the preeclampsia and what has been going on with her." He leaned forward. "But I'm here to help. I will do everything I can to save her."

"Why was she screaming that she couldn't breathe?" All of these medical terms, all of these conditions had turned my anger into fear.

Another doctor said, "I'm Dr. Batise, and I am a pulmonologist. The swelling or fluid retention that your wife was experiencing is a form of edema and due to the congestive heart failure she was experiencing. It developed into acute pulmonary edema. Essentially, all of the fluid that had gathered in her legs and feet began to back up into her lungs and her heart couldn't pump properly. She was literally drowning," he explained solemnly.

This was all too much. All I could do was turn back to the doctor I blamed. "Dr. Walters, she told you that something was wrong. She begged you to listen to her."

"Mr. Logan, preeclampsia is known as a silent killer," he answered. "It masks itself inside of symptoms that are normal for pregnancy."

"Silent?" I screamed. "There was nothing silent about this. She had the symptoms that you're talking about now. She kept telling you, but your arrogance made you choose to ignore her symptoms and her words." With each word I spoke, I moved closer and closer to Dr. Walters.

Angie's father grabbed me again.

When I calmed down, I was able to ask, "So what now?" I looked at each of the doctors in the group. "What do we do for her now? My wife has to go home with me."

The other two doctors genuinely seemed shocked at what I was saying and the care that Angie had received (or had not received) from Dr. Walters, and I believed they wanted to do all they could for her. But then they hit me with the news.

"Right now, your wife has experienced heart, lung, and kidney failure. She's not breathing on her own. We have not been able to control her blood pressure," the cardiologist said.

"If everything is failing, what is working?" I asked.

The doctor shook his head. "Not much, I'm afraid to say. Right now, the machines are keeping her alive and we have to inform you that 80 percent of patients in her situation don't survive."

I understood the numbers, I could do the math, but still I swallowed hard before I asked, "What are you saying to me, Doctor?" My voice cracked as I spoke.

After a moment he said, "She has a 20 percent chance to live."

The doctor continued to talk, but he could have stopped because nothing else registered. I felt as if I were the one with failing lungs. I stood there, leaning against my father-in-law, taking it all in. My head was swirling with all the doctors had said and all Angie had been saying to me.

I had let her down. But that was going to end. I vowed to do everything I could to bring her back. I would breathe for her. I knew that one breath from God could change this whole situation. That's why, in spite of all I'd been told, I had hope. I had hope in the only thing we had. I had hope in God. He was all we had and he was all we needed.

The room had been quiet after the doctor had made that proclamation. I looked up toward the ceiling first, and then around the room at the doctors. "You say my wife has a 20 percent chance to make it?"

Each doctor nodded.

"Well … 20 percent and God is all she needs." I was speaking to myself as much as I was telling them. "You will see me and my family here every day until my wife and my baby leave to go home with me."

My father-in-law and I left the room. There was no need to talk to them anymore. I wanted to get back to my wife.

35

The Breath of Life

(From Angela)

"Jesus, please help me!"

In the next instant after I uttered those words, my spirit lifted from my body and I moved from time into eternity. I left behind my natural body. I left behind all of the pain. In its place an unimaginable and unexplainable contentment washed over me, a tranquility I'd never before known. I was in and at pure peace.

I was aware of myself as spirit, not flesh, as I was being pulled upward. I had no idea how much space I traveled, but my ascension stopped and I came to rest at what seemed to be the top of the room. It had felt as if I'd traveled hundreds of miles, but I was just above the bed. There was no way to measure the distance between here and eternity.

In the flesh I might have questioned that, but in the spirit I didn't have to think—I already knew. All things I was meant to understand, I understood. I didn't have to rationalize; I didn't have to process. It was just the simple yet complete act of knowing.

I knew I was in the spiritual realm, but I wasn't in the place one would call heaven. Yet I felt heavenly. I had previously heard of people reuniting with loved ones or meeting people in the spiritual or heavenly plane. That didn't happen to me; I only met one person—me. The "I" that I speak of was gone. I was no longer I; I was me. This "I" or myself, my ego, the former image I had of myself, was replaced by who I was authentically created to be. I was confident, comfortable, fully self-aware. I was not Ang' or Angie—I was Angela.

I felt enveloped in a white light, yet I could still vividly hear and see what was going on in multiple places at one time. I saw the doctors working on me and heard them talking about my condition.

"Patient going into preeclamptic state with associated increased leg edema, positive proteinuria, and uncontrolled hypertension."

"Arterial blood is showing respiratory acidosis. Attempt to correct with ventilation."

I saw my husband at my bedside, and then my father, my husband, and again my father. I saw my mother, sister, and April pointing through a glass and looking at babies, but I could never see mine. Then they were at my bedside again. My father, who wore a brown blazer, white button-down shirt, and slacks, held my hand while my sister and mother talked to me.

All of a sudden, instead of looking down on them from where I had been perched, I was looking up into their faces. I heard my father say, "I'm here, Ang'. I'm here. Wake up and talk to us." I told myself to squeeze his hand and then I watched him jump up and heard him yell, "Nurse! Nurse!"

Two of them came running into the room.

"She squeezed my hand!" he said. "She squeezed my hand!"

Looking up, I saw hope in his eyes. I saw a waiting room full of my relatives waiting their turn to visit with me. Suddenly, I was back perched at the top of my hospital room almost in a seated position.

The nurse who was with me left me alone and then Dr. Walters walked into the quiet room. He paused for a moment, then took slow steps toward me. Again I went from looking down at him to looking up into his face.

I was completely at peace as he took my hand. "I should have listened to you," he said softly. He stood there for a few seconds, and then he gently put my hand down before the nurse returned to my room.

Back in my perched position, I knew that of all the people I'd seen, the one I hadn't seen was my daughter. A thought came to my head in a jolt: *She's out. Ask for her.* In that instant I was yanked from my vantage point and returned to my body. I opened my eyes.

It took a couple of moments for me to realize I was back within my natural self. I could tell because my thoughts returned. I didn't *know* anymore, but my thoughts were singular. I only thought of my child. And that she was no longer within me, she was no longer in my womb, and I had to see her.

I blinked, though I wasn't capable of much movement or sound, although I was trying hard to move my body. I managed to turn my head slightly, and the nurse who was writing on my chart glanced at me, gasped, and dropped the pen. She ran to my bedside.

I wanted to say something, I wanted to ask for my child, but I wasn't capable of speech. I was able to find enough strength to slowly lift my hand. I pinched my fingers together and moved them around as if I were writing. The nurse nodded, moved quickly across the room, grabbed a piece of paper and the pen she'd just dropped.

No idea how I was able to do it, but while the nurse hit the call button on my bed, I managed to write: *Can I see my baby?*

The nurse read what I wrote and at first frowned as she struggled to make sense of my words. But then it connected and her smile warmed the entire room. "I don't see why not," she said. And with her words I breathed.

Tears streamed down my face as a flood of gratitude overwhelmed me. My tears kept flowing, but I wasn't crying just because I was grateful to be alive, or grateful that I'd be able to mother my child, or grateful to be able to have more time with my family and friends.

There was much more to my tears. I searched my heart to understand the meaning behind these never-ending tears. The answer came from that same place, from that same voice that had been speaking to me for months. I was grateful because inside of this experience I knew what it was like to step into the presence of God. I had the opportunity to know perfect peace. I had the opportunity to feel God hold me.

It was an amazing blessing to be in God's presence in one moment but then in the next to have him answer my prayers. That is what God had done for me. He'd granted my request. He'd been so merciful to allow me the opportunity to be a mother to my child, the child I knew he had given me.

Looking back now on that eight-month experience, I had learned the greatest of lessons. I had lived and learned that a woman's greatest advocate needs to be herself. As women, we must listen to our bodies and to the intuition that is inside of us. That intuition is God's way of speaking to us and through us. We cannot allow people (even doctors) to tell us something different than what we know to be true. We cannot allow anyone's voice to be louder than God's.

My experience gave me that lesson and God helped me learn that lesson. And then he allowed me to return from his womb. He gave me life once again in my natural body. And he gave me everything I needed to really, really breathe.

ACKNOWLEDGMENTS

To our children: We are humbled that God has chosen us to be your parents. A portion of our love for you is written in this book, but the totality of our love for you is written in our hearts, where it shall stay for all eternity. You have brought joy into our lives and the lives of those around you. You will forever be loved.

To our parents: We have come to understand that the journey we went on while becoming parents gave us secondhand experience of the love that parents have for their children. Our firsthand experience was the love that you have shown us. We thank you and honor you for how you have cared for us. We couldn't have asked for better prayer warriors, cheerleaders, coaches, counselors, friends, and supporters. We love you, Raymond Clifton, Earnestine Clifton, Roy Burgin, Lillian Burgin, and Judy Burgin.

To our siblings: Being a sister or a brother means being there for each other, and you all have been there for us. Thank you!

To our friends: We have never been the kind of people who wanted *more* friends; we wanted *real* friends. You all have been the realest of real! We love you and thank you for your support. We have a special thank-you for two friends who were our biggest fans, Carmen Sanders and Christopher Poole. You not only believed in us but encouraged us and prayed for us. We will meet you again in heaven.

To our church family and prayer warriors: We are proof that prayer changes things! We are grateful for everyone from The Ray of Hope Christian Center and the prayer warriors we have at home and around the country who have truly prayed for us. We know that God hears every prayer, and we are thankful for the ones you lifted up on our behalf.

To the BroadStreet team—to Carlton, Bill, and David, and the entire BroadStreet team: Your belief in our testimony and its need to be shared has filled us with gratitude. We are ever thankful for you! Your approach to sharing the good news, the kindness that you have shown to us, and how you walk the talk is a true inspiration. You are wonderful faith and industry leaders.

To our Lord and Savior: We have often been told it was a miracle that I survived my near-death experience during pregnancy and childbirth. And it was. But what was equally a wonder was that you allowed *me* to be in your presence. I marvel at the fact that no matter how small I might be, you love me. I will never be able to fully explain your majesty, grace, and peace, but I will always try. There is truly none like you, God. I will forever thank you for answering my prayer and allowing me to be a mother to my daughter. I will forever be changed by my encounter with you and I will forever be grateful for it.

ABOUT THE AUTHORS

Angela Burgin Logan is the president of Nia Enterprises. A highly sought-after personality, she has appeared on television shows like *The View* and been featured in print and digital publications like *The Huffington Post, Essence Magazine,* and others. As a content creator, Angela produced the feature film *Breathe* and founded the go-to women's online destination LadiesLiveandLearn.com. As a multimedia strategist and influencer, she has created award-winning digital campaigns and worked with brands like A&E/Lifetime Television. Angela is also a pop culture and lifestyle authority who serves as the Director of Social Media for *Uptown Magazine* and *Hype Hair Magazine.* She considers her most important job and greatest honor to be that of mother to her children. She is married to Samson Logan, and the family resides in Buffalo, New York.

Samson A. Logan is a recording artist, actor, and producer who now adds author to his many accomplishments. As a *Billboard* recording artist, Samson has had two top twenty hits, "Atmosphere" and "Future Anniversary," and has performed and collaborated with stars across musical genres, such as gospel legend Shirley Caesar to rap stars like Tupac Shakur. As an actor, Samson has starred in award-winning film, television, and stage productions, such as Tyler Perry's *Diary of a Mad Black Woman* and Je'Caryous Johnson's *Love Overboard.* In addition to producing music projects, Samson has produced film projects, including coproducing the film *Breathe,* which was lauded by top film festivals. He is married to Angela B. Logan and lives in Buffalo, New York.